DR. NEWMAN

AND

HIS RELIGIOUS OPINIONS.

BY

CHARLES HASTINGS COLLETTE.

"They have committed two evils. They have forsaken Me the fountain of living waters, and hewed them out cisterns, broken cisterns, that can hold no water."—*Jer.* ii. 13.

LONDON:

JOHN F. SHAW AND CO.,
48, PATERNOSTER ROW, E.C.
1866.

TO

MAJOR-GENERAL AYLMER, R.A.,

This Book is Dedicated,

AS A SLIGHT TRIBUTE TO, AND RECOGNITION OF,

HIS MANY CHRISTIAN VIRTUES,

BY

THE AUTHOR.

Works by Mr. C. H. Collette.

Dr. Wiseman's Popish Literary Blunders.

"The invariable precision with which the writer, avoiding needless digressions, keeps to the point, and the keen, pitiless logic which runs through his arguments, bear the impress of a legal education. We may add, that these pages are well worth perusal, simply as a specimen of clear, terse, logical reasoning."—*The Critic.*

"It is, perhaps, an advantage, rather than otherwise, that a controversy of the kind should be taken up by a layman, supposing him to be properly qualified: the imputation of professional bias will be avoided in this case; and where questions of evidence are under discussion, a learned lawyer, such as Mr. Collette evidently is, may be of special service to the cause of truth. His literary qualifications for the task he has undertaken are evidently first-rate, and his corrections of the Cardinal are sustained by sound criticism."—*The Clerical Journal.*

"As a lawyer, Mr. Collette has sifted every point of evidence, weighed it, given the exact passages to which the Cardinal goes to prove his case, shows them to be utterly subversive of the opinion and arguments of the Cardinal himself, and then decides that a grosser case of resolute fraud has never been prosecuted in any Court of Law where honest dealing prevails. Mr. Collette has done his work ably and well, and is worthy of the esteem of all honest men for having exposed such infamous means of propping up a system that is at the present moment, to all appearances, tottering to its speedy fall."—*Bell's Weekly Messenger.*

On transmission of 2s. 10d. in postage stamps, or Post Office Order, to Mr. W. PENNY, 57, Lincoln's-Inn Fields, London, a copy will be forwarded post free.

Price 1s.

Union of the Churches: its Difficulties and Possibility.

"Few men are more conversant with Ecclesiastical History in its more modern phases than Mr. Collette, and therefore few could be more qualified to enter fully into the discussion of the subject indicated in the title of this new work from his pen. We believe there are insurmountable obstacles to the success of the movement, and so does the author of the work, of which the first part is before us. It deals with the 'Theories' only of the question; and in doing so the writer displays that extensive research, that mastery of his subject, and that argumentative ability, which have more or less characterised his previous works on controverted ecclesiastical questions."—*Morning Advertiser.*

London: J. PAUL, 1, Chapter House Court, St. Paul's.

Just published, in small 8vo., cloth, price 3s. 6d.

"I Believe in the Holy Catholic Church."

A Controversial Correspondence between C. H. COLLETTE, Esq. (Protestant), and Dr. GERAGHTY (Roman Catholic).

This most interesting correspondence originated from a challenge given by Dr. Geraghty, and the result is a volume replete with theological and historical research on each side of the question.

London: W. MACINTOSH, 24, Paternoster Row.

Works by Mr. C. H. Collette.

In 1 vol., Post 8vo., price 9s.

Henry VIII.: An Historical Sketch.

"We heartily commend this volume to the general perusal of Potestant Englishmen as an antidote of the false aspersions heaped upon the character of Henry VIII., the chosen instrument, whatever may have been his failings, to break the chains which bound England in their numbing fetters, and to clear the way for the glorious liberty of thought and free perusal of God's Word to which these islands owe so much of their prosperity and glory."—*Morning Advertiser.*

"All his facts are honestly stated, and his deductions therefrom are made in a careful spirit."—*Reader.*

"Mr. Collette has made an interesting digest of facts too commonly passed over. His conclusions will, of course, be disputed by many. He has condensed the elaborate matter of Mr. Froude into a more generally readable compass, with such additions as his own researches enable him to make, and has furnished Protestants with a manual of instruction on one of the most important periods of English history."—*London Review.*

LONDON:
W. H. ALLEN & CO., 13, WATERLOO PLACE.

Price 4s.

Novelties of Romanism.

"This work is the fruit of immense industry, of great faithfulness, an acuteness in scholarly controversy which it were well for the Church if her members more frequently displayed. It is an answer complete, searching, and totally unassailable. It is an exhaustive examination of the cause of error, and with it in his hand any clergyman or layman of even moderate understanding may successfully assail the most learned priest among them all. Mr. Collette's labours are not only earnest and intelligent, but stamp him as a man of close erudition, and singular clearness of vision, united with an easy and graceful yet keenly-logical style. Every fact and argument which he uses is a spear piercing the buckler of the enemies of truth. There is here no uncertain hitting, no beating of the air, no rhapsodical utterance or deportation. It is all cold steel, before which our emptily-audacious foe is sure to fly."—*Dublin Warder.*

"By an immense array of facts and documents Mr. Collette proves that the whole system of Romanism is a novelty, an impudent series of additions to the religion of the Gospel."—*The Bulwark.*

"Mr. Collette has a wonderful acquaintance with the constitutions of the primitive Church, and with the writings of the early fathers, and he brings this knowledge, as well as his studies of the later development of heretical usurpation, to bear upon an exposure of the innovations of the various bishops who have held sway in Rome."—*Morning Herald.*

"The object of this work is to show that every one of the specialities of Romanism is a novelty superinduced upon primitive Christianity; and so exact is the learning on which this compendious volume is founded, that the book will endure the test of the sharpest examination of its many literary references."—*The Christian Spectator.*

RELIGIOUS TRACT SOCIETY,
56, PATERNOSTER ROW, and 164, PICCADILLY.

INTRODUCTORY NOTICE.

The names of Dr. NEWMAN, Dr. MANNING, and Dr. PUSEY, have lately come prominently before the public. One has long since gone over to Rome; the second has lately gone; the third, it was by many expected, would have soon followed.

After a long silence, Dr. Newman, "as a wounded brute at bay," is dragged from his "retreat" by the Rev. CHARLES KINGSLEY; hence his "Apologia." This was shortly followed by a "History of his Religious Opinions," which is a reproduction of the "Apologia;" the personal matters between himself and Mr. Kingsley omitted. The two together have been not inaptly designated by his reviewers as "The History of a Clerical Weathercock which has made the grand tour of the Theological Compass." Except from the fact that the "Apologia" did not create the expected sensation, I cannot account for the appearance of the "History."

I have taken these two works as the first part of my review of Dr. Newman's religious opinions.

The second part is a review of Dr. Newman's Letter on Dr. Pusey's last work, entitled "Eirenikon."

The "Eirenikon" is a "peace offering," a hand of fellowship held out by Dr. Pusey to Roman Catholics, and suggested by a letter addressed to him by Dr. Manning.

Dr. Pusey's name has become notorious, a by-word, a designation of a "sect" of High Anglicans believed to be more Romish than Anglican. His name is disagreeably associated with the "Tracts for the Times," as an advocate of the "Confessional," and himself notorious among the "Sisterhood," and we are startled in the outset by an allusion to "our dear friend's tract No. XC.," which he declares to have "done good and lasting service by breaking off a mass of unauthorized traditional glosses, which had encrusted over the Thirty-nine Articles," and that no blame had been attached to his own and the Rev. W. B. Heathcote's vindication of the principles of that ever memorable " Tract " as the natural grammatical interpretation of the Articles! Following in the same course in which Dr. Newman made shipwreck.

I confess to have felt a sickening at heart when my eyes fell on the above declaration. To say that no blame was attached to these vindications is a libel upon the great body of our Church. They were condemned by the almost unanimous voice of the lay as well as clerical members of that Church.

Beyond the above acknowledgment we can gather very little as to the *peculiar* views of Dr. Pusey as contained in the "Tracts." He states his belief in the following words:—

"I believe *explicitly* all which I know God to have revealed to his Church, and *implicitly* anything, if He has revealed it, which I know not. In simple words, I believe all which the Church believes."

This is the exact confession made by Dr. Newman. How a man can believe in that which he "knows not" is a matter beyond comprehension. He does not believe a fact or doctrine, because it is revealed by the WORD of GOD, but because it is proposed by the Church for his belief!—the Church being the communion of Christians, to which he is attached by birth and education. Had he been born a Romanist, he would have uttered exactly the same words. But this apparent humility and submission will not deceive any one. Dr. Pusey has raised a standard of orthodoxy, whose followers have now passed into a "denomination," called *Puseyites*. He dogmatically declares that his standard of orthodoxy is the belief of the Church, and then shelters himself under the assertion that he believes what the Church believes. As a further parallel between himself and Dr. Newman, I may add that they both assert the Church to be infallible. "Infallibility or Infidelity" is Dr. Pusey's motto. Happily Dr. Pusey is in the great minority as to what he alleges to be the belief of the Church of England.

There are a few—only a few—difficulties to be got over towards this contemplated union. These are explained away. Perhaps the "Eirenikon" was issued for this very purpose—to prepare the way. Dr. Pusey points out where they do agree. For instance, as to the "Real Presence," he says: "The doctrine of the Eucharistic Sacrifice depends upon the doctrine of the Real Objective Presence. Where there is the apostolic succession and a consecration in our Lord's words, there, too, it is held by Roman authorities, is the Eucharistic Sacrifice."

On the Seven Sacraments he takes the view of the Newman

school. Dr. Manning charges the Church of England, that while it "sustains a belief in two sacraments, it formally propagates unbelief in the other five." Dr. Pusey considers this a libel. He declares that "the Church of England, while teaching that Baptism and the Holy Eucharist have a special dignity, is careful not to exclude other appointments of God from being in some way sacraments, as channels of grace, or (in the old definition of sacraments) visible signs of an invisible grace. This is, indeed, inseparable from the idea of confirmation, orders, absolution, and marriage."

But he tells us that Dr. Manning "denies the validity of our absolutions." And so he does "our orders;" and without orders what becomes of "our" sacraments? What, then, is the use of "the Church of England multiplying the celebration of its sacraments" if, for want of "orders," the whole are nullified in their proper administration? What one asserts the other denies; and even if Dr. Pusey pretends to believe what his own church denies as savouring of Romanism, his Romish opponent tells him his profession is only a sham, because he does not derive his ordination through the genuine Papal authority. Dr. Pusey may profess the five other sacraments, but he must have learned by this time that, by the example set him by Dr. Newman, there is no "halting between two opinions," and if he desires to hold Romish views, he must do so in orthodox fashion, and follow his "dear friend of Tract XC.," when his "absolution" will become valid without question, and where he will be able to carry on his "confessions" unrebuked, and be empowered to chastise "sacrilegious confessions," the "evil fruits" of which appear to give him so much mental anguish in the Anglican Church.

Dr. Newman reminds Dr. Pusey that there is such a thing as Tradition, besides the Scripture. The latter will not give up the Scriptures, but creates a distinction between the "substance of the doctrine delivered and the manner of delivering it." I have no doubt they will shake hands on this.

It is so far satisfactory to find that Dr. Pusey condemns the "heresy" of the Roman development of the doctrine of "Invocation of Saints." But Dr. Newman will tell him that it is not necessary to hold this doctrine, and Dr. Milner explains away the mere *ora pro nobis;* but Dr. Pusey justly observes that this has led to that "vast system as to the Blessed Virgin which to all of us has been the special 'crux' of the Roman system." He very properly points out that this doctrine "presents itself in many startling forms, co-extensive with the present office of our dear Lord for us." "The intercession of the Virgin is held to be coextensive with His, 'who ever liveth to make intercession for us,' our Divine Lord. And this is taught, not as the gloomy expression of southern feeling, but as the deliberate mind of the present Roman Church." With this expression of opinion, it is indeed surprising that Dr. Pusey and his followers should dally and toy with Romanism, stand themselves on the brink, afraid to take the plunge into the gulf, but entice others, with their imitation of Romish ceremonies, gestures, and vestments; and, what is worse, seeing that such is the result of their example, they persevere in their "ecclesiastical fopperies," and do not stretch a helping hand to save their sinking victims.

Even Dr. Newman despises this class of Anglicans. He says he "used to call them 'the gilt-gingerbread school,' from whom he expected little good, persons whose religion lay in ritualism or architecture, and who played at Popery or Anglicanism."

As a compromise, Dr. Pusey is willing, for the sake of union, to retain "the lawfulness of appealing to the saints to pray for us, as of faith," for on this "there is a large scope for providing that in case of a re-union, our people should not be flooded with these devotions which to us are most alien," forgetting that the very fact of our appealing to saints that they should pray for us, pre-supposes a state that they can *hear our prayers;* once admit this, and the "flood of devotion" follows, which is so much to be deprecated. Avoid all appearance of evil. The simple and harmless *ora pro nobis* is only the stepping-stone to the unbridled system complained of. I repeat, it is the playing at Romanism which is so dangerous.

I admit that many of the acts in which these High Churchmen indulge are in themselves harmless, and they can and do explain them away to their own satisfaction. For instance, Dr. Pusey says, "We know that in kissing the outside of the material Bible we mean only to express reverence for the Word of God; in the traditional custom of bowing to the altar (when the Holy Sacrament is *not* there), we mean only reverence to it, as having been 'the throne of God' (as peers bow before the throne in respect for the absent sovereign). So also, if any should kiss the feet of the crucifix, it would be in reverence to the crucified." But it is these outward acts, harmless in themselves, which lead, with weak minds, to abuses, and eventually all spiritual worship is forgotten, and the votary landed on Roman soil.

To become Romanist, Dr. Pusey points out the fact that there is more to be believed than the "letter of the Council of Trent." There is "that vast practical system which lies beyond the letter of the Council of Trent—things which are taught with a *quasi*-authority in the Roman Church," beyond that which is "actually defined." He thinks, however, that the Roman and Anglican Churches are kept apart much more by this "vast practical system" than the requirements of the Council of Trent decrees. This fact becomes more apparent when we conceive that, beyond the decrees of Trent, a new creed was imposed on the world by an unauthorized (I use the word advisedly) Papal Bull. This established a new system, by permitting what was clearly an innovation, even in the Roman Church — the establishment of Articles of Faith on the authority of a Papal Bull; for it is an erroneous notion to suppose that Pius IV. was authorized by the Trent Council to draw up this new creed. If that creed is binding on the faith of Romanists, then is also the doctrine of the Immaculate Conception, which is proposed for belief on exactly the same authority—an unauthorized Papal Bull. A great principle is here involved, namely, the power of the Pope to impose on the Church for belief a new Article of Faith. On exactly the same authority, we may be called upon to accept all the extravagances and monstrosities contained in all previous Papal Bulls. The doctrine of the Immaculate Conception having been received "as of faith" by the Roman Church entirely on the authority of a Bull of the Pope, Dr. Pusey very justly observes, that a union with the Roman Church "would involve this—that every one should be ready to receive whatever all past Popes had authoritatively uttered, and whatever any future Pope, though unhappily a Borgia or a Julius II., might utter upon any subject whatsoever." Many pages are devoted to the enumeration of dogmas enunciated by Popes in this manner, which are wholly repugnant to the liberty of Christianity; and their repetition by Dr. Pusey gives us some hope that even he, Romish as he is supposed to be, is not so far gone as to swallow this pill, though he may, for the sake of union, "accept the *letter* of the Council of Trent."

On this question of the Immaculate Conception, we have placed before us some very interesting information. We have been led to believe that, with one or two exceptions, the opinions of the Romish bishops were unanimous in their approval of the proposed definition. This is not so. Dr. Pusey has given us an analysis of all their opinions; and there was anything but unanimity. I recommend this part of Dr. Pusey's work to the attention of those who expect to find union in a church whose claim to infallibility is its most alluring bait.

It is Dr. Pusey's remarks on the extravagances of Mary-worship in the Roman Church, and the introduction of the new dogma of the Immaculate Conception, that has induced Dr. Newman to come before the public again; this time not to defend his personal character, but to vindicate Anglican Romanists from the charge of idolatry so clearly brought home by Dr. Pusey. And, in turn, it is this Letter to Dr. Pusey which has furnished me with the subject matter the second part of the present work.

I cannot, however, dismiss the "Eirenikon" without adding a few further remarks. Dr. Pusey dedicates a postscript of some fifty pages to expose the fallacy of the doctrine of the *personal* infallibility of the Bishop of Rome for the time being, a doctrine which, he states, is now being seriously advocated; the Gallican Church, according to the *Dublin Review*, having now withdrawn all their former opposition to the doctrine. What he has written on this subject is sound, as far as it goes. But Dr. Pusey holds to the infallibility of the Church, which may mean anything to suit the moment, and must lead to the most intolerant sentiments; for, of course, he must set up his own standard as the measure of orthodoxy of the church which he alleges to be infallible.

"Hesitate (he writes) how men will for the while, it was truly said by one of the most powerful intellects of the day, there is but one choice, *infallibility* or *infidelity*." *

The "powerful Intellect" here alluded to is Dr. Newman.

All those, therefore, who are not within Dr. Pusey's church are infidels! And this is exactly the charitable conclusion Dr. Newman arrives at in his estimation of his own church.

"There are but two alternatives,—the way to Rome and the way to Atheism." †

Reader, if you are not of the Roman Church, you are on the high road to Atheism, if not already there. If you are not a "Pusey-Anglican," and do not believe Dr. Pusey's church infallible, you are an infidel!

Protestant controversialists are often (and I do not deny without reason) condemned for using strong expressions towards our Roman brethren; but the worst they say of them is that their popular

---

* "Daniel the Prophet," 2nd thousand, p. 393.
† "Apologia," p. 329.

worship is idolatry. But what is this to being called a heretic, an infidel, or an atheist? Who gave these two individuals the right thus to brand their fellow-Christians? Where is their charity? Is that chief of all Christian virtues to be required alone of the infidel or heretic? Dr. Pusey, learn this one lesson from a Layman; we are no more infidel because we do not believe in your infallible Church, than we believe ourselves atheists because we do not belong to Dr. Newman's church. I said, that this doctrine of infallibility leads to intolerance of every other denomination. This is exemplified in the "Eirenikon." Let me give an example. And first of the Evangelical section of our Church Dr. Pusey says:—"I have loved them because they loved the Lord; I loved them for their zeal for souls." But he adds, "I often thought them narrow;" and "that they are often withheld from the clear and full sight of the truth by an inveterate prejudice, that that truth, as held by us" (*i.e.*, the Puseyite school,) "is united with error"! Believing, as the Evangelicans do, that the system of Puseyism is permeated with Romish errors, we can account for the alleged "inveterate prejudice." But of course everybody is wrong but Dr. Pusey and his school; and they do not hesitate to place almost out of the pale of salvation every one outside of their own circle. Hear, again, what this amiable gentleman says of the Dissenters of England, as a "peace offering,"—but, alas! what a perversion of the use of language! Dr. Pusey thinks that the Church of England is the great bulwark against unbelief. But he declares the "Dissenters, in the main, correspond to the Protestant bodies abroad." He says, "When one compares the general condition of the English Dissenters with that of the like bodies abroad—the unbelief in Holland, the Rationalism in Germany, the Socinianism of Geneva, the Arianism, or semi-Arianism, prevalent among the French Calvinists, or the Universalism which is desolating the United States, and (with the exception of one body) the almost entire neglect of baptism there, among those who are the descendants of the English Dissenters —one cannot but think that the degree of faith surviving among them here is very much owing, under the mercy of God, to the English Church, which enfolds them all around, even while they are hostile to it." Every true Churchman will protest against Dr. Pusey's irrational and uncharitable conclusion with regard to his dissenting brethren.

While I believe the Church of England, as the State Church, to be the great barrier against Romanism in this country, as there must be a dominant Church, and therefore the only safeguard of religious liberty, I am also of opinion that the existence of dissent has sobered the Church, and kept it within bounds. But, taking the great body of Dissenters in this country, there is as much true piety as in the Church; and if they chose to retort on us, they have only to point to a Colenso, or to a Manning, Newman, Allies, Oakley, and an army of perverts, fostered or engendered in the bosom of Dr. Pusey's so-called standard of orthodoxy; and it has been a subject of expectation, but would not have created surprise, if Dr. Pusey himself had, with his "non-natural interpretation of the Articles," followed his "dear friend of Tract XC." into the Church of Rome. These High Church Romanizing divines declare that they would rather err with Rome than live in orthodoxy with dissent. We, on the other hand, declare to Dr. Pusey that his book is a libel on the Evangelical ministers of this country—a book calculated to create more disunion and enmity among ourselves, while affecting a pious desire to bring together Christians into communion with each other. And while on this subject, I must draw attention to Dr. Pusey's charitable conclusion. It appears to me a monstrous assumption that an individual should come forward and assert that "the grace of a sacrament belongs to the Church alone," when it is evident that he excludes all classes of Dissenters from that church. These, he dare assert, can receive no grace whatever by a devout and faithful reception of the sacrament of the Lord's Supper. Here is priestly pride and arrogance! Who gave Dr. Pusey the right to judge who is or who is not in the Church? "Heretics," says Dr. Pusey, "are really cut off from the body of Christ." "These," he adds, "receive the sacrament, though not the grace of the sacrament." Let us, for a moment, suppose ourselves Romanists. "You, Dr. Pusey," we would say, "are a heretic; you are really cut off from the body of Christ; you receive a sacrament, though not the grace of the sacrament; this belongs to those alone of the Church, and you are not in the Church." Dr. Pusey would say, this is not Christian charity—and would protest. This is just the language Dr. Manning or Dr. Newman would hold towards Dr. Pusey. Will Dr. Pusey submit? If not, how can he presume to turn on his fellow-Christians who do not conform to his notions of a church, and say that they are cut off from the body of Christ, and have not the grace of a sacrament? Dr. Manning no more considers Dr. Pusey as belonging to "the Church," than Dr. Pusey considers some Nonconformist minister of the Gospel a member of Christ's Church, when, in very fact, that very contemned and despised minister may be a chosen vessel of the Lord to do His holy work—a member of Christ and inheritor of the Kingdom of Heaven, without so-called apostolic orders; and Dr. Manning or Dr. Pusey may be without the gate. God forbid that I should say or suggest that such is the fact; but a Nonconformist minister, if his holy calling did not suggest a more charitable view of Christ's universal religion, might, with equal right, deny the privileges of the Gospel to Dr. Manning and Dr. Pusey. He would ask them to decide between themselves, first, what and where is this Church? before they presume to condemn another as a heretic! And mark the arrogant presumption of this "standard of orthodoxy." He says, "The undoubted presence of the grace of the sacraments is a *proof to us* that we are in the Body of Christ, in which alone He gives it." Where is the evidence? where are the proofs? Drs. Manning and Newman deny the validity of Anglican orders. They say we cannot "perform" or administer a sacrament; therefore, no grace can result from the act. Here is a flat denial of all Dr. Pusey's assumptions and presumptions. Where are his proofs of the undoubted presence of the grace of the sacraments? Is his want—a total absence—of one of the first graces of our Lord's holy religion, charity, a proof? We venture to tell Dr. Pusey that the grace of God in us does not come to us from the fact that we belong to this church or that church, but that we belong to CHRIST. And Dr. Pusey's "prayers for a union" will, we think, avail little before the great God of the universe, who is no respecter of persons, until he divests himself of that spiritual pride which creates for him and his section "a church" out of which he supposes no grace can be conferred.

The most Dr. Pusey can say of Nonconformists is that they are "schismatics;" but Dr. Manning and Dr. Newman will call him both heretic and schismatic. He reminds us, however, of the assuring fact that Dr. Manning admits that, in the English Church, "there are real Christians, a small residuum, whom he supposes to live on and grow in the grace which they received at their baptism." The rest are "in a doubtful state." This Dr. Pusey (unless he indeed hopes himself to be saved through this back-door influence) would declare to be uncharitable, and yet it is the same measure that he metes out to those whom he declares "are cut off from the Body of Christ, and to whom no grace of the sacraments can cleave." This is the man who writes and prays for a union of Christians!

But mark the "self-righteousness" of Dr. Pusey. "Presbyterians have what *they* believe; we, what *we* believe. But they who have observed pious Presbyterians and pious English Catholics, have discerned among our people a spiritual life, of a kind which was not among theirs; in a word, sacramental life." Who gave Dr. Pusey the power to discern the Spirit of God, that works in any of us? What wicked presumption! Does Dr. Pusey assert that he has this "spiritual and sacramental life," and that neither Dr. Chalmers nor Dr. Candlish shared this grace? Thank God, we shall not be judged at the Great Day by Dr. Pusey's standard of "spiritual and sacramental life."

With these observations I commend my work to the consideration of wavering Protestants; I entreat them to look closely into the motives and reasons which have induced some of our perverts to embrace Romanism, and examine them on their own admissions, as I have done with Dr. Newman, and they will soon arrive at a just estimation of their true position. As to Dr. Newman, he has truthfully and succinctly measured his own worth in a letter to Dr. Wiseman, and in which I heartily concur:—"Persons and things," he wrote, "look great at a distance, which are not so when seen close." And he adds of himself, that, "did we know him, we would see that *he* was one about whom there has been far more talk for good or bad than he deserves, and about whose movements far more expectation has been raised than the event will justify." Dr. NEWMAN's modesty has enabled him to exercise the rare gift of appreciating his own character and position. I trust the Reader will find in the sequel a justification of Dr. NEWMAN's opinion of himself.

C. H. COLLETTE.

57, LINCOLN'S-INN FIELDS, LONDON,
March, 1866.

DR. NEWMAN AND HIS OPINIONS.

"Truth is the real object of our reason; and if it does not attain truth, either the premise or the process is in fault."—*Apologia*, p. 380.

"Persistence in a given belief is no sufficient test of truth; but departure from it is at least a slur upon the man who has felt so certain about it."—*Apologia*, p. 120.

THE republication by Dr. Newman of his "Apologia pro vitâ suâ," under the title of "History of my Religious Opinions,"* has given an importance to the first work which its intrinsic merit, I venture to assert, does not deserve. Dr. Newman, nevertheless, stands pre-eminent among the Oxford divines who have seceded from the Anglican Church, by presenting an "Apologia" for the step he had taken twenty years ago—the abandoning of one system of religion for the adoption of another—and who has considered that fact of so great importance as to justify him in publishing, at this late period, a history of his religious opinions. No one could have written more forcibly, more pungently, than did Dr. Newman himself against the Romish system. In 1840 he wrote in the *British Critic* (of which he was for some time editor) in a manner which showed a thorough appreciation of the system. These are his words: "We see Rome attempting to gain converts among us by unreal representations of

* "Apologia pro vitâ suâ." London, 1864; and "History of my Religious Opinions." London, 1865. By John Henry Newman, D.D.

its doctrines, plausible statements, bold assertions, appeals to the weaknesses of human nature, to our fancies, our eccentricities, our fears, our frivolities, our false philosophies. We see its agents smiling, and nodding, and ducking, to attract attention, as gipsies make up to truant boys, holding out tales for the nursery, and pretty pictures, and gilt gingerbread, and physic concealed in jam, and sugar-plums for good children." How true is all this; as true now as it was in 1840. Strong motives, irresistible arguments, were exercised, one would suppose, to divert a mind which could have so accurately conceived and described the working of the Romish system in this country. But after a careful perusal of the two books before me, I cannot discover one substantial argument, one rational explanation, to justify Dr. Newman in taking so important a step as a change of religion, which amounts to a renunciation of his publicly expressed opinions against Rome, and a repudiation of his ordination vows, which also involved a solemn condemnation of the "errors and heresies" of Romanism. There is not one justifying fact advanced to explain the extraordinary change in his religious opinions. There is but one way, which I have well weighed, to account for the phenomenon, and which I will venture to assert in its proper time and place.

The title of the book before us is suggestive of an old French proverb, not worth repeating, simply from the fact that, in the strict sense of the word, "Apologia" does not correspond with the substance and subject of the work. Indeed, our author himself says, that "apologia" is not to be taken in the English sense of "apology," any more than "infant" in law means a little child.* I therefore pass on from the title to the work itself.

Dr. Newman divides the subject matter of the

---

* "Apologia," p. 80.

"Apologia" into two distinct parts. In the first, we have a vindication of the writer's former works, and his personal character principally from the charge of "untruthfulness," made by an open enemy in the person of the Rev. Charles Kingsley. In the second, we are favoured with an autobiography of the author's ecclesiastical education and career, commencing from his boyhood, in February, 1811, when, as he tells us, he found some years after, he had, instinctively and prophetically, as it were, illustrated the first page of his verse-book between the words "verse" and "book" with the figure of a solid cross upright, and next to it is what he meant for a necklace, but which he could not make out to be anything else than a set of beads, with a cross attached—a rosary, in fact—the emblems of (so called) "Catholic devotion." He passes in review a series of years spent in vacillating doubts and imaginary difficulties, the sure token of a weak and ill-regulated mind. "Alas! (he exclaims) it was my position for whole years, to remain without any satisfactory basis for my religious profession, in a state of moral sickness, neither able to acquiesce in Anglicanism, nor able to go to Rome."* "I had no positive Anglican theory. I was very nearly a pure Protestant. Lutherans had a sort of theology, so had Calvinists; I had none."† He then brings us up to the period of his reception into the fostering bosom of his now adopted Church, which act he describes as "coming into port after a rough sea." He has, as he asserts, been ever since "in perfect peace and content," though it is difficult to conceive what he has gained by the change, since he informs us that "he was not conscious to himself, on his conversion, of any difference of thought or of temper from what he had before. He was not conscious of firmer faith in the fundamental truths of revelation or of self-command."‡

* "Apologia," p. 143.   † Ibid. 216.   ‡ Ibid. 373.

These two parts contrast most strongly with each other, so much so that the reader can scarcely be brought to believe them to be the productions of the same mind. There is nothing to identify the spirit of the writer either in style, expression, or train of thought. The second part, when describing his own experiences, I can only compare to the stream whose waters are driven onward in a continuous course, fed from intermediate "strange waters," all converging into one current or channel and irresistibly impelled forward. It passes over *shallows*, betraying a restless and erratic course; but almost imperceptibly it finds itself mixed with the great gulf-stream which swallows it up, and thus loses all original identity and independence of action and existence.

As a theologian, accounting for his religious persuasions, and as a champion of the principles and dogmas of his adopted Church, Dr. Newman is weak, puerile, illogical, and at all times unsatisfactory. I venture to assert that there is no one argument or statement, purporting to account for the change of mind of the author, which will satisfy a Romanist or a doubting Protestant.

I give two examples to illustrate my meaning. On the doctrine of the "Immaculate Conception" Dr. Newman lays down the following extraordinary proposition:—

"I have no difficulty in receiving it: if *I* have no difficulty, why may not another have no difficulty also? Why may not a hundred? a thousand?"*

I have no difficulty in receiving the proposition that Romanism is an imposture and delusion: if *I* have no difficulty, why may not another have no difficulty also? Why may not a hundred? a thousand?

Such is the puerility of Dr. Newman's reasoning

---

* "Apologia," p. 393.

when on points of faith; I find none more logical. The following is another specimen:—

"People say that the doctrine of Transubstantiation is difficult to believe; I did not believe the doctrine till I was a Catholic. I had no difficulty in believing it as soon as I believed that the Catholic Roman Church was the oracle of God, and that she had declared this doctrine to be part of the original revelation. It is difficult, impossible to imagine, I grant;—but how is it difficult to believe?"*

Throughout the "Apologia," or the "History of my Religious Opinions," there is not one single reason given more to the point for believing in the other dogmas of Romanism, than for believing in that huge monstrosity Transubstantiation, which Robert Montgomery aptly illustrated by the line—

"It profanes the soul, and parodies our God."

The reader must pardon me for dwelling a moment on this extract. When Dr. Newman became "a Catholic" he believed at once in Transubstantiation. The belief in the conversion of the consecrated bread and wine into the body, blood, bones, nerves, soul and divinity of our Lord Christ, the very body which was born of the Virgin Mary, and was crucified, and ascended into heaven, was with Dr. Newman immediately consequent on the belief that the Roman Church was the "oracle of God." But whence came the belief that the Roman Church is the oracle of God? Is it declared so to be in the WORD OF GOD? by any apostolical or ecclesiastical tradition of the Christian Church? is it stated to be so in any ecclesiastical writer for 600 years after Christ? I emphatically answer No! There is not one tittle of evidence that the Roman Church is the "oracle of God;" or that she was authorized to declare Transubstantiation to

* "Apologia," p 374.

" be part of the original revelation," or that it is so in fact.

Dr. Newman assumes the major, that the Roman Church is the oracle of God; he then asserts that the Church has declared the doctrine of Transubstantiation to be part of the original revelation, and, *therefore*, he has no difficulty in believing the doctrine itself! It is an undeniable and uncontradicted fact, that the alleged Transubstantiation of the elements was not a doctrine of the Roman Church previous to A.D. 1215, when it was for the first time raised to a *quasi* doctrine by the 4th Lateran Council;* I say " *quasi* doctrine," for even after that date, and up to the Trent Council, Roman doctors freely speculated on the subject. That it was not believed to be a part of original revelation, is admitted by the most learned of the Roman Church.† Indeed, the learned Cardinal Cajetan frankly admits, that that fact which the Gospel has not expressed, viz., the conversion of the bread into the body and blood of Christ, Romanists have received expressly from the Church, and, therefore, not from revelation.‡ It comes to this,—the Roman Church declares itself to be the oracle of God; she invents a dogma, alleges it to be a part of the original revelation without proof, and then imposes it for belief; and Dr. Newman, who hitherto disbelieved the dogma, now believes it, because the Roman Church says that she is the oracle of God! This, then, is a fair sample of the theological depart-

---

* " Unum addit Scotus, quod minimè probandum, quòd ante Lateranense concilium non fuisset dogma fidei."—Bellarm., lib. iii., de Euchar., cap. xxiii, sect. 12, p. 337, tom. iii. Prag., 1721.

† The reader is referred to several authorities extracted from the works of Cardinal Biel, Cardinal Alliaco, Bishop Fisher, Durandus, Cardinal Cajetan, and Cardinal Bellarmine, in proof of this assertion, in the new edition of Humphrey Lynde's " Via Tuta." London, 1850, pp. 33, 35.

‡ " Quod Evangelium non explicavit expressè, ab Ecclesia accepimus, viz., conversionem panis in corpus Christi."—Cajetan, tom. iii. q. 75, ar. i. p. 130, col. 1. Venet., 1612.

ment of the "Apologia." Truly, indeed, has Dr. Newman estimated his own character and importance when he said, "Persons and things look great at a distance, which are not so when seen close;" and he adds that, did we know him, "we would see that he was one about whom there has been far more talk for good or bad than he deserves, and about whose movements far more expectation has been raised than the event will justify."*

In the first part Dr. Newman appears to be in his element; his style is pointed and pungent. We can only adopt his own comparison—he is "the wounded brute at bay."† He is at times sarcastic, at times playful.

As a controversialist, or polemic writer, particularly on the defence, Dr. Newman's style is terse, his points well put, and he deals with his opponent in a manner which secures for him the sympathies of his readers; be it remembered always, the reader who is contented with Dr. Newman's version and manner of presenting his opponent's argument. Many have not time to read both sides of the question; others do not care to read more than what is advanced by their own side. Dr. Newman is quite alive to this, and knows how to take advantage of it. The two following passages may be taken as fair samples of his style:—

"The apostle bids us, 'in *malice* be children, but in *understanding* be men.' I am glad to recognise in Mr. Kingsley an illustration of the first half of this precept; but I should not be honest if I ascribed to him any sort of fulfilment of the second." ‡

"He (Mr. Kingsley) need not commit himself to a definite accusation against me, such as requires definite proof and admits of definite refutation; for he has two strings to his bow;—when he is thrown off his balance

---

* See Dr. Newman's letter to Dr. Wiseman on leaving the Church of England, November, 1845, "Apologia," p. 367.

† "Apologia," p. 289.   ‡ Ibid. p. 6.

on the one leg, he can recover himself by the use of the other. If I demonstrate that I am not a knave, he may exclaim, 'Oh, but you are a fool!' and when I demonstrate that I am not a fool, he may turn round and retort, 'Well, then, you are a knave.' I have no objection to reply to his arguments in behalf of either alternative; but I should have been better pleased to have been allowed to take them one at a time." *

It has been a matter of surprise that, in controversy, there is less charity displayed and more vituperation expended on questions of religion, than on any other subject. The *odium theologicum* has become a proverb. Dr. Newman and the Rev. Charles Kingsley, it would appear, are not exceptions, at least the latter, if we take Dr. Newman's "*consensus*" of his arguments. The "Apologia" appears ostensibly as a reply to Mr. Kingsley's attacks, as well on the works as the personal character of Dr. Newman. The doctor undertakes to vindicate both. The combatants are doubtless men of classical attainments; and we must admit as a self-evident proposition, which Dr. Newman lays down early in his book, "that minds in different states and circumstances cannot understand one another; and that in all cases they must be instructed according to their capacity, and, if not taught step by step, they learn only so much the less." † I do not, however, see the force of the argument or its application; but that is not our affair. I have already expressed my opinion as to Dr. Newman's capacity on theological questions. If Dr. Newman considers, by turning Romanist, he is at the top of the ladder and Mr. Kingsley at the bottom, he may possibly be mistaken.

It is deeply to be regretted that a subject so sacred, so momentous, as the Christianity we mutually profess, should give rise to such bitter feelings, and should have led to the most cruel persecutions. But so it is,

---

* "Apologia," p. 8.   † Ibid. p. 4.

and so perhaps it ever will be, until that happy millennium shall come, when the "wolf shall dwell with the lamb, and the leopard shall lie down with the kid; and the calf, and the young lion, and the fatling together, and a little child shall lead them."*

It is certainly very trying to one's self-respect to be accused of "untruthfulness;" to be told that one "cannot believe what you are saying;" that you are one possessed with "a spirit of almost boundless silliness and simple credulity;" that you are a "child of scepticism and of absurdity;" that you are labouring under a "self-deception which has become a sort of frantic honesty;" † that you are associated with the "odious names" of Liguori, Scavini, and Neyraguet, and other "Romish moralists," and their compeers and pupils; and that you are "at once merged and hurled away in the gulph of notorious quibblers, and hypocrites, and rogues." ‡ It is not pleasant to have it insinuated that to be a "pure, germane, genuine [Roman] Catholic, a man must be either a knave or a fool." Nor is it palatable to be accused of being secretly a [Roman] Catholic "when openly professing to be a clergyman of the Established Church." After this manner does Dr. Newman take a lesson from Junius in his celebrated letters to Sir William Draper, wherein he intimates that "an academical education had given him an unlimited command over the most beautiful figures of speech. Masks, hatchets, racks, and vipers, dance through his letters in all the mazes of metaphorical confusion—the gloomy companions of a disturbed imagination; the melancholy madness of poetry without the inspiration." So Dr. Newman takes advantage of his opponent, and strings together, with-

---

* Isaiah, x ████ † "Apologia" pp. 6, 7, 8, and 20.

‡ In justice to Mr. Kingsley we ought to add that these last epithets are Dr. Newman's own deduction,—logical, we have no doubt; he having been accused by Mr. Kingsley of associating, theologically speaking, with the individuals enumerated.

out the probably justifying context, a series of epithets and passages, of which I have given a sample, for the Rev. Mr. Kingsley's attack, and thus endeavours to secure beforehand the sympathies of the reader, and lead him to believe that he (Dr. Newman) is a persecuted martyr, dragged from the seclusion of his "Oratory;" and in his anguish he exclaims,* "Why will you not let me die in peace? Wounded brutes creep into some hole to die in, and no one grudges it them. Let me alone; I shall not trouble you long."

My task is not to vindicate Mr. Kingsley; he is in safe keeping in his own hands. My present object is to take in view the "Apologia," so far as time and space will permit.

The grave charge which Dr. Newman appears most desirous of repelling is an alleged "untruthfulness" in his actions. "I do not like (he says†) to be called to my face a liar and a knave; nor should I be doing my duty to my faith or to my name, if I were to suffer it. I know I have done nothing to deserve such an insult; and if I prove this, as I hope to do, I must not care for such incidental annoyances as are involved in the process;" and, with this object in view, namely, to repel the charge of untruthfulness, he leaves his opponent and dives into the "Apologia pro vitâ suâ," giving his assailant a flying kick as he passes from one subject to the other. "And now (he says‡) I am in a train of thought higher and more serene than any which slander can disturb. Away with you, Mr. Kingsley, and fly into space. Your name shall occur again as little as I can help in the course of these pages. I shall henceforth occupy myself, not with you, but your charges."

* "Apologia," p. 289.   † Ibid. p. 51.   ‡ Ibid. p. 25.

And so I too leave the "matters personal," to follow Dr. Newman in his own vindication.

I have said that Dr. Newman affects to be deeply grieved at the charge of "untruthfulness;" that he should be accused of being secretly a Romanist when he was openly professing to be a clergyman of the Established Church; that he was, in fact, secretly teaching Romish doctrines. When brought to bay, he "confesses and avoids" and fences. He irreverently and flippantly retorts that "two can play at that." By selecting passages from one or other of the old English divines—Bramhall, Andrews, Hooker, Hammond, Thorndike, Bull, Pearson, &c.—he says he could sanction all his popish tendencies. He also finds the doctrine of *absolution* clearly laid down and sanctioned by our Prayer-book, and private "confession" practised and sanctioned by the same authority; and in the Homilies he professes to find a sanction for every phase of Romanism to justify all his vagaries. If such be the fact, and he was justified in his conscience that what he did was under such high patronage, what need was there of leaving us? But he found that if Bramhall and Thorndike, and others, somewhere in their writings, now and then taught popery (of which, by the way, he gives not the slightest evidence), popery was not the religion of the Church of England, and that popery was abhorred by the people of this country. He found that, if *absolution* was taught in the Anglican Church, it was on a very different system than that of popish absolution, where the priest assumes the office of judge, representing Jesus Christ, making his absolution a judicial act; whereas the Anglican priest prays for the penitent, but leaves the absolution to God, declaring that, "He pardoneth and absolveth all them that truly repent and unfeignedly believe His holy Gospel." Nor does the Anglican presume to take upon himself to accept a person in the tribunal of penance, armed with the Romish invention of "attrition," that is, with no true "contrition" in his heart for the love of God and hatred of sin. Dr. Newman found also that confession was optional. If a penitent was moved to confess his sin, and seek ghostly comfort from the minister of God, he was invited to do so, with a hope of reconciliation with his God. But that was not enough for Dr. Newman. He required more than he could exact in our Church—a compulsory confession—ay, a full and particular confession of every sin, to be made at least once a year, under pain of eternal damnation; so he went over to Rome; but whether he has bettered his position is a secret he has kept close in his own bosom. But the Homilies were his great sheet-anchor. "What (says he) if it should turn out that the very men who drew up the Articles, in the very act of doing so had avowed, or, rather, in one of these very articles themselves, had imposed on subscribers a number of those 'Papistical' doctrines which they were now thought to deny, as part and parcel of that very Protestantism which they were now thought to consider divine?" He alleges that this was the fact. He showed it in his Essay, and now proceeds to show it in his "Apologia,"[*] and we have the same repeated in the "History of his Religious Opinions." Dr. Newman reminds us that the 35th Article recognizes the Homilies as containing "godly and wholesome doctrine as necessary for these times." He then professes to quote twenty-six "separate theses" from these Homilies to prove "that the men who wrote the Homilies, and who thus incorporated them into the Anglican system of doctrine, could not have possessed that exact discrimination between the Catholic and Protestant faith, or have made that clear recognition of formal Protestant principles and tenets, or have accepted that definition of 'Roman doctrine' which is received at this day: hence, great probability accrued

---

[*] Pp. 164—167.

to his (Dr. Newman's) presentiment that the Articles were tolerant, not only of what he called 'Catholic teaching,' but of much that was 'Roman.'"* In other words, Dr. Newman proposes to justify his Romish teaching while an Anglican minister, by the citations he now offers from the Homilies. We have all heard of the Atheist who proposed to prove from the Bible a justification of his belief. He quoted the inspired Psalmist (xiv. 1), who said, "There is no God;" but we turn to the text and we find that "the fool hath said in his heart There is no God;" and it is precisely on this principle that Dr. Newman proceeds to establish his bold allegation.

The propositions are entered under separate numbers in succession, prepared with precision and evident care, each professing to sanction some dogma or practice of the Roman Church.

In order to establish the right of "Excommunication," Dr. Newman quotes from a Homily:—

"That the puissant and mighty Emperor Theodosius was in the primitive Church, which was most holy and godly, excommunicated by St. Ambrose."

But Dr. Newman has overlooked a subsequent passage on this subject:—

"Christ ordained the authority of the keys to excommunicate notorious sinners, and to absolve them which are truly penitent; they [the Popes] abuse this power at their own pleasure, as well in cursing the godly with bell, book, and candle, as also in absolving the reprobate, which are known to be unworthy of any Christian society, whereof he that lust to see examples, let him search their lives."†

We do not find that the Homilies recognize the Popish custom of absolving soldiers and subjects from their oaths of allegiance from sovereigns who differ

---

* "Apologia," p. 167.
† Ibid. p. 495. I quote here the edition 1864 of the Homilies printed by the Society for Promoting Christian Knowledge.

from them on points of religion, or for any other reason.

The doctrine of the seven sacraments is one insisted upon by the Roman Church under pain of eternal damnation.

Dr. Newman would have us believe that the Homilies teach this Roman doctrine.

The following are his statements or "theses:"—

" That ordination is a sacrament."

" That matrimony is a sacrament."

" That there are other sacraments besides Baptism and the Lord's Supper."

Now the Roman Church declares that there are *no more nor no less than seven sacraments, all ordained by Christ,* that is, five—(confirmation, penance, matrimony, extreme unction, and orders)—in addition to the two—Baptism and the Lord's Supper, alone acknowledged by all Protestant Churches. Dr. Newman would have his readers believe that the Homilies specially recognize " orders and matrimony " as sacraments, and others not named, beyond the two admitted by us. I turn to the " Homily of Common Prayer and Sacraments," and I find that Dr. Newman's statement is directly contradicted. The passage, and only passage, in the Homilies referring to this subject is as follows:—

"Now with the like, or rather more brevity, you shall hear how many sacraments there be that were instituted by our Saviour Christ, and are to be continued and received of every Christian in due time of order, and for such purpose as our Saviour Christ willed them to be received; and as for the number of them, if they should be considered according to the exact signification of a sacrament, namely,— the visible signs expressly commanded in the New Testament, whereunto is annexed the promise of free forgiveness of our sin, and of our holiness, and joining with Christ, *there be but two, namely,—Baptism and the Supper of the Lord.* For although absolution hath the promise of forgiveness of sin, yet by the express word of the New Testament it hath not the promise annexed and tied to the invisible sign, which is imposition of hands,—*and therefore absolution is no such sacrament as baptism and the communion are.* And though the *ordering of ministers* hath this visible sign and promise, yet it lacks the promise of remission of sin, as all other sacraments besides do. Therefore, neither it nor any other sacrament else, be such sacraments as baptism and the communion are. But in a general acceptation the name of a sacrament may be attributed to any thing whereby an holy thing is signified. In which understanding of the word the ancient writers have given this name, *not only to the other five commonly of late years taken and used for supplying the number of seven sacraments*, but also to divers and sundry other ceremonies, as to oil, washing of feet, and such like; not meaning thereby to repute them as sacraments in the same signification that the two fore-named sacraments are; and although there are retained by the order of the Church of England, besides these two, *certain other rites and ceremonies about the institution of ministers* in the Church, *matrimony*, confirmation of children—and likewise for visiting of the sick; yet no man ought to take these for sacraments in such signification of meaning as the sacrament of Baptism and the Lord's Supper are, but either for godly states of life necessary in Christ's Church, and therefore worthy to be set forth by public action and solemnity by the ministry of the Church, or else judged to be such ordinances as may make for the instruction, comfort, and edification of Christ's Church."*

Let the reader compare this clear statement with Dr. Newman's garbled version, and estimate the amount of credit that can be attached to Dr. Newman for love of truth and fair dealing.

On the popular subject of saint-worship Dr. Newman reminds us that the Homilies admit—

"That the souls of the saints are reigning in joy, and in heaven, with God."

This is the truth, but not the whole truth. The Church of Rome invites an invocation of these saints. Romanists pray to them, and seek their mercy and intercession, and plead their supposed merits. To believe that saints are reigning with Christ is only to believe with St. Paul, that "to be absent from the body is to be present with the Lord." But did Dr. Newman not know that the Homilies, particularly that "Concerning prayer" and "Against peril of idolatry," most clearly and emphatically condemn the Roman custom of invocation of saints as idolatrous

* Homilies, pp. 376-7-8.

and superstitious, and point to the fact, that Romanists have practically the same opinion of their saints as the Gentiles had of their gods, or "Dii Patroni"?* And though the saints may be reigning with Christ, the Homily points out that they know nothing of our prayers, and invite us to Christ alone as our only Mediator.†

Dr. Newman would insinuate that the compilers, while admitting the purity of the Primitive Church, by inference admit the purity of the modern Roman Church :—

"That the Primitive Church, next to the Apostles' time, as they imply, for almost 700 years, is no doubt most pure.

"But the Primitive Church is specially to be followed."

There being no reference, it is difficult to find the parts supposed to be relied on, and particularly the alleged period of 700 years.

As an historical fact, the great bulk of Roman doctrinal corruptions came in after the 700 years, though some were then maturing.‡ The Homilies do refer to the purity of the Primitive Church; but it was in comparison with the gross and corrupted state of Christianity when they were put forth, A.D. 1562. In the Homily, "Of the right use of the Church," referring to the custom of "penance," as practised in the early Church, there is this passage:§ "And according to this example of our Saviour, in the Primitive Church (which was most holy and godly, and in the which due discipline, with severity, was used against the wicked) open offenders were not suffered once to enter the house of the Lord, &c., until they had done open penance before the whole Church, which primitive custom has been most grossly perverted by the

---

* Homilies, pp. 235, 343, 344. † Ibid. p. 344.
‡ See "Novelties of Romanism," by C. H. Collette. Religious Tract Society. Price 4s. § Homilies, p. 177.

Roman Church by her so-called sacrament of penance, and issue of indulgences.

The next mention of the Primitive Church is in the first part of the Homily, "Against peril of idolatry," pointing out the "peril of idolatry, and superfluous decking of churches." These outward "ceremonies, or costly and glorious decking of the said house or temple of the Lord," are denounced as contrary "to the most manifest doctrine of the Scriptures, and contrary to the usages of the Primitive Church, which was most pure and uncorrupt, and contrary to the sentences and judgments of the most ancient, learned, and godly doctors of the Church," condemning "the corruption of these latter days, which hath brought into the Church infinite multitude of images," &c.;* and the Homily goes on to condemn these images and decorations as "that vice, of all others in the Scriptures, peculiarly called *idolatry*, or worshipping of images."

Dr. Newman is particularly unhappy in his selections from the Homilies.

The next reference to the Primitive Church is in the second part of the same Homily, where the "doctrine concerning the forbidding of images and worshipping of them," taken out of the Scripture, as "believed and taught by the old holy fathers and most ancient learned doctors, and received in the old Primitive Church, was most uncorrupt and pure."† And in p. 199 we are informed, after quoting the well-known passage of Epiphanius, that "it is an evident proof that in those days, which were about 400 years after our Saviour Christ, there were no images publicly used and received in the Church of Christ, which was then less corrupt and more pure than now it is;" and, in summing up the subject, it says that, "by the judgment of the old, learned, and godly doctors of the Church, and by ancient histories ecclesiastical agreeing

---

* Homilies, p. 180. † Ibid. p. 195

to the verity of God's word — images and image-worshipping were in the Primitive Church, which was most pure and uncorrupt, abhorred and detested as abominable, and contrary to true Christian religion."*

And again, when condemning the dedication of churches to saints, &c., we read, "until the time of Constantine, by the space of above 300 years after our Saviour Christ, when the Christian religion was most pure, and, indeed, golden, Christians had but low and poor conventicles, and simple oratories," &c.†

And lastly, while it is true that the Homilies declare that "the Primitive Church is especially to be followed as most incorrupt and pure;" yet it adds the reason, because they "had publicly in churches neither idols of the Gentiles, nor any other images or things directly forbidden by God's word."‡

I believe there is not another reference to the Primitive Church. I now ask Dr. Newman what he means to infer by appealing to the Homilies as upholding the Primitive Church as a pattern of purity? Does he pretend that the Church of his present adoption follows the Primitive Church in those points commended as a pattern by the Homilies? If he does not mean that, then his reference is a delusion, it savours of untruthfulness; it bears the taint of the system alleged against the members of his Church, of using phrases bearing a double meaning, and quoted to mislead and deceive.

In order to sanction the doctrine of "tradition," Dr. Newman presents the following "thesis," as from the Homilies:—

"Again, they speak of a certain truth which they are enforcing, as declared by God's word, the sentences of the ancient doctors, and judgment of the Primitive Church."

* Homilies, p. 222. † Ibid. p. 235 and p. 268.
‡ Ibid. p. 231.

"Of the learned and holy bishops and doctors of the first eight centuries, being of good authority and credit with the people."

"Of the declaration of Christ and His apostles, and all the rest of the Holy Fathers."

"Of the authority of both Scripture and also of Augustine."

What is here intended to be inferred, though Dr. Newman does not declare it, is that the Homilies recognize *tradition* as handed down by the Fathers, as of equal authority with the Scriptures. Such is the doctrine of the Roman Church. Dr. Newman knows full well that throughout the Homilies the Holy Scriptures are put forth as the alone rule of faith; and the fathers and doctors of the Primitive Church are quoted for the sole purpose of confirming that great fact and cardinal point of Protestant teaching. And I could not take, perhaps, a better example than the confirmation by the Fathers of the doctrine and teaching of Scripture, as to the forbidding the use of images in religious worship, and that of the practice of the Primitive Church on that subject above referred to. The very first Homily, "A fruitful exhortation to the reading and knowledge of Holy Scripture," is a refutation of Dr. Newman's insinuation. The very first passage is:—

"Unto a Christian there can be nothing either more necessary or profitable than the knowledge of Holy Scripture; forasmuch as in it is contained God's true word, setting forth His glory and also man's duty. *And there is no truth nor doctrine necessary for our justification and everlasting salvation*, but that is or may *be drawn out of that fountain and well of truth*."*

And with reference to *tradition* this Homily proceeds:

"Let us diligently search for the well of life in the books of the New and Old Testament, and not run to the stinking puddles of men's traditions, devised by men's imaginations, for our justification and salvation."†

Is there any need of further inquiry on this point?

* Homilies, p. 1. † Ibid. p. 2.

On the subject of the Eucharist he says—

"That the ancient Catholic Fathers say that the 'Lord's Supper' is the salve of immortality, the sovereign preservative against death, the food of immortality, the healthful grace."

These words appear as the saying of "some of the Fathers;" and Dr. Newman's application, as a Romanist, of the passage is to show the supposed efficacy of the fact of partaking of the consecrated elements, and the supposed grace conferred "*ex opere operato,*" from the fact of partaking of the sacrament; also, the basis of the doctrine of the conversion of the elements called transubstantiation. But the passage in its entirety explains itself, and if allowed to be completed, gives a very different turn, and an eminently Scriptural and Protestant view,—"All which sayings, both of the Holy Scriptures and godly men," attributed to this "celestial banquet," the Homily takes care to point out, are not said "as specially regarding the terrene and earthly creature [viz. the bread and wine], but always holding fast, and cleaving by faith to the ROCK, whence we may suck the sweetness of everlasting salvation."* The reason, therefore, for quoting part of this passage and not quoting the other part, which explains that which is quoted, is too obvious to dwell upon.

Again, Dr. Newman informs us on the same subject, that the Homilies teach—

"That the Lord's blessed body and blood are received under the form of bread and wine."

"That the meat in the sacrament is an invisible, and a ghostly sustenance."

I cannot find the first passage; but Dr. Newman means to convey that the Homilies here teach the real corporeal presence, as in his Church. But what saith the "Homily" (continuing the passage last above

* Homilies, p. 476.

quoted) in following Christ's institution of this sacrament?

We are warned that we must acknowledge " no other Saviour, Redeemer, Mediator, Advocate, Intercessor, but Christ only; for this is to stick fast to Christ's promise made in His institution, to make Christ thine own, and to apply His merits unto thyself. Herein thou needest no other man's help, no other sacrifice or oblation, no sacrificing priest, no mass, no means established by man's invention;" and we are informed " that faith is a necessary instrument in all these holy ceremonies." " And, truly, as the bodily meat cannot feed the outward man, unless it be led into a stomach to be digested, which is healthsome and sound, no more can the inward man be fed, except his meat be received into his soul and heart, sound and whole in faith. It is well known that the meat we seek for in His supper *is spiritual food, the nourishment of our soul;* a heavenly refection and not earthly, an invisible meat and not bodily, a ghostly sustenance and not carnal; so that to think that without faith we may enjoy the eating and drinking thereof, or that that is the fruition of it, is but to dream a gross carnal feeding, basely objecting and binding ourselves to the elements of creatures."*

Is this fair dealing? Is Dr. Newman truthful in his quotation in this respect?

A leading error of the Roman Church is to make good works *per se* meritorious and deserving of reward; in fact, a means of our justification. Indeed, they go so far as to impose fasting, alms-deeds, prayers, and other good works, as *punishments*—" satisfactions," as they call them—for sins (supposed to be) forgiven in the tribunal of penance, as if " good works," performed as a punishment, can be made so pleasing to the Almighty as to merit a forgiveness of the consequences of sin. The belief in the theory is necessary to the system.

* Homilies, p. 478.

But the contrary doctrine, taught by Augustine, is essentially the present teaching of the Anglican Church—" that we are not justified by preceding good works, because we attain to justification not by merit but by grace;" " for good works are rather the consequence of justification than the predisposing means which lead to justification."* Augustine adds, " The works which are done without faith, though they seem good, are turned into sin;"† and the noted passage of Augustine, " When God crowns our merits [that is, good works] He crowns nothing else but His own gifts," was so offensive to the Romish theory of justification, that it was ordered to be expunged from his works by the compilers of the Expurgatory Index. Hence Dr. Newman's anxiety to show that the Homilies teach the meritoriousness of good works, and for this purpose he quotes a detached passage :—

" That alms-deeds purge the soul from the infection and filthy spots of sin, and are a precious medicine, an inestimable jewel."

The passage is not exactly correct. The Homily says that we are taught by the text, Luke xi. 41, " that merciful alms-dealing is profitable to purge the soul," &c. But the Homily adds, that the meaning of the promise is, " that in doing these things, according to God's will and our duty—not for the worthiness of them, but by the grace of God, ' which worketh all in all '—alms-deeds do wash away our sins, because God doth vouchsafe these to repute us as clean and pure, when we do them for His sake, and not because they deserve or merit our purging, or for that they have any such strength and virtue in themselves."‡

Dr. Newman may or may not subscribe to this

---

* *Opera*, tom. iv. p. 138, H. Venetiis, 1552; and " De Fide et Operibus," c. 14, 1 c., p. 16, D.

† " Sine fide etiam quæ videntur bona opera in peccata vertuntur."—*Cont. duos Ep. Pelag. ad Bonif.*, p. 457, tom. xvi. Paris, 1690.

‡ Pp. 416, 417.

doctrine. It nevertheless is the teaching of the Homilies, and his attempted perversion is an evidence, if not of "want of truthfulness," at least a suppression of truth, and equally tends to mislead.

Alms-deeds and charity are strongly recommended and urged in the Homilies as a godly work; and deservedly so, for Christ promised a reward unto them that give "but a cup of cold water;" but it must be in His name.*

Again, Dr. Newman quotes:—

"The duty of fasting is a truth more manifest than it should need to be proved."

"That fasting used with prayer is of good efficacy, and weigheth much with God."

Fasting in the Roman Church is imposed as a penitential work—a punishment for sin. Periodical fastings with them are imposed as a law. Fasting, therefore, is not generally a spontaneous act with the great bulk of Romanists. The order is executed in pursuance of a command, not from a spontaneous love to serve God for a good end, but to obtain a reward for the act performed, or to cancel the debt due to a sin supposed to be forgiven in the so-called sacrament of penance. When, therefore, Dr. Newman quoted this Homily to prove his orthodoxy, he should have added the explanation given by the Homily as to what it meant. We are instructed in the true value of works and acts.

"Good works come of themselves, and of their own proper nature are always good; as, to love God above all things, to love our neighbours as ourselves, &c. And such like other works there be, which considered in themselves without further respect, are of their own nature mere indifferent, that is, neither good nor evil, but take their denomination of the use or end whereunto they serve. Which works, having a good end, are called good works, and are so indeed; but yet that cometh not of themselves, but of the good end whereunto they are referred. On the other side, if the end that they serve unto be evil, it cannot than otherwise be but that they must needs be evil also.

---

* Mark ix. 41, x. 42.

Of this sort of works is fasting, which of itself is a thing merely indifferent, but is made better or worse by the end that it serveth unto.—To fast, then, with this persuasion of mind, that our fasting and other good works can make us good, perfect, and just men, and finally bring us to heaven, this is a devilish persuasion, and that fast so far off from pleasing God that it refuseth His mercy, and is altogether derogatory to the merits of Christ's death and His precious bloodshedding."*

The prescribed fasting of Rome, say of Lent, preceded or followed by feasting and festivities—a *fasting* as a prescribed penance, as a compounding of punishment, and the like, comes exactly within the condemned category, as " a devilish persuasion." But the Homily proceeds to show what the true end of fasting is, and also, " that time is meet for fasting, for all times serve not for all things;"† showing that " the outward fast of the body is no fast before God, except it be accompanied with the inward fast, which is a mourning and a lamentation in the heart."‡ " Fasting *thus*, used with prayer," adds the Homily—and Dr. Newman omits this all-important word THUS—" is of great efficacy, and weigheth much with God."§

Has Dr. Newman proved his case from the Homilies; and has he bettered his position by adopting the empty, senseless, and prescribed forms of the Roman Church? Let the reader judge.

If Dr. Newman, instead of attempting to pervert the clear teaching of the Homilies, in order to shield himself from the imputation of teaching heretical doctrines while a professed minister of the Church of England, had acted up to the wise and godly counsels contained in these Homilies, he would have been instructed in holy and wholesome doctrines, and preserved from the lamentable exhibition he has made of himself by his misquotations. He would have been satisfied that the compilers of the Homilies had such clear perception of that " exact discrimination between the [Roman]

---

* Homilies, p. 297. † Ibid. p. 306.
‡ Ibid. p. 306. § Ibid. p. 307.

Catholic and Protestant faith," as to come to a very decided conclusion that the Roman Church was a false and apostate church; and we cannot sufficiently admire the boldness of a man who appeals to such an authority as sanctioning his most extraordinary and erratic proceeding.

To go through the Homilies, and transcribe the passages condemnatory of the Romish system called a religion, would be almost to transcribe the Homilies themselves. They are replete with exposures and denunciations of Romanism in every phase. It is, indeed, a matter of surprise that, in this early stage of the Reformation (1562), our divines were able so completely to shake off the superstitions and delusions of a religious system which had for so many years obscured Christianity.

The fatal shoal on which Dr. Newman seems, at least according to his own confession, to have made shipwreck, was in his attempt to reconcile Anglicanism with Popery; and as to the Thirty-nine Articles, to " ascertain what was the limit of their elasticity in the direction of Roman dogma."* The Articles, he said, " do not oppose Catholic teaching; they but partially oppose Roman dogma; they for the most part oppose the dominant errors of Rome. The problem was to draw the line as to what they allowed and what they condemned."† But instead of honestly applying himself to the fair interpretation of these Articles, he sets about " widening and defining them." The prospect, he says, was " encouraging," as there was " no doubt of their elasticity;" and then, with a great deal of sophistical talking, but which ordinary persons would call " a learned way of talking nonsense," he cut out

* "Apologia," p. 160. † Ibid. p. 160.

for himself a *via media*, a middle course, or what we should call 'a halting between two opinions,' "without any positive Anglican theory; very nearly a Protestant, but without any theology."*

What Dr. Newman's idea of a *via media* was at this time, is rather startling for a professed Anglican minister. "I considered," he says,† "that to make the *via media* concrete and substantive, it must be much more than it was in outline; that the Anglican Church must have a ceremonial, a ritual, and a fulness of doctrine and devotion, which it had not at present, if it were to compete with the Romish Church with any prospect of success." One would suppose that Dr. Newman was looking to some secular rival establishments of entertainment, which should produce the most attractive exhibition. The idea of one Christian Church competing with another in ceremonials and rituals! And in what was this competition to consist? The notion is rather strange for a professed Protestant minister; or, if that term is offensive, for a minister of the Anglican Church. The "instances" proposed are "confraternities, particular devotions [the scapulars and rosaries no doubt], reverence for the Blessed Virgin, prayers for the dead, beautiful churches, munificent offerings to them and in them, monastic houses, and many observances and institutions, which he used to say belonged to us [the English Church], as to Rome;" but not one word of spiritual-mindedness, of love to Christ, or zeal for His holy religion. However, during 1841-45 we find him sailing along, taking this *via media* for his course; until his faith, weak, wavering, undecided, met two rude shocks, which shattered the frail bark. Having no ballast, it foundered.

"He that wavereth is like a wave of the sea driven with the wind and tossed. For let not that man think that he shall receive anything of the Lord."‡

---

* "Apologia," p. 216. † Ibid. p. 281. ‡ James, vi. 7.

And what was this shoal on which the waves first cast this frail bark, this floating bubble? It was only a ghost! it was a mirage, the invention of a weak and diseased brain. "Hardly had he brought his course of reading to a close" than this ghost appeared. It appeared to him in the shape of an article written by Dr. Wiseman in the *Dublin Review* of August, 1839, on "The Anglican Claims." At first it made no great impression on him; but a friend (mark how weak and dependent on the opinions of others was Dr. Newman!) pointed out the words "Securus judicat orbis terrarum," as having been uttered by Augustine. This was the ghost,—" the words kept ringing in his ears,"—"Securus judicat orbis terrarum" (*Anglice*— "What every one says must be true"). "These words," Dr. Newman assures us, " decided ecclesiastical questions on a simpler rule than that of antiquity; nay St. Augustine was one of the prime oracles of antiquity;—here then antiquity was deciding against itself."* Did ever any one read such miserable trash! For a mere sentence, the words of St. Augustine, struck him with a power which he never had felt from any words before—they were like the "Turn again Whittington" of the chime.—"By these great words of the ancient father, the theory of the *via media* was absolutely pulverized,"† and his ballast-less vessel was left helpless on the barren strand. The ghost quickly changed its form, and the chime changed to another tune. This time it was "the Church of Rome will be found right after all!" The phantom "now vanished, and his old convictions remained as before." But, nevertheless, he "had seen the shadow of a hand upon the wall." The ghost was seen, which seemed to say, "Tolle, lege—tolle, lege!" and "He who has seen a ghost cannot be as if he had never seen it."‡ Oh sage

---

* "Apologia," p. 212. † Ibid. p. 212.
‡ Ibid. p. 213.

—but superstitious Dr. Newman! By the way, he admits that he was superstitious from a school-boy.

Had Dr. Newman been occupied with the WORD OF GOD instead of, as a Homily says, "the stinking puddles" of the traditions of men, the Spirit would have moved him for good. The hand would have pointed to the warning text of Paul to the Ephesians,* and traced "Tolle, lege—tolle, lege." "Be no more children tossed to and fro, and carried about with every wind of doctrine, by the sleight of men, and cunning craftiness, whereby they lie in wait to deceive; but speaking the truth in love, may grow up into Him in all things, which is the head, even Christ." From the *via media* he would have been guided to the *via tuta* instead of the *via devia*.

An article in the *Dublin Review*, an essentially popish periodical, written by a most subtle Jesuit—Dr. Wiseman—wherein Augustine, an African bishop of the fifth century, is alleged to have conveyed some notion not explained by Dr. Newman, in four Latin words, is sufficient to satisfy Dr. Newman that the Church of Rome may be right after all; that they "decided ecclesiastical questions on a simpler rule than that of antiquity." What that rule is he does not say, and the reader is left in profound ignorance what the four cabalistic words, "Securus judicat orbis terrarum," can possibly mean. Dr. Newman, neither in his "History of his Religious Opinions" nor his "Apologia," thinks it worth his while to explain himself; I have therefore consulted the original, on which I shall make a few observations.

In the article in question, Dr. Wiseman begins by declaring, and taking for granted, that the Church of England is in schism—which he says carries with it the charge of heresy. On this false assumption he builds his whole superstructure, and quotes patristic testimony

---

* iv. 14.

to prove the sin of schism. Our alleged sin and schism consist in emancipating ourselves from the tyranny and exactions of the See of Rome, and reverting back to our original ecclesiastical independence, but without renouncing allegiance to CHRIST, or membership of His Universal Church on earth. Dr. Newman has found it convenient to affirm, or perhaps had not the wit to discover, this fallacy, which strikes at the very root of Dr. Wiseman's arguments. We are not in schism *because* the Roman Church says so, any more than the Roman Church will admit herself to be in schism because the Greek Church brings the like charge against her. The Greek Church was anterior in date to the Roman. They were in communion once; they are not so now. The African Church, in which Augustine was a bishop, was as distinct and separate from the Church of Rome as is the Anglican from the Roman at the present day. But the Roman was the more important Church, as being the seat of empire, and the "more potent principality." Her bishops had a primacy of mere order, not of ecclesiastical rank. There were several distinct communions constituting one Catholic or Universal Church. In the days of Augustine a large and powerful sect sprang up, known as the Donatists. These claimed for themselves exclusively the title of "Catholic," and they denied that title to all other Christian communions; exactly in the same manner as the Roman Church now does. In fact the cases are parallel. The Romanists are the Donatists of the present day.* Augustine, as an African bishop, raised

---

* In order to support his theory, Dr. Wiseman, in his endeavour to draw a parallel between the Donatists and "modern Anglicans," makes Augustine's words apply by anticipation to the latter, clearly misrepresenting their respective positions. He says, "For it so happened that the Donatists, like the modern Anglicans, asserted that they were not the separatists, but that the other Churches were." It is not true that the Anglicans charge other Churches with being "separatists." What we maintain is that we are neither schismatics nor heretics, because we have declared our freedom from the usurp-

his voice against this usurpation and scandal, emanating from his own country. He declared that the Donatists, by making this arrogant claim, separated themselves from the entire Christian Church, and thus made themselves schismatics. It was in expressing this opinion that Augustine used the words which had made an impression on, and scared Dr. Newman.

" Quapropter *securus judicat orbis terrarum*, bonos non esse qui se dividunt ab orbe terrarum, in quacumque parte orbis terrarum." That is, "Wherefore, the entire world judges with security, that they are not good, who separate themselves from the entire world, in whatever part of the entire world."

England, somewhere in the 11th or 12th century, became subject to the ecclesiastical jurisdiction of Rome. This subjection continued to exist more or less until the beginning of the 16th century, when the tyranny and exactions of the See of Rome became so intolerable, that the clergy themselves first petitioned the Crown to emancipate this country from the intolerable yoke under which we suffered. England resumed her independence of the See of Rome, and became exactly what the African Church was in relation to other Christian Churches in the days of Augustine. Rome was deprived by this act of what was called "an inexhaustible well," out of which she drew an enormous revenue. On losing this source of wealth she protested, and still protests, and calls the emancipation an act of schism. But we have yet to learn that this act of emancipation is a "separation from the entire world;" and while we may admit that " securus judicat

---

ation of the local Bishop of Rome, and purged our system of modern innovations on the primitive faith, and retained those doctrines only which the Roman Church herself acknowledges to be orthodox. We admit the Roman Church to be a branch of the Catholic or Universal Church, but grossly corrupted. The whole " article" is based on a series of fallacies, so shallow, so apparent, that Dr. Newman exhibits himself in a most equivocal light in giving this *quasi* approval of Dr. Wiseman's assertions.

orbis terrarum"—"the entire world judges with security"—we are not prepared to admit that the judgment of the Roman Church is the judgment "of the entire world."

Augustine expressed the opinion of the entire universal Church, in condemning the exclusive and arrogant claim attempted to be set up by one particular sect of Christians to be *the* Catholic Church, and agreed that such a universal judgment must be right; therefore Dr. Newman concluded that the Church of Rome—to which there was not the remotest allusion even by inference—"will be found right after all."

Such, then, is the flimsy cobweb which first caught this buzzing—gadding—thoughtless fly.

Dr. Newman pretends to convey the idea, by inference that Augustine looked to Rome as the source of ecclesiastical jurisdiction and power.

But this is more than he dare commit to writing, in plain terms. Augustine signed the famous decree of the Council of Milevis, in Africa, which clearly defined the independent ecclesiastical jurisdiction of the Church of Africa; and there is not one single passage throughout his writings which in the remotest way intimates that he or the African Church were subject to the jurisdiction of Rome. And as to doctrine, his writings show that all the leading errors of Romanism (and against which we protest as innovations in Christianity) were by anticipation condemned as heresies; or by inference by plain declarations of the then admitted teaching of the Christian Church. So much was this felt by the Roman Church, that numerous passages are placed in the Expurgatory Index, and it is admitted by Romanists that in the Venice edition of Augustine's works, various passages were removed, lest, forsooth, the readers might be infected with heresy.*

* See Præfat. Ind. Lib. prohib. ad Lectorem. Genevæ, impress. an. 1629. And for a long account of this expurgated edition, see Clement's "Bibliothèque Curieuse," tom. ii. pp. 268—273.

However, the *via media* theory being "thus absolutely pulverized," Dr. Newman's mind was set afloat again on his stormy sea of doubts and difficulties. Just as he thought that he was righting himself, and sailing along again securely in his *via media*, another storm arose, and set him this time fairly on his beam-ends, and "shattered his faith in the Anglican Church."

For centuries, Jerusalem and the East had been given up to the prey of two fanatical parties, the Latins and the Greeks, who had been squabbling over the superstitious relics of Christianity, fighting for the shell when the kernel was gone. The so-called "Holy places" had been the bone of contention and bitter feuds as to who should be their guards, the Greeks or Latins. To such fanaticism did their fury against each other carry them, that Turkish soldiers were obliged to be put over them to keep the peace, to keep them from tearing each other to pieces. In fighting for the Manger, and the supposed Holy Sepulchre, they forgot CHRIST Himself. Truly might it be said of them, "Why seek ye the living among the dead? He is not here, but is risen." (Luke xxiv. 5, 6.*)

The people were left in the most wretched state of ignorance of the first principles of the Christian religion, and religion itself was brought into contempt in the presence of the Jew and the Turk. A conversion was never heard of. The Bible was a forbidden book; the Services a dead letter, being conducted in a language not understood by the people; and schools were unknown. In this state of moral and religious degradation (Christianity could not be lower), the King of Prussia conceived the idea of forwarding a Protestant mission under a bishop, and of making the experiment what preaching the true Gospel could do to

---

* It is an extraordinary fact that the origin of that short but bloody war with Russia, which carried off so many thousands of brave men, originated in this miserable squabble about the right to guard these so-called holy places.—See Kinglake's *Crimea*

bring back the living Christ to the hearts and minds of the people. He suggested that the first bishop should be nominated from England; and that the scheme should be carried out under the auspices of the Church of England.

The Protestant bishopric of Jerusalem was accordingly founded under the authority of an Act of Parliament and the Queen's license; and thus by the will of this nation, and also *with the special consent of the civil authority of the country* where the mission was to be exercised. It was created for the especial purpose of superintending British congregations " and such other Protestant congregations as might be desirous of placing themselves under the authority of such bishops," and with a view, also, to the conversion of the Jews, and to establish schools and colleges in the East. The religious instruction to be given was to be in strict conformity with the doctrines of the United Church of England and Ireland, and under the superintendence and direction of the Bishop. The Bishop's spiritual jurisdiction was to extend over all who might choose to join his Church and place themselves under the episcopal authority in Syria, Chaldea, Egypt, and Abyssinia, according to the laws and canons of the Church of England.

The first bishop nominated from England was consecrated by the Bishops of London, Rochester, and New Zealand. He was a bishop of the United Church of England and Ireland, a suffragan of the province of Canterbury, and not a colonial bishop. The mission is under the especial patronage of the Archbishops of Canterbury and York, the Bishops of London, Durham, Winchester, Lichfield, Manchester, Carlisle, Ripon, and Rochester, besides many of the clergy, noblemen, and gentlemen of England. The Bishop proceeded to his new sphere of action, with a commendatory letter from the Archbishop of Canterbury to the bishops of the Eastern Churches. It was under this distinguished patronage that this mission was founded in 1841. The building of the church was begun with the full and direct sanction of the Ottoman Porte, and in 1847 the Sultan issued his edict of toleration, by which he gave a legal recognition and protection to all members of Oriental churches who should declare and register themselves as Protestants,—in other words, proselytes,—in his dominions. It is worthy of remark that, in May, 1852, the American missionaries presented an address to Lord Stratford de Redcliffe, the English ambassador at Constantinople, in which they declared that "the Protestant bishop in Jerusalem enjoyed the confidence of thousands as a man of apostolic spirit." His Lordship replied: "I listen with pleasure to the praise so justly bestowed on Bishop Gobat. The example of that distinguished prelate, in all that is truly Christian, can hardly fail, in due season, to produce results which, being matured by patience and untainted with sectarian animosity, are all the more likely to last, and last beneficially for all."

These prophetic words have been realised. The mission has, by the blessing of God, been productive of great results. Churches and schools have been built; throughout the large diocese, numbers of adult converts from the Greek and Latin churches have been made. The schools and colleges are yearly increasing, and the people are beginning to learn a religion of the heart and understanding. The Bible and prayers are now, for the first time, read to the people in their native tongues, and they now, only through this mission, begin to know what true Christianity is; for it must be borne in mind that the services of the different branches of the Greek Church are conducted in a language not understood by the people, and the services of the Latin or Roman Church being conducted, by *compulsion*, in the Latin language, their services are a dumb show.

Since 1847, the Bishop has established in Palestine

alone eight Protestant schools, employing 12 teachers, with 260 scholars. The numbers which have passed through the schools in the interval are not given. Seventeen years ago, when Bishop Gobat went to Jerusalem, there was not one native Protestant; there are now about 500. At the end of March, 1864, the Bishop writes that there had of late been a great movement at Bethlehem; for since his return, at the end of October, nearly 100 heads of families, Greeks and Latins, had joined the Church. When the cholera raged so furiously, the orphan children of the Jews and Turks were brought in great numbers to the Protestant Bishop, in preference to the Greek and Roman priests. He took them in in large numbers, provided for them, and educated them.

Dr. Newman clearly saw the result of such a mission; hence his opposition and "great dismay." He first declared "that there was not a single Anglican in Jerusalem, so we are sending a bishop to *make* a communion, not to govern our own people."* This objection, at least, is now overruled, for a very large communion has been created by the fact of the Bishop's mission. He "augured nothing but evil, if we in any way prejudiced our title to be a branch of the Apostolic Church."† His predictions have, happily, not been realized. He signed a protest, principally founded on the fact that the mission recognized all classes of Protestants who should consent to place themselves under the Bishop; this, he considered, to be a "recognition of heresy," and "the recognition of heresy, indirect as well as direct, goes far to destroy such claim in case of any religious body advancing it; and to admit maintainers of heresy to communion, without formal renunciation of their errors, goes far towards recognizing the same;" and he formally condemns Lutheranism and Calvinism, as "heresies repugnant to Scripture, springing

---

* "Apologia," p. 249. † Ibid. p. 250.

up three centuries ago, and anathematized by East as well as West." This is Dr. Newman's charity. Dr. Newman, who gave you the authority to be a judge? "Judge not, that ye be not judged."* "Why dost thou judge thy brother—we shall all stand before the judgment-seat of Christ."† Dr. Newman may possibly find that the first in his estimation shall be last.

They may retort on Dr. Newman with his own words:—

"A modest man, or a philosopher, would have scrupled to treat with scorn and scoffing, as he does, principles and convictions, even if he did not acquiesce in them himself, which had been held so widely, and for so long,—the beliefs, and devotions, and customs, which had been the religious life of millions upon millions of Christians for nearly twenty centuries [for Lutheranism is reformed Christianity]; for this, in fact, is the task on which he [Dr. Newman] is spending his pains."‡

The Lutheran and Calvinist will retort on Dr. Newman, that in the way which he calls heresy, they worship the God of their fathers, believing all things which are written in the Law and the Prophets.§ But where is Dr. Newman's consistency? At this very period of the "History of his religious opinions" he confesses that the Lutherans and Calvinists had a "sort of theology," and that he actually had none.‖ This is his own confession, at this very period. Who was the greater heretic? The creation of this bishopric, then, was the "blow which finally shattered his faith in the Anglican Church,"¶ and "it brought him to the beginning of the end."** And why? Because the Church "was not only forbidding any sympathy or concurrence with the Church of Rome, but it externally was courting an inter-communion with Protestant Prussia and the heresy of the Orientals;" and, hence he concludes, that by this act the Church of England would not

---

* Matt. vii. 1.   † Rom. xiv. 10.
‡ "Apologia," p. 5.   § Acts, xxiv. 14.
‖ "Apologia," p. 216.   ¶ Ibid. p. 248.
** Ibid. p. 253.

merely cease to be a church, but it "led him to the gravest suspicion that the Church of England *had never been a church all along.*"*

This is all he can assert or advance on the subject which gave the death-blow shattering his faith in the Anglican Church!

We are in the habit of hearing the mission of Austin the Monk, afterwards Archbishop of Canterbury, commended by Romanists: it is commended by Dr. Newman. The fact of his invitation to all the supposed heretical bishops and priests, he found here, to place themselves under him, without any formal re-baptism and confirmation, is not an event which would shatter Dr. Newman's faith in the Roman Church. We lately heard of a Roman bishop, from France, appointed to Cochin China—did that shatter the *ecclesiastical* nerves of the Archbishop of Paris? No, Dr. Newman, you were not an Anglican, but a Roman. You saw with dismay that Rome, with her Latin services and her superstitious worship and use of images, &c., could never make an impression on the Jews and Turks; whereas an Anglican missionary, with open Bible, read with prayers in the language of the people, must eventually supersede,—and is superseding,—the authority, the delusions, and superstitions of the Latin and Greek churches. Dr. Newman may make the fact of this great mission an excuse to declare his alleged want of faith in the Anglican Church; but except on the supposition that he was in fact a papist at the time, no one can see the "sequitur." Dr. Newman now affects an indifference, and pretends that he never heard of any good or harm resulting from the project of a Jerusalem bishopric. I would commend to his special attention the 12th annual report, ending 1864-1865, of "Bishop Gobat's fund for Missions in Abyssinia, Egypt, Syria, and Chaldea," and he will be compelled to tell another

---

* "Apologia," p. 248.

tale. But let Dr. Newman compare the result of *his* last twenty years with the labours of the Bishop of Jerusalem,—the one has led a lazy, idle, profitless life, shut up in an "oratory," the other has carried out an active, vigorous, Christian mission, whose labours have been crowned with marvellous success, he himself gaining the respect and love of all. I do not presume to judge Dr. Newman. His talent may have been hid in a napkin; but of the Bishop of Jerusalem we can say, that he has put his talent out to usury, and brought home to his Master the profit of his labour. "By their fruits ye shall know them."

Dr. Newman having veered round from north to south of the theological compass, settled down at length, as we are now told, as an obedient servant of the Pope, the "arbiter of all true doctrine and holy practice." He tried the Bible,—it disappointed his expectations. "We are told," says he, "that God has spoken. Where? In a book. *We have tried it, and it disappoints.*" As he had previously tried the Thirty-nine Articles, and they disappointed also. Popery—Romanism—was not found in either. He tried the early ante-Nicene fathers, and they disappointed him also. They all were a direct contradiction to Popery proper. He was, as I before remarked, too learned not to discover this fact, a fact too patent indeed to be questioned; so, to reconcile the inconsistency of his proceeding, he invented the theory of DEVELOPMENT.* Christianity was incomplete in the Apostolic age. In the Scriptures and Apostolic writers were found the germs only of Christianity, which, like the sciences, have been developed, century by century, into a Tridentine completeness. So that the further removed we are from the Apostolic age, the more complete—"concrete" is the favourite expression—has become the Christian code under the manipulation of the Roman

---

* "Essay on Development," pp. 125, 126.

priesthood. In the preface of his book he declares the astounding fact, that from 1833, while he had been writing against Popery, "he was only acting as from a pressure from without—it was necessary for our position;" and his attacks on Popery were put forth with "a hope of approving himself to persons he respected, and a wish to repel the charge of Romanism." By his own acknowledgment, therefore, he had been dissimulating. By this acknowledgment, however, he has perpetrated a suicidal act, by destroying (as Mr. Faber remarked) "the entire credibility of his own testimony." It is impossible for us to know when he is serious, for when it serves his purpose he systematically acts on the principle of deliberate insincerity. This book decided his course, as the first public declaration of his faith. But in accepting the Roman creed, Dr. Newman was bound by the declaration of the Trent Council, which, as we have stated, was that each particular doctrine then defined was, as an historically demonstrable fact, held from the beginning, and so defined by all the Fathers in succession. The chorus of the Cardinals, as the last act of the Council, was to declare:—

"We all thus believe: we all think the very same. This is the faith of Peter and of the Apostles; this is the faith of the Fathers; this is the faith of the orthodox. Amen, anathema to all heretics. Anathema, anathema."

Thus the Council closed with cursing their brother Christians, and, if Dr. Newman's theory be correct, with a lie in their mouths.

Dr. Newman went over to Rome while publishing his book, and accordingly, at the close of his preface, he declared that "he recognized in himself a conviction of the truth of the conclusion to which the discussion leads, so clear as to supersede further deliberation;" and so took that occasion to change his religion. If Dr. Newman's "convictions," based on the theory advanced by him, were cogent, then the conclusion come to by the Trent Doctors was erroneous. In any case he is, by anticipation, anathematized by that Council as a heretic.

His first act, he tell us, on his conversion, was to offer his work for revision to the proper authorities. But this offer was declined. How could the Pope and Congregation of Rites falsify their whole system? So Dr. Newman's offer was politely declined. He was too great a catch to be snubbed, so the refusal was based on the alleged ground that the "book was written and partly printed before he was a Catholic," and that "it would come before the reader *in a more persuasive* form, if he read it as the author wrote it." So the authorities desired to reap the benefit of it without taking the responsibility of the original view of the Romish system, now for the first time put forward. The work, however, did not pass unchallenged. Dr. Brownson, a lay Romanist, the editor of an American review, who, as he states, submitted all he wrote to the approval of his ecclesiastical superiors, attacked Dr. Newman in no measured terms, for his theory of doctrinal development, which attack appeared in the *Tablet* Romish newspaper of 11th September, 1852, wherein Dr. Brownson, while repudiating Dr. Newman's theory, hits the right nail on the head. He says (taking a summary of Dr. Newman's position):—

"He [Dr. Newman] could not become a [Roman] Catholic before the invention of the theory of development, because such are the omissions and contradictions of the Fathers, and such the discrepancies between their teachings and those of the present Church of Rome, that it was impossible, without a theory which Roman divines had never recognized, or at least never made use of, to reconcile the Church with the Fathers and the Fathers with one another, or a given Father with himself. He does not say all this in just so many words, but he seems to us to imply it throughout his book."

This was brought to the notice of Dr. Newman, who replied, through Father Glover, "that he had heard of the article, but that he had had no time nor wish to read it. That he had no bad feelings against the writer personally for having written it, but he was sorry that he had done so, *for he had reason to believe that the Essay was doing great good in England.*"

So Dr. Newman was acting on the principle that the end sanctified the means. But Dr. Brownson could not, even at this price, submit to have Romanism branded as a novelty, and thereupon retorts on Dr. Newman for his Jesuitry;—yes, Dr. Newman's *Jesuitry!*—that is the word used by an eminent lay Romanist against you. These are his words published in the *Tablet*:—

"So he [Dr. Newman] looked only at the effects his theory was producing, or supposed to be producing, in a particular locality, without at all troubling himself with the question whether it was true or false; that is, he was willing that the theory, even if false and mischievous, should go uncontradicted, if, for the moment, it *per accidens*, facilitated the conversion of a few Anglicans. This is the only principle we can deduce from the reason he assigns for regretting the publication of our article against his essay, and this is identically the principle Mr. Morris generalizes and sets forth in the work before us, or *what is properly termed Jesuitry!*"

So poor Dr. Newman fell at once into hot water, and is accused even by a Romanist of Jesuitry! This was too much for the Doctor, so he appeals to the *Tablet* in a letter, dated 14th September, 1852. He protests that "it cannot be expected that he should take any formal notice of charges against the soundness of his faith, mixed up with such hearsay evidence [alluding, probably, to Father Glover's report]; such imputations of motive, and such insinuations as are introduced in the extracts from an American Review, as published in the *Tablet* the week previous."

Charges against Dr. Newman for the soundness of his faith! considering that he left the Church of England because there was no certainty of doctrine or teaching in her. This accusation was rather too hard to bear, so he proceeded:—

"I am not conscious to myself of holding anything on the points to which the writer refers which *has not been held by numbers of good Catholics before me* [and pray let my readers bear this acknowledgment in mind], and I never have shown any indisposition to converse or communicate with any theologian who has been kind enough to draw my attention to them."

But mark the passage which follows. It is from the pen of a man who professes to be a reasonable being, acting on convictions after a long and tedious apprenticeship, who has presumed to preach, and teach, and to write hard things and controversial works, professing to be guided in all his acts by a love of truth, and when he is supposed to have acted on conviction, making the degrading avowal that he renounces all judgment or opinion of his own, for he adds :—

"This I trust I may say, that if there be a man in the whole Church who, from faith, obedience, and love towards her, would rejoice and exult in *sacrificing any opinion of his own at the bidding of his ecclesiastical superiors* (if I dare speak of myself), I am the man."

Could a man, supposed to be endowed with reasoning faculties, make a more degrading acknowledgment? This may be the key to all his previous conduct, acting under the order of his ecclesiastical superiors; but it is now confidently believed Dr. Newman never was a Protestant. He carried on a dissimulation for a series of years, as "necessary to his then position." Recollecting, however, that this very charge of dissimulation was brought against him while professing to be of the Church of England, he thinks it necessary to make a protest; so he adds, perhaps conscience-stricken; for it will be observed that Dr. Brownson was not bringing any accusation of this kind against Dr. Newman :—

"I have ever detested the spirit of shuffling and concealing of opinion, so recklessly imputed to me when I was a Protestant. Those who know me will bear me witness that, from a desire to be fair and honest [that is, with a hope of approving himself to persons he respected and a wish to repel the charge of Romanism], what I wrote was ever running to the *extreme* of what I thought, as in that very Essay on Development of Doctrine, which has occasioned the present charges against me."

The imputation was not recklessly made. We have the uncontradicted fact, an accusation made through the public papers at the time, that Dr. Newman had been at a Jesuit college. He was publicly challenged to deny that he was ordained a priest of Rome long before he publicly left the Church of England, and when he left he was not re-ordained. If all this be true—and the charges were publicly made at the time, and uncontradicted—Dr. Newman stands convicted, even on his own acknowledgment, "of shuffling and concealment of opinion."

Dr. Newman's letter concludes thus:—

"It is my comfort and my boast (I say it with thankfulness) that they only among Catholics have felt suspicion of me who have not known me, and that in proportion as they had means of judging of me, they have trusted me.

"I can bear the unkind thoughts of men whom I have never seen, while I am cheered by the countenance of my superiors and friends. Perhaps the able, and (I am sure) excellent writer of the strictures which you [*Tablet*] have published, will live to be sorry, whatever becomes of *me*, for judgments he had no right to form, and no call to put in circulation."

Dr. Newman, it will be seen, skilfully turns the attack of his reviewer on his theory or doctrine as a personal attack on himself. This with a meek, humble, inoffensive, obedient, and submissive individual, it was hoped would obtain sympathy; but Dr. Brownson would not consent to be turned over in that way; so he returned to the charge; and accordingly, in the *Tablet* of 6th November, 1852, he replied as follows:—

"I regret that the illustrious writer (Dr. Newman) should have broken his silence for the first time against me in defence of his personal character, which I have never attacked, instead of his *doctrinal tendencies* which I *have* attacked, and laboured to *prove are subversive of the Christian religion;* for I had supposed it always a characteristic of the [Roman] Catholic doctor to be more sensitive to charges against his doctrine, than to charges against his person. . . . . Doctrinal tendencies which I regard as likely to *prove dangerous to the purity and integrity of the faith.*"

It will have been observed that Dr. Newman asserts that, what he put forth had the sanction of "numbers of good Catholics before him." So Dr. Brownson retorts that what he has written was "at the request of the ecclesiastical authorities of his country, and that he never published an article, written by himself on theological questions, without first submitting it to his own bishop or a competent theologian approved by him."

How these Romans lean upon each other. None have an independent opinion: the layman looks to his priest, and the priest to the bishop; the bishop leans on the Pope, and the Pope himself is not a free agent, for he has his confessor and submits to his guidance; and yet they cannot agree among themselves. Dr. Newman has his backers, so has Dr. Brownson; but they take diametrically opposite views of "Catholic doctrine" as fundamental, and yet they boast of unity. Dr. Brownson thus proceeds:—

"Dr. Newman's doctrine of development was submitted here to a close and rigid examination, not by me only, but by bishops and professional theologians. I have only censured what they bade me censure, and I am responsible only for the manner in which I have done what they instructed me to do. Under these well-known circumstances, Dr. Newman can hardly excuse himself for not replying to the charges I have preferred against the doctrine, either on the ground that the charges are not preferred by a theologian, or that they are charges against his person."

Dr. Newman could not be a Roman Catholic without accounting for the fact that Tridentine doctrines were non-existent in the early stage of Christianity, he only had this developing theory to fall back upon, and he was so far correct; but that, as I stated, contradicted the Tridentine appeal to antiquity. He is asked for an explanation. He does not give it. It is his refusal to satisfy the supposed "orthodox" school that gave dire offence; so Dr. Brownson concludes:—

"The only thing that operates here to Dr. Newman's disadvantage is his refusal to explain himself publicly with regard to his doctrine, which has been publicly controverted, and his apparent disposition to regard attacks on his doctrine as attacks on his person. His silence in this respect is not edifying, and if continued, will lead to suspicion even of his motives. What is asked of him is, to tell us whether we have rightly apprehended his meaning, and if we have not, to set us right; and if we have, to tell us how that meaning can be compatible with Catholic faith. There is no Catholic who wishes to quarrel with him, and all I can assert that I aim at is, to be at once just to him and to Catholic truth. I have no theory of my own that his interferes with, and I seek only to defend the tradition of faith as it has come down to us from the beginning."

Dr. Newman does not respond to this call, but keeps his own counsel; but now, some twelve or fifteen years after, when he thinks all these attacks on him are forgotten, he quietly acknowledges, with reference to this very work,—

"That work, I believe, I have not read since I published it, and I doubt not at all that I have made many mistakes in it; partly from my ignorance of the details of doctrine, as the Church of Rome holds them, but partly from my impatience to clear as large a range for the *principle* of doctrinal development (waiving the question of historical *fact*) as was consistent with the strict apostolicity and identity of the Catholic creed." *

So we are to waive the "question of historical fact"! When Dr. Newman claims antiquity for the Roman Church, it becomes essentially dependent on historical fact. As a Church, the Greek and Eastern Churches are anterior to the Roman; indeed it is believed that Christianity was planted in Britain before it was in Rome; and as to doctrine, those on which the two Churches agree, are of coeval date—those on which they differ, have been engrafted at subsequent periods; and to support which the developing theory is essential. But it is equally fatal to the claim to antiquity so ostentatiously paraded in almost every page of Dr. Newman's present work.

The primary charge, as already observed, brought

* "Apologia," p. 161.

against Dr. Newman, is *untruthfulness*. He is accused of being "secretly a Romanist, when he was openly professing to be a clergyman of the Established Church." This charge is met merely inferentially. Those who took an interest at the time, in the first appearance, about 1833, of the great Tractarian Romanizing movement, originating with a small but prominent cluster of Oxford divines, will well remember that Dr. Newman was pointed out as one of the foremost advocates of the system, identifying himself with the leading characters of the party—Froude, Keble, Pusey, &c. He himself gives the date, 14th July, 1833,* "as the start of the religious movement." Where had Dr. Newman been previous to this date? He had been on a continental tour with his dear and bosom friend, and companion—we could almost add, Father confessor—Hurrell Froude. They were in Rome together: "Froude and I (he says) made two calls upon Monsignore, afterwards Cardinal Wiseman, at the Collegio Inglese, shortly before we left Rome." He thus describes his own feelings:—†

"The thought came upon me that deliverance is wrought, not by the many, but by the few; not by bodies, but by persons. Now it was I think, that I repeated to myself words which had ever been dear to me from my school-days, 'Exoriare aliquis!' now too that Southey's beautiful poem of 'Thalaba,' for which I had an immense liking, came forcibly to my mind. *I began to think that I had a mission.* There are sentences in my letters to my friends to this effect, if they are not destroyed. When we took leave of Monsignore Wiseman—he had courteously expressed a wish that we might make a second visit to Rome,—I said with great gravity, 'We have a work to do in England.'‡ I went down to Sicily, and the presentiment grew stronger. I struck into the middle of the island, and fell ill of a fever at Learforte. My servant thought I was dying, and begged for my last directions. I gave them as he wished, but I said, 'I shall not die.' I repeated, 'I shall not die, for I have not sinned against light, I have not sinned against light.'—My servant, who had acted

---

* "Apologia," p. 100.   † Ibid. p. 98.

‡ Was this prophetic, or in accordance with a newly-imposed vow to propagate "the faith"? I have come to the conclusion that it was the latter.

as my nurse, asked what ailed me. I could only answer, 'I have a work to do in England.'"

He took Palermo on his route, and he admits that he looked back in grateful remembrance for the "comfort he had received in frequenting the churches at Palermo."* What comfort could a Protestant minister receive in visiting Romish churches?†

It was on the following Sunday after his return, 14th July, 1833, that he heard Keble preach the Assize Sermon from the University pulpit, which was subsequently published under the title of "National Apostasy," and which day, as before stated, he "ever considered and kept as the start of the religious movement of 1833."

Now it is a fact that it was considered at the time, and has been often publicly repeated, that Dr. Newman was at this interview with Dr. Wiseman, in company with Froude, formally ordained a priest of the Roman Church, being then in fact a member of that communion. Dr. Newman again visited Rome under the advice of Dr. Wiseman, in 1845,‡ after he had *publicly* renounced the communion of the Church of England. He went ostensibly to be inducted into the priesthood, a ceremony that could have been equally well performed in England. It

* "Apologia," p. 126.

† Dr. Newman appears troubled with a short memory. In order to lead his readers to suppose that he was perfectly innocent of Rome at this time, he, a little before the above extract, says, while in Sicily, on his return from Rome, on this very same journey, while rambling in the country, he came upon a small church. "I heard," he said, "voices, and I looked in. It was crowded, and the congregation was singing—of course it was the Mass, though I did not know it at the time" (p. 126). Here is an ordained clergyman just returning from a continental journey, from Rome itself, where he met and visited Dr. Wiseman, and yet he pretends that he did not recognize the Romish service of the Mass when he heard it! Does Dr. Newman think he will get any one to believe this?

‡ "Soon Dr. Wiseman, in whose vicariate Oxford lay, called me to Oscott, and I went there with others; afterwards he sent me to Rome, and finally placed me in Birmingham."—*Apologia*, p. 368.

has been confidently asserted that Dr. Newman was not then (1845) ordained a priest of Rome; that his journey was a make-belief. Holy orders, in the Roman Church, are accounted a sacrament, which cannot be repeated without sacrilege. Anglican orders are void, in the estimation of the Roman Church. If Dr. Newman was secretly ordained in 1833, the ceremony could not be repeated in 1845, and it was publicly alleged at the time that he was not ordained in 1845, nor ever since.

It is also a fact that Dr. Newman spent the early years of his life in the college of the "Propaganda Fide," at Rome. He was then, it is asserted, a Roman Catholic. When Dr. Newman publicly declared himself a Romanist, and went to Rome ostensibly for his ordination, a day was proposed for the performance of that ceremony. Great curiosity was excited at the time among the English at Rome, to witness the ceremony. Those who were there at the time well remember the circumstance. But for one reason or another it was deferred, until general interest died away, *and no ordination, so far as the public are aware, took place.* One only conclusion was come to; namely, that Dr. Newman had been already ordained a priest of Rome, and was actually a priest while officiating in the Anglican Church. This challenge was, at the time, publicly made, and has never been denied.

When Dr. Newman was ordained a minister of the Church of England, he pledged himself, in his ordination vows, to preach against those peculiar doctrines of Rome which separate the two churches, as "damnable heresies and superstitions;" when he was ordained priest of the Roman Church, he submitted an implicit credence in all these so-called heresies and superstitions, previously ostensibly denounced by him as such, and he then "promised, vowed, and swore most constantly to hold and confess" these same heresies and superstitions, "whole and entire, *and to procure, as far as lay in his power, that the same should be held and taught, and preached by all* who might be under him or entrusted to his care by virtue of his office."

Dr. Newman is now openly an officiating priest in the Roman Church. It was, therefore, with more than ordinary curiosity that we anxiously awaited the announcement by Dr. Newman, in his Biography, as to the exact time when, in fact, he had formally taken the vows of the Roman Church as a priest. One would have supposed that the precise date when this important occurrence took place, and the circumstances attending it, and by whom the ceremony was performed, would be duly notified. But we look in vain for this information; all we are told* is, that in 1845 he was "received" into the Church of Rome; and he says, "for a while after my *reception* I proposed to betake myself to some secular calling;" but he nowhere mentions his re-ordination.

So far, then, as this "Apologia" is concerned, the mooted question remains unanswered,—when was Dr. Newman ordained a priest of the Roman Church?—our curiosity remains unsatisfied. His subsequent volume " History of my Religious Opinions"—is equally silent on the subject!

We are met with a very powerful argument in opposition to the theory of a feigned submission to the Established Church, and that Dr. Newman could have been a disguised Romanist, in the fact, that for a series of years, anterior to his public withdrawal from the Church of England, in one or other of his works, we find him condemning the errors of Romanism as deadly heresies. He said of the Romanists, that their communion was infected with heresy; " that we are bound to flee it as a pestilence. They have established a lie in the place of God's truth; and, by their claim of immutability in doctrine cannot undo the sin they have

---

* " Apologia," pp. 336-7, 373.

committed."* "I spoke (he says) successively of the Roman Church as being bound up with the cause of Antichrist, as being one of the many Antichrists foretold by St. John, as being the spirit of Antichrist, and as having something very antichristian, unchristian, about her." "I thought the Church of Rome was bound up with the cause of Antichrist by the Council of Trent."

He admits to have made declarations to the same effect at various times in various successive years. How is this, we ask again, to be reconciled with the supposed hypocritical proceeding attributed to him? Happily it does not devolve on me to give a decision, for Dr. Newman himself gives the solution;—he admitted in his last solemn act, before he *publicly* left the Church of England, that he had been deliberately asserting what he himself at the very time disbelieved!

His book on "Development" was his last production while ostensibly a minister of the English Church. In the "advertisement" prefixed to this Essay† he says, that in making such declarations "he was not speaking his own words, but was only following almost a *consensus* of divines of his church." And the reason he assigns for this deception on the public was, that "such views were necessary for our position;" that is, the otherwise anomalous position of himself and his associates; and he actually seeks to excuse himself for holding himself forth under false colours, and desires that these strong expressions against Romanism should be ascribed to a hope of approving himself to persons whom he respected, and to a wish "to repel the charge of Romanism"!

His explanation in his "Apologia" is not quite so open-spoken as in his "Development," written at the time. It nevertheless is sufficiently clear. He says, in addition to the above:—

* "Apologia," p. 124. † Pp. vi—ix.

"As a matter, then, of simple conscience, *though it went against my feelings*, I felt it to be a duty to protest against the Church of Rome. But besides this, it was a duty, *because the prescription of such a protest was a living principle of my own church*, as expressed in not simply a *catena* but a *consensus* of her divines, and the voice of her people. Moreover, such a protest *was necessary* as an integral portion of her controversial basis; for I adopted the argument of Bernard Gilpin, that Protestants 'were *not able* to give any *firm and solid* reason for the separation besides this, to wit, that the Pope is Antichrist.' But while I thus thought such a protest to be based upon truth, and to be a religious duty, and a rule of Anglicanism, and a necessity of the case, *I did not at all like the work*. Hurrell Froude* attacked me for doing it, and besides, I felt that my language had a vulgar and rhetorical look about it. I believed, and really measured my words, when I used them; but I knew that I had a temptation, on the other hand, to say against Rome as much as ever I could, *in order to protect myself against the charge of Popery.*"†

"In addition (he says) I was embarrassed in consequence of my wish to go as far as possible in interpreting the Articles in the direction of Roman dogma, without disclosing what I was doing to the parties whose doubts I was meeting, who might be thereby encouraged to go still further than at present they found in themselves any call to do."‡ We should be glad to know what are Dr. Newman's ideas of honesty! But unfortunately for him, the bubble burst too soon, for he lets out that the immediate cause of his giving up his living was the unexpected (a premature, of course) conversion to Romanism of one of his pupils.§ Dr. Newman has the boldness to remind us that "we Englishmen like manliness, openness, consistency, and truth."|| Did he, as an Englishman, practise these virtues himself at this time?

"In spite (he says) of my ungrounded fears of Rome and the decision of my reason and conscience against her usage; in spite of my affection for Oxford and Oriel, yet I had a secret longing love of Rome,

---

* Froude seems to have been Newman's evil genius.
† "Apologia," p. 128.   ‡ Ibid. p. 162.
§ Ibid. p. 246. || Ibid. p. 227.

the mother of English Christianity." And again he informs us that he (in 1850) wrote an account of his "reasonings and feelings in 1839," which are as follows : *—" It was difficult to make out how the Eutychians or Monophysites were heretics unless Protestants and Anglicans were heretics also ; difficult to find arguments against the Tridentine Fathers which did not tell against the Fathers of Chalcedon ; difficult to condemn the Popes of the sixteenth century without condemning the Popes of the fifth. The drama of religion and the combat of truth and error were ever one and the same. *The principles and proceedings of the Church* [of Rome] *now were those of the Church then ; the principles and proceedings of heretics then were those of Protestants now.* I found it so almost fearfully." A startling announcement, indeed, for a minister in an essentially professing Protestant Church to make ! On the eve of his leaving (April, 1845), he wrote to " an intimate friend," announcing his determination, and adds, "How could I remain at St. Mary's a hypocrite ?"† And before this, in writing to a friend, in December, 1841, three years before he left the Church of England, he says, "for myself, this only I see, that there is indefinitely more in the Fathers against our own state of alienation from Christendom than against the Tridentine decrees."

What hope can we have of a man who admits that he was not able to give any firm and solid reason for his separation but that the Pope was Antichrist ? This last stumbling-block ceased to exist on passing from one system to the other. He had already, it appears, reconciled himself to all the peculiarities of Romanism. "In spite (he says) of my ingrained fears of Rome, and the decision of my reason and conscience against her usages, in spite of my affection for Oxford and Oriel, yet I had a

* "Apologia," p. 209. † Ibid. p. 366.

secret longing love of Rome, the mother of English Christianity [a statement Dr. Newman knows, as an historical fact, to be untrue], and I had a true devotion to the Blessed Virgin, in whose college I lived, *whose altar I served*, whose immaculate purity I had in one of my earliest printed sermons made much of;"* and consequently he " had no changes to record;" he " had no anxiety of heart whatever;" he "has been in perfect peace and contentment."†

" I was not conscious to myself, on my conversion, of *any difference of thought or temper* from what I had before. I was not conscious of firmer faith, nor had I any trouble about receiving those additional articles which are not found in the Anglican creed. Some of them I believed already, but not any of them was a trial to me. I made a profession of them upon my *reception* [he never speaks of his ordination], with the greatest ease, and I have the same ease in believing them now."

And again he says :—

"When, in 1845, I wrote to Bishop Wiseman, in whose vicariate I found myself, to announce my conversion, I could find nothing better to say to him than that I would obey the Pope as I had obeyed my own bishop in the Anglican Church. My duty to him was my point of honour, his disapprobation was the one thing which I could not bear."‡

A conversion implies a *change*. Here there appears to have been none. Again, one naturally asks for a reason for such conversion when a public declaration of a new faith has been made, and particularly from one who volunteers an autobiography, an " Apologia," a history of his theological experiences, thoughts, and actions; from one who deliberately informs us that§ " from the age of fifteen dogma has been the fundamental principle of my religion. I know no other religion. Religion, as a mere sentiment, is to me a dream and a mockery. What I held in 1816, I held in 1833, and I hold in 1864. Please God I shall hold it

---

* " Apologia," p. 279.   † Ibid. p. 373.
‡ Ibid. p. 123.   § Ibid. p. 120.

to the end." Dogma then was, and is, his study, his existence. It is in *dogma* that the two churches, England and Rome, essentially differ; and yet Dr. Newman changes his religion and assumes, or is supposed to assume, a new code of dogmas, without giving one word of explanation, one valid reason for the change! and tells us that he was not concious of any change. A fit scholar and disciple we have here ready to hand to become associated with as a compeer and pupil of the "notorious quibblers, hypocrites, and rogues," of the school of "Romish moralists!" These are Dr. Newman's own epithets, not mine.

The first act of Dr. Newman, when he first returned from Rome, was to set on foot the movement which led to the publication of the "Tracts for the Times," he himself writing some of them; among others, the ever-memorable "Tract XC." "I had (he says) out of my own head, begun the Tracts."* His main object now appeared to be to reconcile the Thirty-nine Articles with his Romish notions. "I wanted (he candidly confesses) to ascertain what was the limit of that elasticity [of the Articles] in the direction of Roman dogma."† The doctrine of Apostolic succession he had been taught long before (in the year 1823) "in the course of a walk round Christ Church meadow."

Dr. Newman complains of being "incessantly misrepresented."‡ He is indignant that he should be accused of duplicity, in representing himself to be what he is not,—a minister of a Protestant church, while in fact "a virtual, or actual Roman Catholic." But how does he meet the charge? Does he deny it? He puts the case himself. "Father Newman and the Vicar of St. Mary's are one and the same. There has been no change of mind in him; what he believed then he believes now, and what he believes now he believed

---

* "Apologia," p. 109.   † Ibid p. 160.
‡ Ibid. p. 291.

then." Exactly so; and this was the general belief then, which by the way he admits, by saying that it was not Mr. Kingsley alone "who entertains, and has entertained, such an opinion of me and my writings,"* and that belief has been to our minds confirmed by subsequent events. What explanation does Father Newman give? He says, "to dispute this is frivolous. To distinguish between the past self and his present is subtlety, and to ask for proof of their identity is seeking opportunity to be sophistical."† Under such an answer, Dr. Newman can exercise the full scope of the system of "amphibiology" and permissive "mental reservation," for a good cause, of course, that is, the "good of the Church," the "necessity of his position." But there is a proverb, what every one says is—is right. Dr. Newman admits that it was not Mr. Kingsley alone who entertained, and has entertained, such an opinion of him and his writings. He further admits that it is the impression of large classes of men, the impression twenty years ago, and the impression now,—in fact, that the impression was general, that he was doing the work of Rome, whilst wearing the livery of the Church of England. He admits that he scouted the name of Protestant, and was aware that many of the doctrines which he professed were generally known as badges of the Roman Church, as distinguished from the faith of the Reformation. If all these are facts, there remains a still greater fact to be stated; and that is, Dr. Newman does not allege that the public was wrong in their estimation, or that his own acts did not justify the charge. He at length declared himself to be what the public had long known him to be in heart,—a Romanist; and the public was not deceived in their estimation of Dr. Newman's character. What was this but hypocrisy and duplicity? He now, with the simplicity of injured innocence, says that sort of charge is a matter he cannot properly

* "Apologia," p 41.   † Ibid. pp. 40-41.

meet, because he cannot duly realize it! He tells us that he never had any suspicion of his own honesty. Did any Jesuit make any other admission when carrying out the directions of his superior? And (says Dr. Newman) "when men say I was dishonest, I cannot grasp the accusation as a distinct conception, such as it is possible to encounter."* The charge is very clear, but I admit it difficult to conceive, as applied to a professed minister of the Gospel. Even his last act was to declare that two things were plain; first, that every one was prepared for such an event; next, that every one expected it of him.† And yet he never had a suspicion of his own honesty! Dr. Newman is full of inconsistencies, to say the least of it.

We now leave the charge of *untruthfulness* against Dr. Newman for the consideration of the reader. He may now be able to appreciate the statement of Mr. Kingsley, which, in fact, has stung Dr. Newman more deeply than anything said of him,—that we may "henceforth be in doubt and fear, as much as an honest man can be, concerning every word Dr. Newman may write." The evil genius of Dr. Newman was Froude, by whom he was "easily persuaded" to accompany him to the South of Europe.

Richard Hurrell Froude was a student and commoner of Oriel College, Oxford, and elected Fellow in 1826, received priest's orders in the Church of England 1829, and died 1836. While in this church, Dr. Newman informs us that Froude—

"Professed openly his admiration of the Church of Rome, and his hatred of the Reformers. He delighted in the notion of a hierarchical system, of sacerdotal power, and of full ecclesiastical liberty. He felt scorn of the maxim, 'The Bible, and the Bible only, is the religion of Protestants,' and he gloried in accepting traditions as a main instrument of religious teaching. He had a high, severe, idea of the intrinsic excellence of virginity; and he considered the Blessed Virgin its great pattern. He delighted in thinking of the saints;

---

* "Apologia," p. 280.   † Ibid. p. 362.

he had a vivid appreciation of the idea of sanctity, its possibility, its heights; and he was more than inclined to believe a large amount of miraculous interference as occurring in the early and middle ages. He embraced the principle of penance and mortification. He had a deep devotion to the Real Presence, in which he had a firm faith. He was powerfully drawn to the Mediæval Church, but not the Primitive."[*]

This is what Dr. Newman playfully calls "going ahead across country,"[†] and which Froude had "no scruple in doing"! This is the man who, as Dr. Newman informs us, was his "dear and familiar companion," and with whom he was in the closest friendship,[‡] and who, as he tells us "taught him to look with admiration towards the Church of Rome, and in the same degree to dislike the Reformation; who fixed deep in him the idea of devotion to the Blessed Virgin, and led him gradually to believe in the Real Presence." From Froude he says he learned to "admire the great mediæval Popes."[§] He once thought that the essence of the offence of Romanism consisted in the honours which the Roman Church paid to the Virgin Mary and the saints; and the more he grew in devotion both to the saints and to "Our Lady," the more impatient he was at the Roman practices; "as if those glorified creations of God must be gravely shocked—if pain could be theirs—at the undue veneration of which they were the objects;" but that Hurrell Froude, "in his familiar conversations, was always tending to rub these ideas out of his mind;"[||] and yet, in another place, with a peculiarly short memory, Dr. Newman pretends that his "opinions on religion were not gained, as the world said, from Roman sources, but were the fruit of his own mind."[¶] Was Dr. Newman a child, to be thus led by a confirmed Papist? Did it occur to him that it was the

---

[*] "Apologia," p. 86; and also p. 24, "History of my Religious Opinions."
[†] "Apologia," p. 106. [‡] Ibid. p. 124.
[§] Ibid. p. 126. [||] Ibid. p. 125.
[¶] Ibid. p. 181.

very height of dishonesty in a professed minister of the Church of England, who had taken the vows to drive away these strange and heretical doctrines, to remain in the Church and receive his wages as a faithful servant? Is this honest and fair dealing in the sight of God and man? And it is under the wing of this Jesuitical spirit that Dr. Newman desires to shield himself. Yes, and he shields himself too under the further excuse that he could pick out of one or other of the Anglican divines—Bramhall, Andrews, Hooker, Hammond, Bull, Thorndike, Pearson, &c.—one or other of his Popish predilections!* and in a most irreverent manner he states "that two can play at that," when accused of Popery, and when the "Articles, Homilies, or Reformers" were brought in witness against him. And this is the man who boasts "that at all times he had a deep conviction that honesty was the best policy." But who can minister to a weak and diseased mind? A Hurrell Froude could lead him with a thread; and so submissive had he become, that he tells us that "if the Holy See ever decided that there was the true apostolic succession in the Church of England, he would believe it." In whatever estimation we may hold Dr. Newman's conduct while a professed member of the Church of England, he is now very open and plain-spoken. He states that "persistence in a given belief is no sufficient test of truth." This is true, and Dr. Newman, no doubt, felt the force of the statement, when he now publicly declares, that what he held in 1816 he held in 1833, and now holds in 1864; bearing in mind that he lays particular stress, that "dogma" had ever been his great fundamental principle; but he goes on to say, "that departure from any given belief is a slur upon the man who has felt so certain about it." To relieve himself, therefore, of the imputation consequent on his supposed conver-

---

* "Apologia," p. 181.

sion from the church whose ministry he had so long served, he declares that he was "not conscious of any change in himself of thought or feeling as regards matters of doctrine," on leaving one system for another. But in order to veil his real sentiments while in the Church of England, as we have shown, he now declares that he had a temptation to say against Rome as much as ever he could, in order to protect himself against the charge of Popery, and that he was embarrassed in consequence of his wish to go as far as was possible in interpreting the Articles in the direction of Roman dogma, without disclosing what he was doing to the parties whose doubts he was meeting. He actually denies that the Thirty-nine Articles "were drawn up against Popery." These Articles, he declares, were not drawn up antagonistic to "any religious doctrine at all, but a political principle."* What! Dr. Newman, was the great truth contained in the 6th Article,—"Holy Scripture containeth all things necessary to salvation,"—drawn up to combat a "political principle"? or was the declaration that Christ "is the *only* Mediator between God and man;" and "that we are accounted righteous before God only for the merit of our Lord and Saviour Jesus Christ by faith, and not for our own works or deservings;" or the declaration, that "works of supererogation cannot be taught without arrogance or impiety," enjoined to combat a "political principle"? or was the precise declaration that "Christ alone was without sin;" and that "the Romish doctrine concerning purgatory, pardons, worshipping and adoration of angels, as well of images as of relics; and also invocation of saints, is a fond thing vainly invented, and grounded upon no warranty of Scripture, but rather repugnant to the Word of God"? and that "transubstantiation overthrows the nature of a sacrament, and hath given occasion to

---

* See his "Religious Opinions," pp. 80, 81.

many superstitions," enjoined to combat " a political principle" ? We may admire Dr. Newman's candour; but in secular transactions such duplicity, as he himself admits to have carried out, would receive its appropriate designation; and we have yet to learn that deceit is consecrated when practised under the garb of " religion." If this is his notion " of keeping his hands clean and his heart pure," we differ on notions of morality. Dr. Newman asks for " a fair stage and no favour," but he becomes remarkably irritable when Mr. Kingsley takes him at his word, and exhibits his duplicity in terms (to our minds perfectly justifiable), but which happily is not our province or mood to repeat. But of this fact we are now certain, that when Dr. Newman was an officiating minister in the Anglican Church, he was in heart and soul a Romanist, if not also a Romish Priest.

When Dr. Newman took his vows as a priest, to be ready with all faithful diligence to banish and drive away all erroneous and strange doctrines contrary to God's word, will he dare assert that he was called upon to drive away erroneous " political principles" ? We are quite prepared to admit that the Church of Rome has become a *political system* ; that dominion and power is its aim; but that view of the subject is dismissed by our Articles in a few but emphatic words:—

"THE BISHOP OF ROME HATH NO JURISDICTION IN THIS REALM OF ENGLAND."

Dr. Newman, while officiating as an " Anglican minister," asked himself a simple question, " Can I be saved in the English Church ? Am I in safety were I to die to-night ?"* Now that Dr. Newman has left that church, does he really believe that no one can be saved

* " Apologia," p. 363.

in that church? He dares not boldly say that he really believes that there is no salvation out of his present church. It is true, however, that he does now declare the Roman Church to be the only true church. But the characteristic of Dr. Newman's mode of proceeding is to make hardy assertions, and jump to certain conclusions, without one single argument or proof in support of what he advances. For instance, without one word of proof or explanation, he says, "On the one hand, I came gradually to see that the Anglican Church was formally in the right; then that no valid reason could be assigned for continuing in the Anglican; and again that no valid objections could be taken to joining the Roman." Again, "as I have already said, there are but two alternatives, the way to Rome and the way to Atheism."* This is strong indeed. So we, who are not on the road to Rome, are on the road to Atheism!

While yet a professed member of the English Church, he said, "I fear that I must confess that, in proportion as I think the English Church is showing herself intrinsically and radically alien from Catholic principles, so do I feel the difficulties of defending her claims to be a branch of the Catholic Church."† If by "Catholic" he means "Roman," then he is right in fact, though his honesty may be doubted, for remaining one single day in that church with such notions. That he did mean Romish or Popish, he seems to admit; for shortly after he gives his reason for resigning his living,—"because I think the Church of Rome the Catholic Church, and ours" [he was writing to a friend, then also of the Church of England] "not part of the Catholic Church, *because not in communion with Rome;* and because I feel that I could not honestly be a teacher in it any longer."‡

---

* These statements are all repeated in Dr. Newman's last reprint —"History of my Religious Opinions," 1865, pp. 200 and 204.

† "Apologia," p. 350.   ‡ Ibid. p. 351.

As to the latter assertion, he has elsewhere told us in fact, that the immediate cause of his leaving was because he could no longer shield his real sentiments from public reprobation. The bubble prematurely burst. One of his "nurslings" went over to Rome too soon. Like most conspiracies, the scheme was prematurely disclosed. Now, what grounds had he for thinking the Church of Rome *the* Catholic Church? From one end of his book to the other there is not one single attempt to prove that the Roman Church is that true church. Dr. Newman makes a series of idle assertions, and dignifies his work with the title of a history of his religious opinions; opinions advanced without reasons, and statements made without proofs. "It seems a dream," he says, "to call a communion Catholic, when one can neither appeal to any clear statement of Catholic doctrine in its formularies, nor interpret ambiguous formularies by the received and living Catholic sense, whether past or present."* What can he possibly mean? Here is a man who now frankly admits a fact, which he at the time studiously attempted to conceal, that his great object, while in the English Church, had been to endeavour to ascertain the extent of elasticity of the Articles of the Church of England in the direction of "the Roman dogmas,"† and of reading and interpreting them in a non-natural sense, and is astounded that he should be accused of untruthfulness, or that his honesty should be called in question. He gravely tells us "that he never had any suspicions of his own honesty;" and when men said that he was dishonest, he could not grasp the accusation as a distinct conception, such as it was possible to encounter.‡ Indeed, Dr. Newman! The result speaks for itself. He was ultimately compelled to declare himself a Romanist. His excuse is that there is no clear statement of

* "Apologia," p. 350.   † Ibid. p. 160.
‡ Ibid. p. 280.

Catholic doctrine in the formularies of the Church of England to which appeal can be made, nor a living infallible authority to interpret ambiguous formularies! Now let us see how far he has bettered his position in the Roman Church, as to certainty and practical utility to one who seeks truth from a love of it. I maintain that the formularies and decrees of the Roman Church, and by which he professes to be governed, are so undefined, uncertain, and loosely worded (and as would appear purposely so), that to some no explanation can be offered at all, and to others opposite and contradictory interpretations can, and are given; even extending to points of doctrine which one would suppose should be made clear by a self-styled infallible church. First take her Creed, which Dr. Newman, as a priest, has subscribed as being the "true Catholic faith, without which no man can be saved;" which he promised, "vowed, and swore" most constantly to retain and profess, entire and inviolate, and, as far as in him lay, to be retained, and taught and preached.

The first article of this Creed is, " I most steadfastly admit and embrace apostolical and ecclesiastical traditions, and all other observances and constitutions of the same [Roman] Church." If we ask one priest and then another to define what he includes in the above article, we should get widely distinct answers, according to circumstances and the person who puts the question. There are numerous ecclesiastical traditions which have been wholly abandoned; and many adopted as such, of comparatively recent origin. Who is to define what is or what is not a *tradition* within the meaning of this article, when the Roman Church herself has not done so? It is easy to say, "I believe in all the traditions of the Church," but no one can say what those traditions are. Where is the authority to which appeal is to be made to decide this question? The Church! What is the "Church," and how does it speak? Where is it to be found when required?

Dr. Newman tells us that he "must ever profess to be guided by Scripture and by tradition."* Can Dr. Newman say by what traditions he is guided, which are not defined in Scripture? The traditions relative to points of faith, spoken of by Irenæus, and other early Fathers, were all reduced to writing, and formed what we now call the New Testament, as they expressly declared. Dr. Newman knows full well that the early Christian divines looked to the Scriptures alone for their rule and guide. But I ask Dr. Newman again on whose authority are *traditions* made binding on our consciences? Who is responsible for their correctness and purity? Where are they to be found? If Dr. Newman is really guided by this tradition, he can find no difficulty in answering all these questions, and defining what are the points necessary to be believed, which are not read in the Scriptures or proved thereby? Again, what is included in the words "all other observances and constitutions" of the Roman Church? Can Dr. Newman give us any idea whatever? And yet all these undefined observances and constitutions are thus raised to the dignity of articles of faith by being made a part of the creed of the Roman Church. It must be admitted that a decree of a Pope solemnly promulgated, and recorded in the book of Canon Law, is a "constitution" of the church that sanctions it. Let me give an example:—Boniface VIII. issued a decree, and which is to be found in every edition up to the present day, of the Canon Law of the Church of Rome, wherein he laid down as follows:—"We declare, say, define, and pronounce it to be necessary to salvation for every human creature to be subject to the Roman Pontiff." Again, the decree of Innocent III., forming the third canon of the fourth Lateran Council, commanding the extirpation of heretics,

---

* "Apologia," p. 393.

though declared by some and denied by others, to be a substantial decree of a general council, is part of the Roman canon law of the present day. Are these two precepts "observances and constitutions" of the Roman Church? Dr. Newman may find it convenient to say no, but the words of his Creed have a restricted meaning. "Observances and constitutions" are wide terms. He may say they refer only to the "decrees" of a general council. This is a plausible answer; but what means the article which follows—" I *likewise* undoubtedly receive and profess all other things delivered and defined, and declared by the sacred canons and general councils"? This embraces something beyond the "other observances and constitutions" named in the first article of the Creed. And this leads us to ask which are the general councils here alluded to? Who has fixed the number? And are all Romanists agreed on the point? Some hold eight, some ten, some eighteen, as general councils, and some only parts of decrees of some of these. Dr. Newman appears to hold to eighteen,* but does not name them. But if it be true, as Bellarmine tells us, that the records and decrees of councils have been most negligently kept, and contain many errors,† what existing infallible authority is there to rectify the omissions and errors of mutilated and perverted records? Is there any certainty as to what are and what are not contained in these canons?

Take the next article. Dr. Newman is bound to "admit the Holy Scripture according to that sense which the Roman Church has held and does hold." Can he, on the authority of any credible witness, state the "sense" which he is here bound to admit on any given chapter or text? Is the sense of the Church to be found anywhere? Does any priest pretend to be

* "Apologia," p. 396.
† "Libri conciliorum negligenter conservati sunt, et multis vitiis scatent."—Bell. *de Concil.*, lib. i. c. ii. sect. i. Prag. 1721.

able to give that sense? Then, again, that sense can only be according to the " unanimous agreement of the Fathers." Dr. Newman is now bound not to interpret Scriptures except according to the unanimous agreement of the Fathers. Is Dr. Newman, or any other Romanist, able to produce such unanimity on any text? If he cannot, how can he profess to be guided by the Scriptures at all? I am dealing, be it remembered, with articles of faith.

Again, if there is any doctrine which is, one would suppose, clearly defined, it is Transubstantiation; the alleged literal, carnal conversion of the consecrated elements of bread and wine into, not merely the " Soul and Divinity," but also the *real substantial* body, blood, bones, and nerves, of the self-same body of Christ that was born of the Virgin, and was nailed to the Cross; which definition entirely excludes a spiritual interpretation of our Lord's words, " This is my body," on which the doctrine is supposed to be founded. Notwithstanding this plain declaration and definition, Veron, in his " Rule of Catholic Faith"* (one of the books, by the way, presented to Dr. Newman shortly before he withdrew from the Church), lays it down that—" Not only may the body of Christ, though really present under the Eucharistic symbols, be called a *spiritual* body, and Christ himself a *spirit*, but the body of Christ may be said to be present under the appearances of bread and wine, in *a spiritual manner, or spiritually,* and not in a *corporeal and natural* manner, or, which is the same thing, *not corporeally or carnally.*" The italics are as in the original. If this be so, Dr. Newman will find a difficulty in reconciling the Roman definition and Veron's interpretation as " a clear statement of Catholic doctrine."

Take another article of the Creed. " Likewise, that

---

* Translated by Father Waterworth, Birmingham, 1833, p. 99. This book is one of those specially recommended to perverts, and is declared in the Preface to be of " undoubted authority."

the saints reigning together with Christ *are to be honoured and invocated.*" The original words are, " Similiter et sanctos una cum Christo regnantes, venerandos atque invocandos esse." This is precise language as a command of the Roman Church. These saints, supposed to be reigning with Christ, *are to be* (not *may be*) invocated; and accordingly, fully two-thirds of the Roman prayers are made up of invocations and prayers to saints. Nevertheless, Dr. Newman dogmatically lays it down, " Invocations are not *required* [*sic*] by the Church of Rome."* If so, can the " statement of the [Roman] Catholic doctrine" be clear? But Dr. Newman sees, but hides, the difficulty of the doctrine and its requirements, which is anything but clear, as is imagined. The invocation is restricted to saints actually reigning with Christ. How is a Romanist to know, for certainty, that his or her patron saint, or the saint invocated, is in that happy state? What finite being or assumed infallible authority can answer the question? Can Dr. Newman, who professes to belong to a church where certainty reigns, answer the question? The idolatry of the Roman Church ran riot on this head; so much so, that Alexander III. passed a decree that no one should be acknowledged as a saint, and invoked as such, unless he had been declared to be a saint,—in other words, duly canonized as such, by the Bishop of Rome. The reason given was, lest idolatry be committed by invoking one not in a state of happiness, one who might possibly be damned. But it was not, as admitted by Veron himself,† decided by the Roman Church until the beginning of the 15th century, at the Council of Florence (A.D. 1439), " whether the souls of the blessed are received in heaven and enjoy the clear vision of God before the resurrection and the last day of final judg-

---

* " Apologia," p. 363.
† " Rule of Catholic Faith," as above, p. 82.

ment." Some admit, some reject the Council of Florence as a General Council, and the validity of its decrees. If not general, the question as to the state of departed souls is still an open question, and may be doubted. We know that the early Christian writers held opposite opinions on this subject. But Romanists admit that no one can be invocated until canonized. Is canonization an article of faith? If not, the ceremony and supposed result can be rejected and disbelieved. Now Veron again lays it down, "That the canonization of saints is not an article of faith; in other words, it is no article of our faith that the saints whom we invoke are really saints, and in the number of the blessed." . . . "It is clear (he continues) that there is no evidence to prove, either from the written or unwritten word of God, that these persons were saints;"* and may, therefore, without the charge of heresy, be rejected as such. Let me repeat the words of the Roman Creed—"Likewise that the saints *reigning with Christ are to be invocated*,"—and which Dr. Newman is sworn to teach. Now, compare this with Veron's statement. I confess that to me the whole doctrine and theory (setting aside the fact that saints must be omniscient and omnipresent to hear the prayers at one time from all quarters of the globe) appear to be full of difficulties, uncertainties, and inconsistencies. The Church of England, on the other hand, is precise. Prayers, by her, are directed to God alone, through Christ our Lord. The *certainty* of this channel is admitted by Romanists. And yet Dr. Newman pretends that in the Anglican Church he cannot appeal to any clear statement of doctrine.

The Creed further says—"I also affirm that the power of indulgences was left by Christ in the Church, and that the use of them is most wholesome to Christian people." Can Dr. Newman assert that

---

* Veron, as above, pp. 84, 85.

indulgences, as now practised by his church, have any kin or similarity to the custom as practised by the early Church? Can he define its effects? Will he dare deny the fact that numerous Popes have issued bulls granting indulgences which extended not only to the forgiveness of temporal punishments due to sin but to the sins themselves? "Indulgentias et remissiones peccatorum" are words of ordinary occurrence in Popes' bulls, and these indulgences are even dogmatically declared to be applicable to souls in purgatory! Indeed, the granting of indulgences to remit the temporal punishments due to sin in this world and in purgatory, is also of almost daily occurrence. But what says Veron again in his "Rule of Catholic Faith"?—"With regard to the power of granting indulgences, it is not of faith [that is, it may be entirely discredited] that there is in the Church a power to grant such indulgences as actually will remit at the tribunal of God, either in this life or in the life to come, the temporal punishment which may remain due after our sins have been pardoned."* Again, he says, "There are Catholic writers who deny in plain and undoubted terms that indulgences are of any use to the dead."† And he gives us to understand that we may entirely reject the whole theory on which the doctrine of indulgences is built, namely, the existence of a celestial treasure of superabundant merits of Christ and departed saints. So that the whole doctrine is left in an entire fog. We are to believe that the power of indulgences was left in the Church, but how they are dispensed, their practical utility or extent, are mysteries undefined!

Again, the Roman Creed requires Dr. Newman to receive seven sacraments, properly so called, the Decree of Trent enforcing the belief with an anathema. It is admitted that, in order to constitute a sacrament, three

* Veron, as above, p. 52. † Ibid. pp. 57-8.

essentials are necessary. 1. The Institution of Christ; 2. Form; 3. Matter. It is further admitted that two of these, Baptism and the Lord's Supper, embrace the three essentials. The remaining five are—1. Confirmation; 2. Penance; 3. Extreme Unction; 4. Orders; and 5. Matrimony.

Let us now see Rome's certainty in these so-called sacraments:—

1. *Confirmation.*—" When did Christ ordain this sacrament?" This question is asked in a popular catechism—" The Abridgment of Christian Doctrine," revised and recommended by the Romish Bishop, Dr. Doyle. The answer is, "*The time is not certain;* but divines *most probably* hold it was instituted at Christ's last supper, *or*, between His resurrection and ascension."* Confirmation, therefore, wants the *evidence* of institution by Christ; there is *no certainty* in the matter. But let us go to a higher authority—the " Catechism of the Council of Trent,"† under the head " Confirmation"—" Instituted by Christ." The effrontery is something astounding:—

"But to impress the faithful with a deeper sense of the sanctity of this sacrament, the pastor will make known to them *by whom it was instituted;* a knowledge the importance of which with regard to all the sacraments we have already pointed out. He will, accordingly, inform them that, not only was it instituted by our Lord Jesus Christ, but as S. Fabian, Bishop of Rome, testifies, the chrism and the words used in its administration were also appointed by Him: a *fact of easy proof* to those who believe confirmation to be a sacrament, for all the sacred mysteries are beyond the power of man, and could have been instituted by God alone."

Could any reasonable man have conceived that this is all a self-styled infallible church could advance in proof of the validity of this so-called sacrament? But this is not all. Reference is made to Fabian's second Epistle, in a foot-note, as the authority. There are

* P. 77, stereotyped Edition; Dublin, 1833.
† I transcribe from the edition translated into English by Donovan, Professor, &c., Royal College, Maynooth. Dublin, 1829, p. 196.

only three epistles attributed to Fabian, and they are, all three, now universally admitted to be notorious forgeries of the ninth century! Fabian is supposed to have lived A.D. 236. The alleged matter, "chrism," resting on the same evidence, goes with the alleged "institution by Christ." As to the Form:—The ancient custom was to confirm by the laying on of hands. This form is wholly abandoned by the modern Roman Church. It forms no part whatever of the ceremony. The *Pontificale Romanum* does not say a word of laying on of hands. They have substituted, "I sign thee with the sign of the Cross, and I confirm thee with the chrism of salvation, in the name of the Father, &c." The only truly traditional apostolic custom, which would otherwise be the "*form*," they have abandoned! And this is the church which Dr. Newman recommends for certainty of doctrine in its formularies!

2. *Penance* in the Roman Church is a most complicated affair. True repentance, from the love of God and hatred of sin, forms no part of this sacrament. They admit that God forgives their sin thus repented of *without* confession and absolution—two parts of this so-called sacrament. We come to the tribunal of penance with an *imperfect repentance*, which they call *attrition* and sorrow for sin, from the fear of its consequences, that is, the punishment that follows. This, with private confession to a priest, with the priest's absolution, who acts judicially in the matter, and imposes, at his discretion, "satisfaction" or temporal punishments; these constitute the sacrament. Perhaps Dr. Newman will point out where and when Christ instituted this piece of machinery. He cannot. The *matter* of the sacrament is stated to be the "acts of the penitent, contrition, confession, and satisfaction."* In the first place, *contrition* is not necessary:

---

* Catechism, as above, p. 258.

contrition is the repentance from the love of God, and the forgiveness takes place without the sacrament. Again, these acts are not *material* substances and *visible signs;* and therefore the Council of Trent calls them "quasi materia"—"the matter as it were." It is thus admitted not to be the thing itself; it wants, therefore, two essentials—institution and matter. The form is stated to be "I absolve thee." As that form was never used for 1,000 years after Christ, this alleged essential is a modern innovation. Where, then, is Dr. Newman's certainty of this sacrament?

3. *Extreme Unction.*—It is scarcely pretended that this so-called sacrament was instituted by Christ. The "Catechism of Christian Doctrine" puts the question, and answers it:—

"Q. When did Christ institute it?

"A. *The time is uncertain. Some think* it was instituted at His Last Supper; *others* that it was between His resurrection and ascension"!

But the Council of Trent (Session xiv. can. i.) expressly avoids the word "instituted" as applied to this so-called sacrament, but uses the word "insinuatum"—*insinuated!* It lacks, therefore, the essential of a sacrament—institution by Christ.

4. *Matrimony.*—As to institution, Dr. Doyle, in the same Catechism, asks,*

"Q. Where was it made a sacrament of the new law?

"A. When and where Christ instituted this sacrament *is uncertain.*"

It further lacks "matter," which Dr. Doyle, in the same Catechism, says is "the mutual consent of the parties, &c." How can a "consent" be *matter!* So that there is as little *certainty* about this so-called sacrament as the others.

5. *Orders.*—As to *matter* and *form*, Peter Dens, in his

* P. 405.

"Theologia," on Orders,* states four different opinions as to the "matter and form of the priesthood." According to the Trent Catechism, the *matter* of the sacrament consists in the delivery to the person ordained, of the chalice with the consecrated wine, and of the paten with the bread. Now, Dens† very properly advances three objections to this. "1. Because Scripture nowhere speaks of the delivery of the vessels. 2. Because, even during the first ten centuries, that custom was not known in the Latin Church. 3. Because the Greek Church has not that custom." As to the form, which is "Receive the power of offering Christ, &c.," it is a fact that down to the Council of Florence, A.D. 1439, the form of ordination was laying on of the hands by the bishop. This was, by that council, altered to the above form of words. Indeed, the Roman canon law lays down that the ordination would be valid without the imposition of hands.‡ It lacks, therefore, institution by Christ. Indeed, Dens admits, in the place above cited, that "it must be premised that Christ did not definitively institute the *matter* and *form* for the sacrament of Orders, as in other sacraments, but only in general."

So that, in fact, these five alleged sacraments are, even according to Romish admissions, surrounded by doubts and uncertainties, and yet Dr. Newman has the boldness to declare that he has left our communion because we "cannot appeal to any clear statement of Catholic doctrine in its formularies." I do not see that Dr. Newman has bettered his position in this respect, though he may claim for himself an infallible tribunal (which, when wanted, can never be found) to clear difficult questions.

If we ask Dr. Newman about "Purgatory," how, to what extent, and in what manner, and what is the

---

* N. 4, vol. vii. p. 43; Dublin ii. 1832. † As above, p. 45.

‡ "Sine impositione manuum."—*Corp. Juris Canon.*, tom. ii. p. 265. Paris, 1612.

evidence that the souls therein detained are assisted by the suffrages of the faithful, what can he answer, but with Veron, that there is no certainty in the matter at all, and as little certainty, in fact, of the existence of any such *place* or *state*; and which of the two, *place* or *state*, they dare not define.

Dr. Newman is now called upon to believe, as another article of faith, that the Roman Church is the "mother and mistress of all churches," which, as to the former, is historically false; and as to the latter, it is not the fact that she is the mistress of all churches. The article, which compels Dr. Newman to admit that there are other churches besides the Roman Church, equally imposes upon him the admission as an article of faith, of two palpable falsehoods.

And lastly, Dr. Newman is bound to "embrace and receive all and every one of the things which have been defined and declared in the holy Council of Trent concerning original sin and justification." This is a bold declaration. If Dr. Newman can define the meaning of the Council of Trent on justification, he is a cleverer man than many in his church who have gone before him. It is an admitted fact that, previous to the Council of Trent, there were in the Roman Church two contending parties, the Dominicans and Jesuits, holding opposite opinions on justification; the Dominicans with Luther holding the views clearly taught by Augustine, the great luminary of the African Church in the fifth century. In fact, the Augustinian doctrine is the present Protestant doctrine. The doctrine created a civil war in the bosom of the Roman Church. The subject came under consideration of the Council of Trent at the 6th session, A.D. 1547. The discussion was smart and bitter, and "among the members of the Council were many who held opinions on this point [justification] entirely similar to those of the Protestants."* With

---

* Ranke, "History of the Popes," book ii. s. 5.

the time-serving shifts that guide Rome in most of her deliberations, in order to satisfy both parties and reconcile discordant opinions, the decrees on justification were purposely drawn up obscurely and some parts inconsistent with others. This led to further disputes, and each party claimed a victory. No sooner was the session ended, than Dominic a Soto, the leader of one faction, published a book in support of the views of his party, which was answered by Andreas Vega, his chief opponent, and they claimed the authority of the decrees of Trent in support of their respective opinions. The war continued, which led to an open rupture between the Dominicans and the Jesuits, and which continued between the Jansenists and the Jesuits up to a recent date. These facts are too notorious to require further reference. Will Dr. Newman set himself up as an infallible authority, and decide between the contending parties, and say who rightly interpreted the decrees of Trent? So conscious did the doctors of Trent feel of the doubtful character of their decrees, that their last act was to declare that—

"If, in receiving these decrees, any difficulty should arise (which it does not believe), which may require declaring or defining, the Holy Synod, besides other remedies appointed in this Council, trusts that the most blessed Pontiff will take care, either by assembling of those whom he shall think expedient to handling the matter, especially from those provinces in which the difficulty has arisen, or even by the celebration of a General Council, if he shall deem it necessary, or by any other better way which shall seem good to him, to take care of the necessities of the provinces, for the glory of God, and the tranquillity of the Church."*

This was the last act of a self-styled infallible council, appealing to a fallible tribunal to explain or expound its own decrees. A committee of cardinals now exists to meet this requirement. So that Dr. Newman, after all,

* "Concil. General." Labbe. et Coss. Concil. Trid., Sess. xxv. tom. xiv. col. 919. Paris, 1671.

has but a fallible certainty of understanding the decrees of his own church, and a fallible set of men to expound them! His words are, indeed, worthy of repeating, given, as they are, as a reason for leaving the Church of England to go to Rome:—

"It seems a dream to call a communion Catholic, when one can neither appeal to any clear statement of Catholic doctrine in its formularies, nor interpret ambiguous formularies by the received and living Catholic sense, whether past or present."*

I maintain that the whole Roman system is one mass of absurdities and contradictions. Their own doctors and divines are at variance with each other, even on first principles—they are scarcely agreed on anything. If you quote the opinion of one divine, however eminent he may otherwise be, even that of a Pope, if convenient, his opinion is repudiated as that of a private doctor; and yet, one of their greatest boasts is, that there is a uniformity of teaching throughout their church! and perhaps there is no question on which there are more diverse opinions than on the question of infallibility itself, on which, it may fairly be supposed, all ought to be agreed. Dr. Newman himself felt the difficulty of this question, but he could not pass it over. He labours upon it, but is obliged to give the real difficulty the "go-by." He says, "I am not here determining anything about the essential seat of that power [infallibility], because that is a question doctrinal, not historical and practical." Not practical! How is one to appeal to infallibility? how are we to recognize its oracular decisions, if we cannot define the seat of infallibility itself? It is essentially a practical question; but I deny that it is a "question doctrinal." Nothing can be a doctrine unless it is formally proposed for belief as such. This is a rule laid down by Veron. Now, infallibility never has been proposed as a

* "Apologia," p. 250.

doctrine by the Roman Church. She never has by any decree or other constitution claimed to be infallible, much less has she defined the seat or extent of infallibility; and yet Dr. Newman presumes to lay down in precise terms the extent, "now in its fulness," of this "tremendous power." The whole is a creation of his own imagination, which may be accepted or repudiated by his co-religionists at pleasure, as was his theory of Development.

I must enumerate some of the points on which the Church of Rome, according to Dr. Newman, alleges to claim to act with infallible authority:—

"It claims to have a sure guidance into every meaning of every portion of the Divine Message in detail, which was committed by our Lord to His apostles."

It is really to be lamented that the Roman Church, with this power, has not issued any infallibly true and correct interpretation of Scripture, and thus at once settled all our doubts and difficulties; but that would be too *practical*.

"It claims to know its own limits, and to decide what it can determine absolutely and what it cannot."

Doubtless, as a Nasmyth's hammer can be regulated to crack a nut or flatten a ton of iron.

"It claims, moreover, to have a hold upon statements not directly religious, so far as this, to determine whether they indirectly relate to religion; and, according to its own definite judgment, to pronounce whether or not, in a particular case, they are consistent with revealed truth."

For instance, it claims the existence of "Purgatory" to be a doctrine of the Church; but it can tell us nothing about it, or how the doctrine is "consistent with revealed truth." That, again, would be too practical!

"It claims to decide magisterially, *whether infallible or not* [this is odd], that such and such statements are, or are not, prejudicial to the Apostolic *deposition* of faith in their spirit or in their consequences, and to allow them or condemn and forbid them accordingly."

Setting herself as sole judge, the Church of Rome proceeds to anathematize, or, in other words, damn to all eternity, those who do not accept such statements as she chooses to assert are prejudicial to the faith; of course, invented by herself,—say the Immaculate Conception, which she calls apostolical.

"It claims to impose silence at will on any matters of controversies of doctrine, which, on its own *ipse dixit*, it pronounces to be dangerous or inexpedient, or unimportant."

"It claims that, whatever may be the judgment of Catholics upon such acts, these acts should be received by them with those outward marks of reverence, submission, and loyalty which Englishmen, for instance, pay to the presence of their sovereign, without public criticism on them, as being in their matter inexpedient, or in their manner violent and harsh."

Passing on to the "Catholic Church," he adds:—

"It claims, not only to judge infallibly on religious questions, but to animadvert on opinions in secular matters which bear upon religion; on matters of philosophy, of science, of literature, of history,—and it demands our submission to her claim."

"It claims to censure books, to silence authors, and to forbid discussions."

Dr. Newman, of course, then approves of Bacon's works being prohibited, and of Macaulay's History of England being a "tabooed" book from a gentleman's library.

"It must, of course, be obeyed without a word; and perhaps, in process of time, it will tacitly recede from its own injunctions. In such cases the question of faith does not come in; for what is matter of faith is true for all times, and never can be unsaid."

Having raised his imaginary "Frankenstein;" he bows his head and declares "I profess my own absolute submission to its claim."* He receives it "as it is infallibly interpreted by the authority to whom it is thus committed, and implicitly as it shall be, in like manner, further interpreted by that same authority till the end of time." This is a very cheap submission,

* "Apologia," p. 389.

for, as we have said, the Church of Rome has defined nothing whatever about infallibility!

"Such," exclaims Dr. Newman, "is the infallibility lodged in the Catholic Church, viewed in the concrete, as clothed and surrounded by the appendages of its high sovereignty: it is, to repeat what I said above, a supereminent, prodigious power, sent upon earth to encounter and master a great evil."

Well done, Dr. Newman, you have indeed become confiding and garrulous in your old age! But, alas! this huge and grand fabric is razed to the ground by the suggestion of a bare possibility that infallibility may be at fault nevertheless; for he warns us that—

"It does not follow, because there is a gift of infallibility in the Catholic Church, that therefore the power in possession of it is in all its proceedings infallible. 'Oh, it is excellent (says the poet) to have a giant's strength, but tyrannous to use it like a giant.'"!

Very poetical indeed! and the whole is as imaginative as poetical effusions generally are. When Dr. Newman added this fatal saving clause, he no doubt had in his mind (infallibility extending to *science*) the condemnation of Galileo and his theory of the diurnal motion of the earth, and the stability of the sun as the centre of the solar system, by the then reigning Pontiff and the Sacred Congregation of the Roman Church, specially empowered to decide in such matters, as false, heretically untrue, and *contrary to faith*. If infallibility indeed extends to science, we have discovered that, in this instance at least, it has been grievously at fault, and we may fairly conclude that this "great fabric of a vision" should have some more substantial proofs of its effect than the bare assertions and claims made by erratic individuals, who place themselves at the head of God's creation as the elect and sole members of the only true Church on earth. Dr. Newman tells us that there "is nothing to surprise the mind *if* the Creator should think fit to introduce a power into the world invested with this prerogative." "Much virtue is there in an *if*"! Nothing to surprise the mind! We may not be surprised at anything Dr. Newman chooses to believe; but as the Creator has not been pleased to invest any individual, or set of individuals, with the powers enumerated, we Protestants look sceptically on. But listen to Dr. Newman's logic. He says,

"When I *find* that this is the very claim of the Catholic Church, not only do I feel no difficulty in admitting the idea, but there is a fitness in it which recommends it to my mind."*

But what if his church does not claim it, and that he has been running after a Will-'o-the-wisp—a shadow—another ghost? But what am I saying? A man who disbelieved in transubstantiation until he discovered the Church of Rome was the oracle of God, and then at once swallowed this theological abortion, is capable of executing any extraordinary ecclesiastical jugglery, or spiritual sleight-of-hand tricks.

The effect of this "claim" on Dr. Newman's mind is an implicit obedience and acceptance of everything enumerated by this oracle, however extravagant, however absurd, however ridiculous, as we shall presently see. "I profess (says he) my own absolute submission to its claim." "I believe the whole revealed dogma as taught by the Apostles, as committed by the Apostles to the Church, *and as declared by the Church to me*,"—after the system of the old nursery story, "This is the house that Jack built," &c.; and in this Dr. Newman and Dr. Pusey go hand in hand. "In simple words (says the latter), I believe all the Church believes."

But how does Dr. Newman receive this doctrine? "I receive it, as it is infallibly interpreted by the authority to whom it is thus committed, and (implicitly) as it shall be, in like manner, further interpreted by that same authority till the end of time."

* "Apologia," p. 382.

Now, if Dr. Newman had given us some idea how he got at this authority, he would have conferred a practical benefit on society; but that is exactly what he does not do, and cannot do. He is therefore compelled to lay down the absurd proposition, that the seat of infallibility is not a practical question. Having swallowed the whole theory, he immediately branches out into an extraordinary confession, the result of this implicit submission to a supposed infallible authority:—

"I submit to the universally received traditions of the Church" [By universally received does he mean received by the Roman Church alone, or by universal Christendom?], "in which lies the matter of those new dogmatic definitions which are from time to time made, and which in all times are the clothing and the illustration of the Catholic dogma, as already defined." It is necessary sometimes to assume a learned way of talking nonsense, and of all occasions the present seems to require it. Dr. Newman continues: "And I submit myself to those other decisions of the Holy See, theological or not, through the organs which it has itself pointed out" [the Church of Rome never having done such a practical act], "which, waiving the question of their infallibility, on the lowest ground, came to me with a claim to be accepted and obeyed." What all this may mean or embrace it is impossible to tell, and I doubt much if Dr. Newman knows himself; but in order, like a prudent man— even in his old age—to meet future emergencies and calls on his faith (I should say credulity), he adds, "Also I consider that, gradually, and in the course of ages, Catholic inquiry has taken certain definite shapes, and has thrown itself into the form of a science, with a method and a phraseology of its own, under the intellectual handling of great minds." With a mind, therefore, open to accept anything and everything, from the Immaculate Conception to the Pope's personal infallibility, if it come to that—a theory really now mooted and proposed to be accepted as a doctrine—he "feels no temptation at all to break in pieces the great legacy of thought thus committed to us for these latter days."

The "great legacy of thought"! These Romanists certainly have "a method and phraseology of their own." But the "great legacy" really appears to be a gift to swallow any theological proposition, possible or impossible to conceive, without any thought at all.

We have here, however, the idea of the development principle, which has rendered Dr. Newman so notorious, and which has enabled him to overcome difficulties which presented themselves, in accepting palpably modern innovations.

We cannot pass by Dr. Newman's extraordinary work on Development without some notice.

Dr. Newman once thought, or professed to think, as we have seen,—and he seriously promulgated the idea—that the Roman communion is infected with heresy; that we are bound to flee it as a pestilence; that Romanists have established a lie in the place of God's truth; and, by their claim to immutability in doctrine, cannot undo the sin they have committed. Without one word of apology for this sweeping denunciation, Dr. Newman reads Mr. Kingsley a lecture on his "intellectual blindness,"* for entertaining similar views on their present relative positions.

"A modest man or a philosopher would have scrupled (he says) to treat with scorn and scoffing, as Mr. Kingsley does, in my own instance, principles and convictions, even if he did not acquiesce in them himself, which had been held so widely and for so long—the beliefs and devotions, and customs which have been the religious life of millions upon millions of Christians for nearly twenty centuries, for this in fact is the task on which he is spending his pains."

---

* "Apologia," p. 5.

If Dr. Newman's allegation as to twenty centuries' prescription be true, Mr. Kingsley must be, as alleged,* "so constituted as to be stone-blind to his own ignorance." We shall presently see, that he asserts his "stronghold to be antiquity." † But the assertion made—the claim to antiquity for the Roman Church—is just what Dr. Newman has not proved, and cannot prove. To solve his own doubts and difficulties, as to which is the true Church, England or Rome, he (as he tells us) "determined to write an Essay on doctrinal development," ‡ and then, if, at the end of it, his convictions in favour of the Roman Church were not weaker, to make up his mind to seek admission into her fold. He ostensibly acted on this resolution in the beginning of 1845, and worked at his Essay steadily until the autumn.

When finished the work appears to have been so satisfactory to himself, that he, on its publication, (outwardly) quitted the Church of England, and was admitted as a member of the Romish communion. We would confidently appeal to this very work to refute Dr. Newman's present appeal to "antiquity" and to "twenty centuries' prescription." The theory of development is in direct antagonism to the repeated dogmatic assertions made by the doctors assembled at the Trent Council, in their decrees. They promulgated the alleged fact, that all her doctrines were declared in the Scriptures, taught by the Apostles, and handed down by the tradition of the universal Church. They professed simply to have declared what was of faith from the beginning, by simply defining and declaring what those doctrines were. Dr. Newman, however, was too well read in ecclesiastical history to accept such a proposition, whatever he may now advance as "necessary for his

---

* "Apologia," p. 5. † Ibid. p. 208.
‡ Ibid. p. 360.

position." He accepted the doctrines, but he could not accept as a matter of fact the allegation so confidently advanced, which he knew could not be established by proof; so he invented the theory of development. Religion, like arts and sciences, was to him a system of progression. He maintained that there are "gaps in the structure of the original creed of the Church,"* and in order to fill up these gaps, developments have arisen in after-ages, "not provided in Revelation as originally given."† This supplementary notion is applied to the doctrines of papal supremacy, image-worship, the worship of saints and angels, Mary-worship, and purgatory. But how are we to account for the strange omission of all these by the Fathers of the Church, whose genuine works may be fairly accepted as the records of the then existing opinions and practices? Dr. Newman's ingenuity was not at fault even here. The primitive Christians were so much occupied, he says, with "the actual superstitions and immoralities of Paganism before their eyes," that they "were not likely to entertain the question of the abstract allowableness of images in the Catholic ritual," or "to determine the place of St. Mary in our reverence," or "to recognize purgatory," or "to acknowledge the sovereign jurisdiction of the Pope," or to "inculcate the meritoriousness of monachism,"‡ or "to denounce the Protestant view of justification." Here, however, we have peeping out the "*amphibilogia* of the Roman casuists;"§ for the existence of which, as practised in the Roman Church, he declares himself "in no way answerable." Dr. Newman makes a boast of his honesty; he declares,||

"He has ever been fair to the doctrines and arguments of his opponents; never slurred over facts and reasonings which told against himself; has never given his name or authority to proofs which he

---

* "Apologia," p. 102.   † Ibid. p. 99.   ‡ Ibid. p. 145.
§ Appendix, p. 20. || Ibid. p. 24.

thought unsound, or to testimony which he did not think at least plausible; who has never shrunk from confessing a fault when he felt he had committed one—who loved honesty better than name, and truth than dear friends."

And having thus allowed him to sound his own trumpet, I assert that any tyro in ecclesiastical history would be able to demonstrate to Dr. Newman the fallacy of his position. These practices, now called doctrines, did not appear in the writings of the early Fathers of the Church, simply because they were neither practices nor even contemplated as part of the Christian code or creed. But setting aside this negative evidence, we have the positive evidence that the writings of these Fathers teem with passages which directly contradict the supposition that any of these modern papal developments existed in the Primitive Church. The inquiry is an interesting subject, but too extended for our present purpose; but we may rest satisfied with the fact that, negatively, none of the "developments" mentioned by Dr. Newman can be found in the writings of the genuine early Fathers for the first five centuries; while, positively, passages are abundant to prove that no such doctrines formed part of the creed, or even practice of the early Christian Church.

Dr. Newman's "Apologia" is full of assertions without proofs. We have seen that "dogma" is his "fundamental principle in religion."[*] He declares[†] that his "stronghold is antiquity." ... "In the middle of the fifth century, I found, as it seemed to me, Christendom of the nineteenth century reflected." He says our business is to make ourselves "more holy, more self-denying, more *primitive*."[‡] "For myself, this

[*] "Apologia," p. 120.　　[†] Ibid. p. 208.
[‡] Ibid. p. 263.

only I see, that there is infinitely more in the Fathers against our [the English Church] own state of alienation from Christendom than against the Tridentine decrees." In upholding Anglicanism, he says* that he "was forging arguments for Arius or Eutyches, and turning devil's advocate against the much-enduring Athanasius and the majestic Leo." He declares† "Rome to be the mother of English Christianity;" and, again,‡ "her zealous maintenance of the doctrine of the rule of celibacy I recognized as apostolic, and her faithful agreement with antiquity in so many points besides, which were dear to me, was an argument, as well as a plea in favour of the great Church of Rome."§ And he declares that he is "fully confident that the Church of Rome was the only true church,"|| and that the very "novelty made it [the Anglican Church] suspicious;"¶ and he considers it plain—

"That a theory such as this, [viz.] whether the marks of a divine presence and life in the Anglican Church were sufficient to prove that she was actually within the covenant, or only sufficient to prove that she was at least enjoying extraordinary and uncovenanted mercies, not only lowered her level in a religious point of view, but weakened her controversial bias."

Very charitable indeed! The Church of England enjoying an "extraordinary and uncovenanted mercy of God"! What is Dr. Newman's authority for this? However, we have in all this the broad and bold assertion that Anglicanism is a novelty, and Romanism based on antiquity. It is true, he repeatedly informs us that he is not writing "controversially;"** but he, nevertheless, tells us that *dogma* is "the fundamental principle of his

---

* "Apologia," p. 210. † Ibid. p. 279. ‡ Ibid. p. 126.

§ Dr. Newman is particularly unhappy in his selection of the doctrine of 'celibacy,' as illustrative of his idea of antiquity. And his historical allusion to the alleged fact that Rome was the mother of the English Church is a downright misrepresentation.

|| "Apologia," p. 268. ¶ Ibid. p. 967.
** Ibid. pp. 266, 209.

religion." It is therefore pretended to be asserted that the "dogmas" of the Roman Church are old, and Anglicanism is a novelty! As Dr. Newman does not advance one tittle of evidence to support his proposition, we will press the matter home a little, on his theory of dogmas. In the first place, he admits* that

"In both systems [the Roman and the Anglican], the same creeds are acknowledged. Besides other points in common, we both hold that certain doctrines are necessary to be believed for salvation; we both believe in the doctrines of the Trinity, Incarnation, and Atonement; in original sin; in the necessity of regeneration; in the supernatural grace of the sacraments; in the Apostolical succession; in the obligation of faith and obedience, and in the eternity of future punishment."

And yet he maintains that we are outcasts, dependent on uncovenanted mercies! And why, forsooth? Because we do not believe in the "dogmas" of his church, which, we allege, have been added;—namely, the supremacy, transubstantiation, prayers for the dead, purgatory, indulgences, the invocation of saints, and worship or religious *cultus* of images, or in the five additional sacraments, compulsory oral confession, and compulsory celibacy of the priesthood, &c.

When the Church of England separated from Rome, she cast off an usurped supremacy, which took its first rise only in the seventh century, and ended in a system of tyranny and exaction beyond the power of endurance. It is a remarkable fact that the Roman clergy themselves, in England, first originated the movement of a separation from Rome. In their petition to the throne, in 1528, to remove the burthensome tax on their incomes, imposed on them by the Bishop of Rome, is the following:—"May it please your Highness [Henry VIII.] to ordain, in this present Parliament, that the obedience of your Highness and of the people be withdrawn from the See of Rome."† The separation took

---

* "Apologia," p. 147.
† Strype's "Eccles. Mem.," vol. i. p. 158, fol. edit.

place before the reformation of the Church itself. The Church in this country assumed its original ecclesiastical position as an independent church; and the work of our Reformers, which soon followed, was to bring back the Church itself to a more primitive state. This is a question of doctrine. The leading principle of our Reformers was, as Jewell said,* to approach, " as much as possibly they could, to the Church of the apostles, and the ancient Catholic bishops and fathers ;" and, as Neal said,† "To depart no further from the Church of Rome than she had departed from the practice of the Primitive Church." As our Reformers cut at the root of Romish corruptions and superstitions, the inventions of a corrupt and sordid priesthood, no wonder that Dr. Newman should now shrink from their dangerous society.‡ "Anathema (says he) to a whole tribe of Cranmers, Ridleys, Latimers, and Jewells; perish the names of Bramhall, Ussher, Taylor, Stillingfleet, and Barrow, from the face of the earth."§ Strange that Dr. Newman should have so soon forgotten Hurrell Froude's "almost dying words," addressed to himself:—"I must enter another protest against your cursing and swearing. What good can it do? And I call it uncharitable to an excess;" and to which we give a hearty amen! But Dr. Newman is imbibing only the spirit of his adopted church, which hurls "curses, anathemas, and maledictions" on all who refuse to embrace her novelties. That Dr. Newman, on his change, "added articles to his creed," he candidly admits ; ||" but the old ones, which he then held with a divine faith, remained." It is to these new or additional articles to which we take exception, and for

* Jewell's "Apology," p. 124. London, 1685.
† Neal's "History of the Puritans," i. 38. London, 1837.
‡ "Apologia," p. 210.
§ The passage goes on—"ere I should do aught but fall at their [the much-enduring Athanasius and the majestic Leo] feet in love and in worship." || "Apologia," p. 124.

the adoption of which we nowhere find any rational explanation. That they are novelties, Dr. Newman could not deny; indeed he was too well read in ecclesiastical history to advance any denial. He was therefore driven to use most extraordinary expedients.

Dr. Newman's mode of reasoning, if we can dignify the process with that term, is truly astounding. Papal supremacy is with him, as Bellarmine has it, "the sum and substance of Christianity;" and De Maistre asserts that "without the Pope there is no true Christianity." The unqualified acceptance of the Pope's supremacy is an absolute necessity; but how are we to make it square with our preconceived notions of ecclesiastical history? Its acknowledgment rests (Dr. Newman says) on exactly the same foundation as the doctrine of the Trinity! Dr. Newman argues as follows:—You admit the *doctrine of the Trinity*. That doctrine is incomprehensible; of course it is—it is a mystery. But there is "less difficulty" in admitting the *supremacy* than in admitting the *Trinity*; therefore, to be consistent, we must admit also the supremacy of the Pope of Rome!* But an intelligent reader will say,—then we must, on the same process of reasoning, admit all the other doctrines and dogmas invented by the Roman Church, against which we protest as *novelties*, or as Dr. Newman calls them, *developments*. Of course we must; and herein alone is the Doctor consistent in driving home his theory. He places in one category all the leading Scriptural doctrines of Christianity and modern Papal developments under one head. Here they are in his own words, and a strange medley they present to a Bible-read Christian! He assures us that the Incarnation of Christ, the Mediation, the Atonement, the Mass, the merits of Martyrs and Saints, the Invocation and *cultus* of them, the centre of ecclesiastical unity in the Holy See, the authority of Councils,

---

* "Essay on Development," p. 167.

the Sanctity of Rites, the veneration of holy places, shrines, images, vessels, furniture, and vestments, Penance, Purgatory, Indulgences, the Real and material Presence in the Eucharist, Adoration of the Host, the virtue of relics, Original Sin, and Celibacy, all rest on the same basis in the way of well-developed evidence, so closely compacted together as to be quite inseparable.*

"You must accept the whole," says Dr. Newman, "or reject the whole; reduction does but enfeeble, and amputation mutilate. It is trifling to receive all but something which is as integral as any other portion: and, on the other hand, it is a solemn thing to receive any part; for before you know where you are, you may be carried on, by a stern logical necessity, to accept the whole. Moreover, since the doctrines altogether make up one integral religion, it follows that the several evidences which respectively support those doctrines belong to a whole and must be thrown into a common stock, and all are available to the defence of any."†

What can be advanced in reply to a man who seriously proposes such an extraordinary system of logic? You believe in God—you believe in a Trinity; therefore you must believe in the Pope's supremacy, transubstantiation, purgatory, image-worship, and anything else the Church of Rome has or may in future impose upon us for belief. And in this category, and precisely in the same manner, he now includes the modern doctrine of the "Immaculate Conception"! The process of ecclesiastical digestion is certainly as wonderful and complicated as the material process attending the nourishment of the body. This sudden universal reception of everything Rome teaches has, nevertheless, proved to be the common course and resort of all those of our clergy who have gone over to Rome, though their previous lives and professions had been standing protests against Popery. They all have, by some extraordinary process, been enabled to annihilate

---

* See Faber's "Letters on Tractarian Secession to Popery," Letter V. Dalton, Cockspur-street. London, 1846.

† "Essay on Development," pp. 154, 155.

all their former prejudices; and with one act of subscription to accept and acknowledge, exactly on the same footing of belief, all the ancient truths of Christianity and all the modern Romish additions. The Rev. Mr. Allies, the son-in-law and examining chaplain of the late Bishop of London, Dr. Blomfield, was shocked to find a lay tribunal decide an ecclesiastical proposition then in controversy between the High Church and Low Church parties in the well-known case of Gorham *v.* the Bishop of Exeter, contrary to his notions of orthodoxy. Although Mr. Allies had previously been, in his official capacity, a standing protest against Rome, he at once turned Papist, and without wincing, swallowed the whole of the decrees and canons of Trent and the twelve additional articles of Pope Pius's creed subsequently imposed on Christendom, exemplifying, in fact, the propositions boldly laid down by Dr. Newman, which all must follow who enter the Roman Church. Dr. Newman forgets, or finds it convenient to forget, that the fundamentals of Christianity are clearly proved from the BIBLE, which both parties admit to be written by Divine inspiration. *That* is our foundation of belief for their acceptance as dogmas not to be doubted. Once adopt Dr. Newman's principle, and there is no absurdity which we may not be called upon to accept as doctrine to be believed as necessary to our salvation; and that even contrary to all preconceived notions, prejudices, and even evidence. That we should have to believe contrary to evidence, we need give but one example. Dr. Newman, in his "Apologia," admits that the greatest difficulty he had to overcome was to reconcile himself to the "*undue reverence*"[*] and religious worship paid to the Blessed Virgin Mary by the Roman Church.

"I thought," he says,[†] "the essence of the offence of the Roman Church to consist in the honours which she paid to the Blessed Virgin

---

[*] "Apologia," p. 125.   [†] Ibid. p. 125.

and the saints.—Instead of setting before the soul the Holy Trinity, and heaven, and hell, the Church of Rome does seem to me, as a popular system, to preach the Blessed Virgin, and the Saints and Purgatory.*—I could not go to Rome (he asserts) while she suffered honours to be paid to the Blessed Virgin and the Saints, which I thought incompatible with the Supreme incommunicable Glory of the one Infinite and Eternal." †

In his "Essay on Development" he admits that, "in the first ages, there was no public or ecclesiastical recognition of the place which S. Mary holds in the economy of grace. This was reserved for the fifth century." With these admissions, we can scarcely appreciate the assertion so confidently made that the invocation and *cultus* of the saints, of whom the Blessed Virgin stands forth as the head, is to be admitted exactly on the same evidence as the belief of the Incarnation of Christ, His Mediation, and the Atonement! This is a bold way of getting over a difficulty. It is breaking through a hedge instead of passing through the gate—the "cutting across country." This was his excuse when he left the Church of England. The extracts we have given are his feelings before he left her communion, but we look in vain throughout the "Apologia" for an explanation how the transition of thought took place, and when, and under what circumstances, he discovered that the Romish worship of the Virgin was compatible with the worship of the Supreme Being, and how he became reconciled to the monkish extravagance of this Romish adoration. All the explanation we can find is that "he had a secret longing love of Rome, the mother of English Christianity, and he had a *true devotion to the Blessed Virgin.*" Such explanations, while they are peculiarly characteristic of the system of Dr. Newman's anomalous position, are anything but satisfactory to the student "halting between two opinions."

That we may thoroughly appreciate the tone of

---

* "Apologia," p. 224. † Ibid. p. 258.

mind and tenor of thought of Dr. Newman, we may here point out the fact that he applies the very same process in order to conform his mind to a belief in the legends and miracles so copiously related in the Roman Breviary, and other books of Romish devotion, so called.

Any one who has glanced his eye over the narration, in Romish works, of the wonderful cures that have been effected, as alleged, by so-called relics, and has read these wonderful " ecclesiastical miracles," sickens at the thought that there are individuals who give credence to such "pious frauds" and "old wives' fables," to sustain which there is not the slightest proof that can stand a rational investigation. But hear Dr. Newman:—

"It is plain," he says,* "there is nothing extravagant in this report of relics having a supernatural virtue; and for this reason, because there are such instances in Scripture,† and Scripture cannot be extravagant"!

Now how can we deal with a man who *argues*—the courtesy of controversy obliges me to use the word—in this manner, except by falling back on the assertion so strongly deprecated by Dr. Newman (and by myself too, for I protest against calling names), that a man must be either a " fool or a knave" for advancing such a proposition. We feel wholly at a loss how to express our pity for the state of degradation to which an otherwise gifted mind has fallen, because subjected to the pressure of Romanism, and its inseparable consequences. We would wish the Doctor had pushed his theory a little further, and had told us by what infallible process we are to ascertain real from false relics—real from false miracles—for we presume that he will not admit " supernatural virtues" to attach to false relics. Nor will he deny that priests have been

---

* "Apologia," Appendix, p. 41.
† See 2 Kings xiii. 20, 21 ; Acts xix. 11, 12 ; John v. 4.

detected in palming off false miracles, attributing supernatural effects, from what we call natural causes. Indeed he is obliged to confess " that the present advance of science tends to make probable that various facts have taken place in the order of nature, which hitherto have been considered by Catholics as simply supernatural." A convenient way of accounting for the pious frauds perpetrated at so-called " holy wells," &c.

But let this pass. To go on to so-called " Ecclesiastical miracles" in comparison with " Scriptural miracles." Now considering (to say the least of them,) the *wonderful* stories that are related in the Breviary and books of saints, and particularly in the book of the Bollandists, he must indeed be a bold man who can unflinchingly assert that he believes these narrations to be as true as the miracles related of Christ and the Apostles; and that he accepts them all exactly on the same evidence as he accepts the doctrines of the Trinity and the Incarnation, and who can allege that they are as likely to have happened, and are to be received by all with the same authority as the miracles performed by our Saviour and His disciples, as recorded in Holy Writ. And yet Dr. Newman seriously advances these propositions. Dr. Newman does not hesitate to avow himself to be champion of the Roman Church, even to support her palpable and well-established frauds! He takes a bold stand, and we can but admire him for his consistency, in this at least, in publishing the principles on which he professes to act. He says:*—

" As to the Catholic religion in England at the present day, this only will I observe—that the truest expedience is to answer right out when you are asked; that the wisest economy is to have no management; that the best prudence is not to be a coward; that the most damaging folly is to be found out shuffling; and that the first of virtues is to 'tell the truth, and shame the devil.'"

---

* " Apologia," Appendix, p. 71.

Acting then on this principle, Dr. Newman does not mince matters. His "wisest economy is to have no management, no half-measures, no shuffling." A great blot in the Roman system is to be accounted for,—"the best prudence is not to be a coward." There they are, admittedly most wonderful stories, and they are solemnly recorded and adopted by the Roman Church. It is a part of their system, and must all be received as a whole. "You must accept the whole or reject the whole." So Dr. Newman takes a plunge. He says:*—

"I will take one of those subjects, of which I spoke on the opening of this lecture, as offensive to Protestants—namely, our belief in the miracles. We accuse our enemies [the Protestants] of untruth in most cases. We do not accuse them, on the whole, of untruth here. I know it is very difficult for prejudice such as this to open its mouth at all without some mis-statement or exaggeration; still, on the whole, they do bear true—not false—witness in the matter of miracles. We do certainly abound—we are exuberant; we overflow with stories which cause our enemies—from no fault of ours—the keenest irritation, and kindle in them the most lively resentment against us. Certainly the Catholic Church, from east to west, from north to south, is, according to our conceptions, hung with miracles. The store of relics is inexhaustible; they are multiplied through all lands, and each particle of each has in it at least a dormant, perhaps an energetic virtue of supernatural operation. At Rome there is the true Cross, the crib of Bethlehem, and the chair of St. Peter; portions of the crown of thorns are kept at Paris; the holy coat is shown at Trèves; the winding-sheet at Turin. At Monza the iron crown is formed out of a nail of the Cross, and another nail is claimed for the Duomo of Milan; and pieces of our Lady's habit are to be seen in the Escurial. The Agnus Dei; blessed medals; the Scapular, the cord of St. Francis, all are the medium of Divine manifestations and graces. Crucifixes have bowed the head to the suppliant, and Madonnas have bent their eye upon assembled crowds. St. Januarius' blood liquefies periodically at Naples, and St. Winifred's Well is the scene of wonders even in an unbelieving country. Women are marked with sacred

---

* I am now quoting from Dr. Newman's Lecture delivered at Birmingham, "On the present position of Catholics in England." He refers to this lecture, and quotes largely from it, in the "Apologia," Appendix No. 5, p. 284; but as he omits important passages, as rather too startling, I prefer to quote from the original itself.

stigmata; blood has flowed on Fridays from their five wounds, and their heads are crowned with a circle of laceration. Relics are for ever touching the sick, the diseased, the wounded, sometimes with no result at all, at other times with marked and undeniable efficacy. Who has not heard of the abundant favours gained by the intercession of the Blessed Virgin, and of the marvellous consequences which have attended the invocation of St. Anthony of Padua? These phenomena are sometimes reported of saints in their lifetime as well as after death, especially if they were Evangelists or martyrs. The wild beasts crouched before their victims in the Roman amphitheatre; the axe-man was unable to sever St. Cecilia's head from her body, and St. Peter elicited a spring of water for his gaoler's baptism in the Mamertine. St. Francis Xavier turned salt water into fresh for five hundred travellers; St. Raymond was transported over the sea on his cloak; St. Andrew shone brightly in the dark; St. Scholastica gained by her prayers a pouring rain; St. Paul was fed by ravens; and St. Frances saw her guardian angel. I need not continue the catalogue. It is agreed on both sides; the two parties join issue over a fact: that fact is, the claim of miracles on the part of the Catholic Church; it is the Protestant's charge, and it is our glory."

Then at page 298 he says:—

"I think it impossible to withstand the evidence which is brought for the liquefaction of the blood of St. Januarius at Naples, and for the motion of the eyes of the picture of the Madonna in the Roman States. I see no reason to doubt the material of the Lombard crown at Monza; and I do not see why the holy coat at Trèves may not have been what it professes to be. I firmly believe that portions of the true Cross are at Rome and elsewhere; that the crib of Bethlehem is at Rome, and the bodies of St. Peter and St. Paul also. [I believe that at Rome, too, lies St. Stephen, that St. Matthew lies at Salerno, and St. Andrew at Amalfi. I firmly believe that the relics of the saints are doing innumerable miracles and graces daily, and that it needs only for a Catholic to show devotion to any saint in order to receive special benefits from his intercession. I firmly believe that saints in their lifetime have before now raised the dead to life, crossed the sea without vessels, multiplied grain and bread, cured *incurable* diseases, and stopped the operation of the laws of the universe in a multitude of ways.]* Many men, when they hear an educated man so speak, will at once impute the avowal to insanity, or to an idiosyncrasy, or to imbecility of mind, or to decrepitude, or to fanaticism, or to hypocrisy. They have a right to say so if they will; and we have a right to ask them why they do not say it of those who bow down before the mystery of mysteries—the Divine Incarnation.

---

* This portion between [ ] is left out by Dr. Newman in his "Apologia." See Appendix, p. 57.

If they do not believe this, they are not Protestants; if they do, let them grant that He who has done the greater may do the less."

Dr. Newman proceeds to say:—

"Ecclesiastical miracles are *probable* because Scripture miracles are *true*. As to the former of the two, I say that if Protestants are surprised at my having no *difficulty* in believing ecclesiastical miracles, I have a right to ask them why they have no difficulty in believing the Incarnation;" and he declares "we Protestants are most inconsistent and one-sided in refusing to go into the evidence for ecclesiastical miracles, which, on the first blush of the matter, are not stranger than those miracles of Scripture which they happily profess to admit."

Well done, Doctor Newman! will you permit us to analyze chemically the ingredients of the bottle alleged to contain the blood of St. Januarius, or examine the apparatus which causes the Virgin of Rimini to wink her eyes? We have never yet heard of the invitation being tendered. Until such an investigation be seriously offered, do not say we *refuse* to go into evidence.

It would be doing Dr. Newman an injustice, were I to omit his entire argument in favour—or as he would put it—in proof of his so-called Ecclesiastical miracles, and I do this at the expense of wearying my readers. In the appendix of the "Apologia,"* he argues—one must permit the word—thus:—

"We affirm that the Supreme Being has wrought miracles on earth ever since the time of the Apostles; Protestants deny it. Why do we affirm? why do they deny? We affirm it on a first principle, they deny it on a first principle; and on either side the first principle is made to be decisive of the question. . . . . Both they and we start with the miracles of the Apostles; and then their first principle or presumption against our miracles is this—'What God did once, He is not likely to do again;' while our first principle or presumption for our miracles is this—'What God did once, He is likely to do again.' They say, 'It cannot be supposed He will work many miracles;' we, 'It cannot be supposed He will work few.'

"The Protestant, I say, laughs at the very idea of miracles or supernatural powers as occurring at this day; his principle is rooted in him, he repels from him the idea of miracles; one is just as likely as another; they are all false. Why? Because of his first principle,

---

* P. 49.

there are no miracles since the Apostles. Here, indeed, is a short and easy way of getting rid of the whole subject; not by reason, but by a first principle which he calls reason. Yes, it is reason, granting his first principle is true; it is not reason, supposing his first principle is false.

"There is in the Church a vast tradition and testimony about miracles; how is it to be accounted for? If miracles *can* take place, then the *fact* of the miracle will be a natural explanation of the *report*, just as the fact of a man dying accounts satisfactorily for the news that he is dead; but the Protestant cannot so explain it, because he thinks that miracles cannot take place; so he is necessarily driven, by way of accounting for the report of them, to impute that report to fraud. He cannot help himself. I repeat it: the whole mass of accusations which Protestants bring against us under this head—Catholic credulity, imposture, pious frauds, hypocrisy, priestcraft,—this vast and varied superstructure of imputation, you see all rests on an assumption, on an opinion of theirs, for which they offer no kind of proof. What then, in fact, do they say more than this—'*If* Protestantism be true, you Catholics are a most awful set of knaves!' Here, at least, is a most sensible and undeniable position.

"Now, on the other hand, let me take our own side of the question, and consider how we ourselves stand relatively to the charge made against us Catholics; they hold the mystery of the Incarnation,—and the Incarnation is the most stupendous event which ever can take place on the earth; and after it, henceforth, I do not see how we can scruple at any miracle on the mere ground of its being unlikely to happen. . . . . When we start with assuming that miracles are not unlikely, we are putting forth a position which lies embedded, as it were, and involved in the great revealed fact of the Incarnation. So much is plain on starting; but more is plain too. Miracles are not only not unlikely, but they are positively likely; and for this simple reason, because, for the most part, when God begins, He goes on. We conceive, that when He first did a miracle, He began a series; what He commenced He continued: what has been will be. Surely, this is good and clear reasoning. To my own mind, certainly, it is incomparably more difficult to believe that the Divine Being should do one miracle and no more, than that He should do a thousand; that He should do one great miracle only, than that He should do a multitude of lesser besides. . . . If the Divine Being does a thing once, He is, judging by human reason, likely to do it again. This, surely, is common sense. If a beggar gets food at a gentleman's house once, does he not send others thither after him? If you are attacked by thieves once, do you forthwith leave your windows open at night? . . . Nay, suppose you yourself were once to see a miracle, would you not feel the occurrence to be like passing a line? Would you, in consequence of it, declare, 'I will never believe another if I hear of one'? Would it not, on the contrary, predispose you to listen to a new report?" . . . . .

Now let me illustrate Dr. Newman's theory by a few extracts from the Roman Breviary, the volume of volumes, which contains an abridgment of the divine offices of his church, appointed for the several canonical hours of each day during the course of the year, and which he designates as "that most wonderful and most attractive monument of the devotions of the saints."* Dr. Newman and all others in his church, who enjoy any ecclesiastical revenue,—all persons, of both sexes, who have professed in any of the regular orders, —all subdeacons and priests, are bound to repeat, either in public or in private, the whole service of the day out of this book. The omission of any one of the eight portions of which that service consists is declared to be a mortal sin!

The edition from which I quote is the "BREVIARIUM ROMANUM," published in 1845, in Dublin, by Richard Coyne, printer and bookseller to the Royal College of Maynooth, with the license and approbation, under his hand and seal, of the late Most Rev. Dr. Murray, dated 6th July, 1845; and which purports in its title-page to be published "by the order of Pope Pius V., according to a decree of the Sacred Council of Trent," and afterwards sanctioned by the authority of Popes Clement VIII. and Urban VIII.

I can only give a few extracts; but these will be fair samples of the contents of the book. It may facilitate my readers in finding the passages, to state that the work is in four volumes or parts, corresponding to the four seasons of the year—Pars Verna, Pars Æstiva, Pars Autumnalis, Pars Hiemalis — I shall specify, with the pages, from which my extracts are taken.† I shall begin with Dr. Newman's Patron Saint.

* "Apologia," p. 154.
† I follow the selection given in the *Catholic Layman*, but I have carefully verified every line with the original.

On 26th May, the Feast of *St. Philip Neri*, Confessor,* the fourth, fifth, and sixth lessons contain the history of that saint; and all faithful priests are encouraged to cultivate the love of God, by believing what is therein narrated; first praying solemnly that God would mercifully grant that they might *profit by the example* of his virtues.

After narrating that St. Philip was born at Florence, and had betaken himself to Rome, where he instituted the congregation of the Oratory, the fifth lesson proceeds thus :—

"Wounded by the love of God, he continually languished; and with such ardent love did his heart beat, that, when it could no longer be contained within its boundaries, the Lord miraculously enlarged his bosom, by breaking and raising up two of his ribs! Moreover, when performing the sacred offices, or fervently praying, he was sometimes seen lifted up into the air, and shining on all sides with a wonderful light!"

That he was rescued from a pitfall by an angel (as the narrative goes on to state), and was favoured frequently with apparitions of heavenly spirits, and even of the Blessed Virgin herself, or that he saw several souls surrounded by splendour ascending into heaven; or that, having restored many sick and dying people to health, he actually recalled one dead man to life, will probably seem but commonplace and every-day occurrences in comparison with the previous story, about the love of God having broken his ribs; or (what is related with equal gravity), that in consequence of having preserved the most spotless purity, he arrived at so refined a sense of smell, that he could even distinguish those who preserved their chastity by their odour! and, of course, detect others *ex fœtore*.

On the 19th of October, the Feast of *Peter of Alcantara*,† the lessons are equally edifying :—

---

* Pars Verna, pp. 554-5.
† Pars Autumnalis, pp. 402-3.

" The love of God and his neighbour diffused in his heart, after some time excited in it such a burning flame, that he was obliged to break out from the confinement of his cell into the open fields, to moderate by the coolness of the air, the burning heat engendered in it! He was frequently seen suspended in the air, and shining with a wonderful effulgence! He passed over rapid rivers without wetting his feet! A staff fixed by him in the ground immediately grew up into a flourishing fig-tree! While he was making a journey by night in a heavy fall of snow, he took refuge in a ruined house without a roof; but for him the snow remained suspended in the air, and acted as a roof, that he might not be smothered by it!"

The manner of his passing the rivers is not particularly stated, but we may assume it was in the orthodox fashion of other saints, of whom we read in the same volumes. For instance, we find that *St. Francis de Paulo* crossed the Strait of Sicily *on his own cloak*, taking another monk as a passenger!* So also *St. Raymond de Pennafort*, who, being about to return from the island of Majorca to Barcelona, spread his cloak upon the sea, and performed the voyage of a hundred and sixty miles in six hours, finishing by entering his monastery through the closed doors.† So also *St. Hyacinth, the Pole,* ferried over, in like manner, on his cloak, a number of his companions across the flooded Vistula.‡

St. Andrew Avellini seems to have been an equally useful travelling companion in his own way; for, returning home one tempestuous night, after confessing a sick man, when the rain and wind had extinguished their torch, not only neither he nor his companions were the least wet, but the whole company had the advantage of seeing their way in a pitch dark night by the radiance of the saint's person.§

St. Stanislaus, of Cracow, seems also to have possessed this *light-emitting* quality. This bishop, we are gravely informed, purchased a plot of land from one

---

* 2nd April, Pars Verna, p. 466.
† 23rd January, Pars Hiemalis, p. 476.
‡ 16th August. Pars Æstiva, p. 572.
§ 10th November, Pars Autumnalis, p. 456.

of the public functionaries, on which to build a church. Some time after the bishop was called upon for payment; to which application he replied, that the money was already paid, and required but three days to substantiate his point. The holy bishop repaired to the cemetery, where the man of business had been buried *upwards of three years*, took off his mantle, spread it on the tomb, and called upon his old friend to come up, and in an instant he came forth, walked to the magistrates' office, deposed on oath that the money was paid, went back, and slept in the Lord! After performing this remarkable miracle, poor St. Stanislaus was barbarously murdered by the king, who was his enemy, and seems to have been too hardened to profit by this great miracle, and his body was quartered and scattered about the fields. The wild beasts would have made a repast of the holy relics but for the watchfulness of some eagles, who never allowed any of them to touch them, until the canons of Cracow, led by the light thrown out by the scattered limbs, collected them the ensuing night! The most wondrous part of the tale remains, however, to be told; for the different parts of the body, when properly adjusted together, suddenly united as closely as kindred drops, and not a mark was left of the effects of the knife! What a pity it was that poor Stanislaus derived no benefit from all these marvellous interpositions; for though his body was so wonderfully put together again, he seems to have been past resuscitation himself, though, to make up for it, *after his death he did many miracles*, no doubt equally faithworthy as those so particularly narrated.*

This recalls to my mind the miraculous joining together of the links of the chain of St. Peter, recorded in the Breviary lessons for the feast of *St. Peter ad Vincula*.†

---

* 7th May, Pars Æstiva, pp. 321-2.
† 1st August, Pars Æstiva, p. 503.

Eudocia, the wife of Theodosius the younger, being on a pilgrimage to Jerusalem, received as a present the chain with which St. Peter was said to have been bound in prison, when he was liberated by the angel. This chain, *set in jewels*, was forwarded by the pious empress to her daughter, then at Rome. The young princess, rejoiced with the gift, showed the chain to the Pope, who repaid the compliment by exhibiting another chain, which the holy Apostle had borne under Nero; but no sooner had the Pope brought the two chains into contact, than, lo! it came to pass, that the links at the end of the two chains miraculously became joined together, and had all the appearance of a single chain wrought by the same artificer!

The Pope, no doubt, at once claimed the whole, which is still to be seen as one of the standing miracles at Rome, and is occasionally held out as one of the inducements to the faithful to visit the holy city.

A somewhat similar miraculous conversion of property is recorded of another pontiff, Pope St. John.*

His Holiness being on a journey, near Corinth, and in want of a quiet and comfortable horse, borrowed one which the wife of a certain nobleman used to ride. The animal carried the Pope with the greatest docility, and when the journey was over, was honourably returned to its master. So wicked had the horse become, however, that he always afterwards threw his mistress, "as if," says the Breviary, "*feeling indignant* at having to carry a woman, since the Vicar of Christ was on his back"! It is needless to add, that the horse was subsequently presented to his Holiness as unfit to be ridden by a less dignified personage.

St. Denis' story is well known; it is however related in the Breviary,† and perhaps is the longest walk

---

* 27th May, Pars Verna, p. 558.
† Pars Autumnalis, p. 389, 9th October, Lectio vi.

of a dead man on record, after that of St. Stanislaus's "man of business." We give it in the very words of the Breviary:—

"He took up his head after it was cut off, and carried it in his hands for two thousand paces."

Have any of my Roman Catholic readers the courage to ask their priest whether this is not in his Breviary,—in that very book so often seen under his arm, in his walks and journeys, and which he is seen reading with such indefatigable assiduity, and whether he *believes* it to be true? Does Dr. Newman really believe it to be true?

But, again, in this wonderful book we read to the following effect:—

Paul the Hermit, is there stated to have* retired to a cave in the desert parts of the Thebais, on account of the persecution of Decius and Valerius, where he lived to the age of 113. Being near his death, Anthony, another Egyptian anchorite, paid him a visit by a supernatural command from heaven. They at once saluted one another by their proper names, though previously strangers to each other, and began to talk about spiritual matters, when a raven, who had been in the habit of bringing Paul half a loaf of bread daily, brought a whole loaf for him and his visitor! After the raven had departed, "Ah," said Paul, "the Lord has sent us our dinner. It is now sixty years since I have received daily half a loaf; to-day my allowance has been doubled." They then proceeded to eat their dinner at the fountain, and spent the night in divine praises. In the morning, Paul admonishing Anthony about his death, which was then approaching, exhorted him to bring him a cloak which he had got from St. Athanasius, and which he wished to have as his winding sheet. Anthony was

* Pars Hiemaliis, pp. 450-1, 4th, 5th, and 6th lessons.

coming back with the cloak when he saw the soul of Paul ascending into heaven, surrounded by the holy company of the prophets and apostles, and choirs of angels. In the cave he found the corpse of Paul, with crossed knees, erected head, and hands stretched out on high, which he wrapped in the cloak as desired. He was, however, at a loss how to dig a grave, being himself an old man of ninety, having no spade or other instrument to do it with. When, lo! *two lions* ran swiftly from the interior of the desert to the body of the blessed old man, and gave Anthony to understand, very intelligibly, as well at least as they could, that they greatly deplored Paul, and then set to work with their claws, and striving to outdo one another, eagerly dug a hole in the earth big enough conveniently to contain the body, and then departed! When they were gone Anthony buried the body in the grave prepared by these singular grave-diggers, and formed a tomb over it after the manner of Christians. He then took possession of Paul's coat, which was made of palm-leaves, in the manner of basket-work, and wore it regularly as long as he lived as a holiday dress on Easter and Whitsunday.

I may here briefly refer to a few other specimens of *pious lions* recorded in the same book; and I doubt not there are others, if I had time to search further.

St. Venantius * was ordered to be cast to the *lions*, but they, forgetting their natural ferocity, cast themselves at his feet!

St. Prisca also, after suffering many other cruelties, was brought into the amphitheatre and cast to a *lion;* but he, forgetting his savage nature, humbly cast himself at her feet! † This and other miracles were, however, sad to say, wrought in vain; for poor Prisca's persecutors, after unsuccessfully trying to starve, burn,

---

* 18th May, Pars Verna, p. 544.
† Pars Hiemalis, p. 461.

and tear her to pieces with iron nails, at last succeeded by bethinking themselves of the more summary process of cutting off her head!

A still more striking instance, however, is to be found* where SS. Primus and Felicianus having been cast into the theatre, and two lions let loose on them, the noble animals not only prostrated themselves at their knees, but fawned upon them with their heads and tails. The poor saints, however, were, as usual, despatched with the axe.

A very similar story is told† of SS. Vitus, Modestus, and Crescentia, who were also cast to a lion, who prostrated himself and licked their feet.

In the same volume‡ we have a slight variation in the spectacle, in the case of SS. Abdon and Sennen, who having been cast to the *bears* and *lions* for spitting on the images, in the time of the Emperor Decius, the wild beasts were afraid to touch them, whereupon the never-failing sword was successfully resorted to, in spite of the miracle.

Whilst on the subject of wild beasts, we ought, however, not to omit mentioning the case of the celebrated *St. Januarius* and his companions,§ who, after having escaped unhurt from a burning furnace, and various other trials, were also thrown to the wild beasts in the amphitheatre, which (as before), forgetful of their natural ferocity, prostrated themselves at the feet of Januarius. This, however, did them but little good, for the prodigy having been attributed to magical incantation, they, like St. Prisca and the rest, were despatched with the sword.

The story then goes on to tell the exploded fable of St. Januarius's blood, which, kept in a glass phial, in a coagulated state, liquefies and bubbles up, just as if

---

* Under date 10th June, Pars Æstiva, p. 361.
† Same vol., p. 375, 15th June.
‡ 30th July, Pars Æstiva, p. 496.
§ 19th Sept., Pars Autumnalis, p. 343.

it were recently shed, as often as it is placed in sight of the martyr's head!

This favourite standing miracle is annually enacted at Naples, before thousands of admiring spectators; but it has been well asked—Would it not be more charitable to allow one of our chemists to view the blood, and observe its change, not surrounded by priests, candles, and the smoke of frankincense, and thus convert us all at one stroke?

Thus I might proceed throughout this book, which I may safely call *the* book of " lying wonders;" and these are only a few of the edifying and instructive "lessons" which every Roman Catholic priest is bound to read daily, under pain of mortal sin, and taught to pray that he may emulate. Might I not venture to ask, if my readers can believe that any intelligent or educated priest, in the nineteenth century, can sincerely give credit to such old wives' fables?—and if they do not believe them, *how long* will they submit to the humiliating indignity of reciting with their lips what they must disbelieve in their hearts, if they dared utter the truth? Dr. Newman cannot—dare not—repudiate any one of these " lying wonders."

But if my readers are not already nauseated, I would further observe that these wonders are by no means restricted to the Breviary. The lives of the saints, in authentic editions edited by Romish priests in this country, are replete with such fables, and all seriously proposed to the belief of the faithful! Take Dr. Wiseman's lives of St. Alphonsus Liguori and others canonized in 1839 (London, 1846). I give two extracts as fair samples. In p. 102 of the life of St. Francis di Girolamo, he writes:—

"That wonderful gift also, which *authentic testimony* proves several saints to have possessed, namely, the power of being present in more than one place at times—between which no physical interval is perceptible—was not denied to our saint."

And of St. John Joseph of the Cross, Dr. Wiseman says :*

"The zeal of our saint did not *pass unrewarded*; it was on this occasion that he first experienced those ecstasies and raptures with which he was thenceforward so eminently favoured. One day being searched for in vain through the convent, he was at length discovered in the chapel raised up in an ecstasy, so high from the ground that his head touched the ceiling."

Did Dr. Wiseman really pretend that this acrobatic feat was the reward of the zeal of the saint? If so, I would inform the simple doctor that I have seen a man walk along the ceiling with his head downwards! but I should be ashamed to hint that the feat was the result of any inward ecstasy or rapture like the above.

As Dr. Wiseman was the great apostle of the Romish Church in this country, I will give two further specimens of alleged miracles which he proposes to our belief.

I have before me Dr. Wiseman's edition, that is the edition (London, 1852) published under his sanction, and under his authority and name, of Liguori's "GLORIES OF MARY." In this book innumerable miracles are said to be performed through the instrumentality of the Blessed Virgin, to attest her all-powerful and omnipresent existence; and the revelations made to various individuals to whom she personally appeared, thickly crowd every chapter. But to this book I shall have to refer elsewhere; and therefore I will but notice one of many similar miracles related. In page 64 we are informed :—

"Bernardine de Busto relates that a bird was taught to say, 'Hail, Mary!' A hawk was on the point of seizing it, when the bird cried out, 'Hail, Mary!'—in an instant the hawk fell dead. God intended to show thereby that, if even an irrational creature was preserved by calling on Mary, how much more would those who are prompt in calling on her, when assaulted by devils, be delivered from them."

It is a favourite Romish theory, that the miracles

* P. 124.

performed by his church, or, to be more correct, members of his church, are one of the divine attestations of the sanctity in, and the truth of, that church. I exclaim, in all seriousness, "God help them!" if we are to take the cases cited as *proofs* or *examples*.

If, however, we turn to the Word of God and seek there for the true marks of an apostate church and people, do we not there find the Roman Church clearly portrayed? We read, "Now the Spirit speaketh expressly that in the latter times some shall depart from the faith, giving heed to seducing spirits and doctrines of devils; speaking lies in hypocrisy; having their consciences seared with a hot iron; forbidding to marry, and commanding to abstain from meats" (1 Tim. iv. 1, 2). And that "the time will come when they will not endure sound doctrine; but after their own lusts shall they heap to themselves teachers, having itching ears; and they shall turn away their ears from the truth, and shall be turned unto fables" (2 Tim. iv. 3, 4). "Whose coming is after the working of Satan, with all power and signs and lying wonders" (2 Thess. ii. 9). For "this cause God shall send them strong delusion, that they should believe a lie" (2 Thess. ii. 11).

Viewing the system of Popery in the light of Holy Scripture, we discern most clearly its spiritual deformity, and contrariety to the truth as it is in Jesus; and for this reason it is we ardently desire to save unstable minds from being entrapped by her delusions; and I look upon the fact of there being advocates of these "delusions and superstitions" in the present day, as the greatest miracle of the nineteenth century.

Having thus performed an unwelcome task, I must remind the reader that Dr. Newman has the boldness to assert that in the "accounts of mediæval miracles there is no *extravagance* in their *general character;*"*

---

* Appendix, p. 42; the italics are in the original.

but, to save his credit, he adds that he "cannot affirm that there was always *evidence* for them." Alas! how our hopes are withered. With strange inconsistency, he places the *evidence* in their support at a very low estimate. "Miracles, to a Catholic, are historical facts, and nothing short of this, and are to be regarded and dealt with as other *facts*."* Dr. Newman forgets his logic,—a *fact* remains a *fact*, whatever the evidence may be to support it or to bring it to our comprehension or belief. But he destroys the illusions by placing his church's miracles on a level, in point of evidence, with any other circumstance recorded in our histories. Take an instance advanced by Dr. Newman: †—

"There is our Queen again, who is so truly and justly popular; she roves about in the midst of tradition and romance; she scatters myths and legends from her as she goes along; she is a being of poetry, and you might fairly be sceptical whether she had any personal existence. She is always at some beautiful, noble bounteous work or other, if you trust the papers. She is doing alms-deeds in the Highlands; she meets beggars in her rides at Windsor; she writes verses in albums, or draws sketches, or she is mistaken for the housekeeper by some blind old woman, or she runs up a hill as if she were a child. Who finds fault with these things? He would be a cynic—he would be white-livered, and would have gall for blood, who was not struck with the love her subjects bear her. Who could have the head, even if he had the heart, could he be so cross and peevish, who could be so solemn and perverse as to say that some of these stories may be simple lies and all of them might have stronger evidence than they carry with them? Do you think she is displeased at them? Why, then, should He, the Great Father, who once walked the earth, look sternly on the unavoidable mistakes of His own subjects and children in their devotion to Him and His?"

And this is Dr. Newman's apology for his Romish miracles. But forgetting what has been said, Dr. Newman feigns to be indignant at the bare possibility of the priests' words being doubted as to the truth of these alleged miracles,—their character is at stake. The priests assert the miracles to be true; is that not sufficient, ye unbelievers? "It is a great thing

---

* "Apologia," Appendix, p. 52.   † Ibid. p. 54.

exclaims Dr. Newman) to have our character cleared; and we may reasonably hope that the next time our word is vouched for occurrences which appear to be miraculous, our facts will be investigated, not our testimony impugned. Even granting that certain occurrences which we have hitherto accounted miraculous, have not absolutely a claim to be so considered, nevertheless they constitute an argument still on behalf of revelation and the Church." I confess that "I do not seem to see it."

I have dwelt more largely on this part of my subject, as I conceive it will better illustrate the true temper, the sample of argument,—reasoning if you like,—adopted by Dr. Newman in his "Apologia" for embracing the Roman religion. I designated this part of his work as feeble, puerile, illogical, and unsatisfactory, and I believe that I am fully justified in making the assertion. And nowhere does Dr. Newman advance any deeper or more cogent reasons for becoming a Romanist, and adopting the peculiar dogmas of his newly-adopted creed, than he does for accepting the "mediæval miracles" of his church, all of which he confesses to embrace with as firm a hold as he does the fundamental doctrines of Christianity! I cannot bring myself to believe that he places any credence in the former,—does he then believe the latter?

It is true that his mind had always, from his youth, a superstitious bent. In p. 56 he says, that when he was a boy he was "very superstitious, and for some time previous to his [so-called] conversion, when he was fifteen, he used constantly to cross himself in going into the dark." The admission that the fact of crossing was a *superstitious* act, is important and true. Has Dr. Newman changed his mind in this respect? Again, he admits that he used to wish the Arabian tales were true. "My imagination ran on unknown influences, on magical powers and talismans. I thought life might be a dream, or I an angel, and all this world a deception,—my fellow-angels, by a playful device, concealing themselves from me, and deceiving me with a semblance of a material world." A mind thus constituted is a fit receptacle for any and every extravagance which a corrupt church might present in the wonderful and extravagant. Dr. Newman, certainly, does not shirk the consequence of his tendencies. He says, "I do not shrink from uttering my firm conviction that it would be a gain to the country were it vastly more superstitious, more bigoted, more gloomy, more fierce in its religion, than at present it shows itself to be."* This is entirely a matter of opinion and taste. We can now fully appreciate the bent of Dr. Newman's mind; but our Anglo-Romish brethren can scarcely claim such a man as a convert, or find reason to congratulate themselves on the acquisition.

Dr. Newman appears to have been attacked by the Rev. Mr. Kingsley on a weak point, namely, the *Moral Theology* of the Roman Church.

Of all the systems falsely called "Moral Theology," the code of the Roman Church, which passes under that head, is perhaps the most *delusive*. It is perfectly true that the vast mass of Jesuit writings passing under the above designation, is not officially acknowledged by the Roman Church, nor perhaps recognized by all Roman Catholics. We know of their official condemnation by the French Parliament in 1762, and it is a great fact that the Jesuits themselves have been successively driven out from every country in Europe but England, on account of the seditious and immoral principles taught by them. But I assert that the whole Roman Church is responsible for a great mass of their doctrines and teaching, which have been summarized in the volumes passing under the title of

* "Apologia," p. 117.

Liguori's Moral Theology, and which have, with the other works of this theologian, undergone twenty years of the strictest examination by the Sacred Congregation of Rites at Rome; and it has been declared by that authority that there is not one word worthy of censure throughout his entire works. This examination was undertaken with a view to his canonization—the very greatest honour to which a Roman priest (for it appears that priests alone arrive at that dignity) can attain. Liguori, therefore, has been very properly selected. Many of us have heard of Liguori's " Moral Theology," but few have taken the trouble, or had the opportunity, of studying the original. A plausible writer, like Dr. Newman, would fain persuade us that it is merely prejudice on our part when we condemn St. Alphonso and his system. "I cannot think (says Dr. Newman) what it can be, in a day like this, which keeps up the prejudice of this Protestant country against us, unless it be the *vague charges* which are drawn from *our books of Moral Theology;* and with the notice of the work in particular which my accuser especially throws in our teeth." And in reply to this last assault, Dr. Newman proposes, " in a very few words, to bring his observations to a close."

Dr. Newman attempts to justify Liguori's theories on *lying;* for it is not Liguori that is attacked, as Dr. Newman adroitly argues, but the Roman moral system, of which he is an exponent—by the alleged fact that great Protestant writers have promulgated the same doctrines; and he refers more particularly to the justification held forth of equivocating and lying, under peculiar positions, by Paley, Milton, Jeremy Taylor, Johnson, and others. Let the reader have the full benefit of Dr. Newman's own justification before we make the comparisons.

" Now, I make this remark first :—Great English authors—Jeremy Taylor, Milton, Paley, Johnson, men of very distinct schools of thought —distinctly say that, under certain special circumstances, it is allowable to tell a lie. Taylor says: 'To tell a lie for charity, to save a man's life, the life of a friend, of a husband, of a prince, of a useful and a public person, hath not only been done at all times, but commended by great, and wise, and good men. Who would not save his father's life, at the charge of a harmless lie, from persecutors or tyrants?' Again, Milton says: 'What man in his senses would deny that there are those whom we have the best grounds for considering that we ought to deceive—as boys, madmen, the sick, the intoxicated, enemies, men in error, thieves? I would ask by which of the commandments is a lie forbidden? You will say by the ninth. If, then, my lie does not injure my neighbour, certainly it is not forbidden by this commandment.' Paley says: 'There are falsehoods which are not lies, that is, which are not criminal.' Johnson: 'The general rule is, that truth should never be violated; there must, however, be some exceptions. If, for instance, a murderer should ask you which way a man is gone.'"*

This is what Dr. Newman styles an "*argumentum ad hominem*," and were we, who "are so fierce with St. Alphonso, to meet Paley or Johnson to-morrow in society, would we look upon them as liars or knaves, as dishonest and untrustworthy?" He is sure we would not. Why then, he asks, do we not deal out the same measure to [Roman] Catholic priests? Dr. Newman has a knack of turning observations, applied to a system, to persons. "I ask (he says), if you would not scruple in holding Paley for an honest man, in spite of his defence of lying, why do you scruple at St. Alphonso?" Liguori is merely explaining a system; he is only one of many who believe in it. Dr. Newman has made out his case as from Paley, and the others. Now let us make out ours from Liguori, and let the reader discover, if he can, the alleged parallel or justification.

Dr. Newman says that "it cannot be denied that Alphonso Liguori lays down that an equivocation, that is, a play upon words, in which one sense is taken by the speaker, and another sense intended by him for the hearer, is allowable, *if there is a just cause*, that is, a special case, and may even be confirmed by an oath." †

---

* "Apologia," p. 417.   † Id. ibid.

This is true as far as it goes; but Dr. Newman should have given Liguori's examples and definition of a "just cause." But we allege that Liguori does not stop at a mere play upon words, but that he justifies fraud and deliberate perjury.

On the question "whether it is lawful to use equivocation in an oath," after refining on the distinctions of double-speaking, or amphibologia, and mental reservations, Liguori lays it down, "as a certain and a common opinion amongst all divines," that "for a just cause it is lawful to use equivocation in the propounded modes, and to confirm it [equivocation] with an oath."*

To state some minor cases or "propounded modes," Liguori says (we are only on equivocation and permissive lying):—

"A poor man absconding with goods *for his support*, can answer the judge that he has nothing."

The reader must bear in mind, that in courts of law abroad, the accused and witnesses are interrogated by the judge, and not by the counsel of the parties.

"He who receives a loan, but afterwards returns it, can deny that he received a loan, he *understanding thereby that he should pay it.*"

"He who hath promised marriage, but thence (*sed inde*) is not bound to marriage, can deny the promise—*that is, so as to be bound by it.*"

"He who comes from a place falsely supposed to be infectious can deny that he came from that place—to wit, as a pestilent place, *because that is the mind of the inquirer.*"

"If any one being invited as a guest, be asked whether the food is good, which in truth is unsavoury, he can answer that it is good—*to wit, for mortification.*"

"It is lawful to conceal the truth when there is a cause; viz., when any one seeks money from you, you can answer, 'Oh, that I had it,' or 'I would delight to have it.'"

"Can a creditor assert by a deed, with an oath, that nothing was paid to him, though a part was paid; but he may have credit on another account, which he may not be able to prove? We answer that he can, provided he does not swear that that quantity was due to him on that deed, lest other former creditors might incur loss."

---

* Liguori, "Moral Theol.," tom. ii. p. 316, *et seqq.* Mechlin, 1845.

As a general rule, Liguori lays down—

"That when there is a just cause of necessity or utility, any one can use double-speaking on an oath, although of his own accord he comes forward to swear."

Having proposed the case, "Whether it is a mortal sin to swear with double speaking or restriction not purely mental, *without a just cause*," and after giving some conflicting opinions on the subject, Liguori gives his own opinion, that this is only a venial sin.

"The reason of this more probable opinion is, because in such an oath, already truth and justice are present; only judgment or discretion is wanting, which deficiency is only venial," but "for a just cause it is lawful to use restriction, not purely mental, even with an oath, if it can be understood from the circumstances." *

But every theory, it must be observed, resolves itself into a "just cause." What is a "just cause," we are not left in doubt,—"any honest end, in order to preserve good things for the spirit, or useful things for the body." †

We have given a few minor samples of what may be considered a "just cause," according to the estimation of Liguori. Dr. Newman, by his apparent frankness, would mislead an uninstructed reader on this subject. He would give us to understand that the license of Rome's *Moral Theology* went no further than taking advantage of a doubtful pun or play upon words having a double meaning. And "*upon this* point" he proposes to give his opinion as plainly as any Protestant can wish; and therefore he avows at once, that in this department of Morality, much as he admires the high points of the Italian character, he likes the English

---

* "E contrario licitum est, justa causa uti restrictione non pure mentali, etiam cum juramento, si illa ex circumstantiis percipi potest."—*Moral Theolog.*, tom. ii. p. 318, n. 152.

† "Justa autem causa esse potest quicumque finis honestus ad servanda bona spiritui, vel corpori utilia."—*Ibid.*, tom. ii. p. 316. Mechlin edit., 1845.

character better.* Did it not strike Dr. Newman, that the English character on points of Moral Theology, to which he gives the preference, is due to their Protestant religion, in acting up to their solemn protest against all the innovations and corruptions of the Roman Church, relying on the WORD of GOD for their rule and guide?

I will now take a further example from Liguori, which does not exactly come within the supposed harmless permission of playing on the double meaning of words.

We are told in the Church of Rome, that the seal of confession is sacred. This we can understand, and a confessor being interrogated of a crime divulged in the confessional, acts up to the principles professed by his Church, by refusing to answer, and he is esteemed a martyr should punishment follow. But Rome's Moral Theology does not rest here. Dens, in his *Theologia*, a Maynooth College text-book, proposes the following question, to which he gives the reply:—

"What, therefore, ought a confessor to answer, being interrogated concerning a truth, which he has known through sacramental confession?

"*A.* He ought to answer that he does not know it; and if necessary confirm the same by an oath." †

It is this system of deliberate perjury that Liguori indorses; not only indorses, but assigns a reason for the lawfulness of the act. The priest in the confessional ceases to represent the character of a man. He represents JESUS CHRIST himself. So the Trent Catechism lays down:—" They [the Priests] are called not only angels, but Gods, holding as they do the

---

* "Apologia," p. 417.

† "Quid igitur respondere debet confessarius interrogatus super veritate, quam per solam confessionem sacramentalem norit?

"*R.* Debet respondere, se nescire eam; et si opus est, idem juramento confirmare."—*Dens, Theologia*, tom. vi.: De Fractione Sigilli Sacramentalis, No. 160. Dublin, 1832.

place and power and authority of God on earth."* Liguori avails himself of this—what shall I call it—delusion?—let us rather say imposture—and says "a confessor can affirm, even with an oath, that he does not know a sin heard in confession, by understanding *as man, not as the minister of Christ.*"†

"And the reason [alleged] is, that he who interrogates has not a right to be informed of a matter unless that matter is communicable; such is not the knowledge of the confessor." But suppose the question be changed in form by one who was aware of this theological license to commit perjury, and should ask "whether he heard it as a minister of Christ." Here the confessor may change his character by a playful illusion, and may still affirm with an oath that he does not know the sin heard in confession. "Because the confessor always is understood to answer as man; he cannot speak in his capacity as minister of Christ. Hence when any one is bound to conceal the infamy of another, he may lawfully say, I do not know it (licite dicat, Nescio, non habeo scientiam utilem ad respondendum), that is to say, I have not a knowledge which is useful for answering; or I do not know it so as to

---

* "Nam cum episcopi et sacerdotes, tanquam Dei interpretes et internuntii quidam sint, qui ejus nomine divinam legem et vitæ præcepta homines edocent, et ipsius Dei personam in terris gerunt, perspicuum est eam esse illorum functionem, quâ nulla major excogitari possit. Quare merito non solum angeli, sed Dii etiam, quod Dei immortalis vim et numen apud nos teneant, appellantur. Quamvis autem omni tempore summam dignitatem obtinuerint, tamen Novi Testamenti sacerdotes cæteris omnibus honore longe antecellunt. Potestas enim tum corpus et sanguinem Domini nostri conficiendi et offerendi, tum peccata remittendi, quæ illis collata est, humanam quoque rationem atque intelligentiam superat: nedum ei aliquid par et simile in terris inveniri queat."—*Catech. Concil. Tridentini*, pars ii.; De Ordinis Sacramento, § 2, p. 327; edit. Paris, 1848.

† "Hinc inferetur—I. confessarius affirmare potest etiam juramento, nescire peccatum auditum in confessione, subintelligendo, ut hominem non autem ut ministrum Christi."—*Liguori, Moral Theology*, tom. ii. p. 319, No. 153, edit. Mechlin, 1845.

make it known. And if any one rashly should ask from a confessor whether he may have heard such a sin in confession, he can rightly answer, *I have not heard it* (non audivi); that is to say, as man, or so as to manifest it." These are the mental reservations which are supposed to justify the oath! But Dr. Newman may object that this is an exceptional case. We cannot admit this, even setting aside the awful reflection, that the minister professes to represent our Lord in the confessional, and is prepared to issue from that tribunal with a lie, to be confirmed even by an oath. GOD IS TRUTH! But we can afford Dr. Newman even this advantage, for Liguori proceeds in the same place to declare that " a witness not legitimately interrogated by a judge can swear that he does not know a crime, which in reality he does know, by understanding that he does not know the crime concerning which legitimately he can be inquired of, or that he does not know it so as to give evidence concerning it." Here, again, we can understand that in some extreme cases, a witness might prefer to suffer the prescribed punishment, rather than divulge his knowledge so as to criminate a relative or friend; but where is the authority for teaching that the witness can lawfully *swear* that he does not know a *crime* committed by another; for this license is given to the witness as well as to the accused (Reus aut testis à judice, &c.). And who is to be a judge as to the legitimacy or propriety of the interrogation? Is an equivocation here again permitted? Liguori gives two grounds: a person may exercise a discretion as to the propriety of his being interrogated, *first*, " when the crime appears to himself to be free from blame; " second, " or if he know a crime which he is bound to keep a secret, when no scandal may have gone abroad." *

---

* " Reus aut testis a judice non legitime interrogatus, potest jurare, se nescire crimen, quod revera scit; subintelligendo, nescire crimen,

Liguori admits that where the accused is legitimately interrogated by a judge, he cannot equivocate, because he is bound to render obedience to the just commands of his superior, and likewise in " important contracts ;" because, if it were not so, another would suffer injury. I am happy to give this acknowledgment ; but, alas! the advantage is immediately taken away by Liguori himself, for he adds :—

"Make an exception where the crime is altogether concealed. For then he can, yea the witness is *bound to say that* the accused did not commit the crime (imo tenetur testis dicere reum non commisisse). And the same course the accused can adopt *if the proof be not complete* (si non adest semiplena probatio) ; because then the judge does not legitimately interrogate."—Tom. ii. p. 320, n. 154.

It would be an insult to the common sense of my readers to dwell on the phases of this system of moral theology, and the awful consequences to society were it generally accepted in England ; for however much Dr. Newman may admire " the high points of Italian character," he has very good reason to admit that he likes the " English character better." But Dr. Newman has no right to object to this system as a peculiarity in the Italians. Liguori's works were submitted to twenty years' strict scrutiny by the properly constituted Roman authorities previous to his canonization, and the result was that they declared that there was not one word in them worthy of censure, and, therefore, clearly binding on the conscience of every member of the Roman Church.

Dr. Newman tries the *tu quoque* argument, and declares that his readers would be startled if informed that Paley, Jeremy Taylor, and other English divines have laid down " a maxim about the lawfulness of lying."* Will Dr. Newman venture to assert that

de quo legitime possit inquiri, vel nescire ad deponendum." "Idem, si testis ex alio capite non teneatur deponere, nempe si ipsi constet crimen caruisse culpa ; vel si sciat crimen, sed sub secreto, cum nulla præcesserit infamia."—Tom. ii. p. 319.

* "Apologia," p. 420.

either of these divines has laid down any such maxims as are propounded by his church, under the cloak of religion and moral theology, falsely so called? These divines have, it is alleged, in some extreme cases, given a certain license to equivocate or evade, and that is the extent to which he can draw his parallel. But does any honest man pretend that a witness, in a trial for murder, can swear that he does not know of the crime, because, according to his judgment, the crime appeared to himself to be free from blame, or because the scandal had not gone abroad, or that the crime was altogether concealed, or because the proof is not complete? Liguori puts an extreme case: He asks "whether an accused, legitimately interrogated, can deny a crime even with an oath, if the confession of the crime would be attended with great disadvantage." The great disadvantages are stated to be "danger of death, or the prison, or perpetual exile, the loss of all property, the danger of the galleys, and such like." It is certainly difficult to prejudge what each of us would do under such trying circumstances; but one would suppose that *the moral law* was clear. But Liguori says that the case is "sufficiently probable (satis probabiliter) that the accused may deny the crime, even with an oath, at least without great sin, by understanding that he did not commit it so that he is bound to confess it, only let there be a hope of avoiding the punishment. The reason is, because *human law* cannot lay men under so great an obligation with so severe a penalty." If Liguori had placed the excuse on a higher ground,—namely, chance for repentance, that would have been at least a worthy motive; but no, the sufficient justification to deny the crime, even with an oath, would be if there is "a hope of avoiding punishment."

But here another question arises,—Can such a perjured person be absolved by a priest in the confessional? Or is he absolved from the crime attaching to perjury unless he confesses to a priest and gets absolution?

What says Dr. Newman to these questions? Here is a tough bit of moral theology for him to "tackle," to answer which, we fear, neither Paley nor Jeremy Taylor will assist him. "St. Alphonso, who has the repute of being so lax a moralist, having (as Dr. Newman informs us) had one of the most scrupulous and anxious of consciences himself," deems it necessary to grapple with these difficult questions. So he solves it thus:—

"But here it is inquired if such an accused person, or one who, making a contract, deceives by swearing with equivocation, may be absolved unless he makes known the truth. Some, not improbably, answer in the negative; but more probably Sanches (and others) *say that he can be absolved;* because in such an oath—which cannot be called a perjury—he has not sinned against commutative justice, but against legal justice, and due obedience to a judge whose command of unfolding the truth is *transient, and only lasts while* the judge *interrogates.* And the same thing, Sanches says, in the same book, concerning a lying witness; and, therefore, each of them can be absolved; but he should reveal the truth. But both are bound to render satisfaction to the other, if they are able, in another way; but if they are not able? But the Salamanca doctors say that they are bound again to make known the truth in trial. But I [Liguori, this most scrupulous and conscientious man] would even excuse them, if they were altogether unable to make satisfaction for the present, or even the future."

The reader must pardon me for a moment. I am, in my profession, accustomed to draw contracts, and bind man and man to solemn obligations in business. Suppose I meet a Roman Catholic, one of the contracting parties. How do I know that in this contract he will not deceive the other, by swearing equivocally, when brought to trial, to save himself from imprisonment or other inconvenience? It is, we are told, vulgar prejudice, and uncharitable, not to believe a Roman Catholic on his oath. Yet we are told that he may perjure himself, and may be absolved, for such an oath, they tell us, is not a perjury; and if he went to a father confessor of the Liguori school,—for there are numerous priests here of the Redemptorist order,—he would be excused, if he could not make satisfaction. Well, Dr. Newman, what is your opinion, under the circumstances? "I pause for a reply."

In the confessional we are treading on "consecrated ground," where everything seems to be regulated by a law peculiar to Roman theology, on which neither Paley, nor Jeremy Taylor, nor Johnson dare to tread, but where Liguori and Dr. Newman, in his character of Father Newman, are permitted to enter and revel. Liguori, on this delicate subject, proposes another question, equally startling, and, I trust, peculiar, or restricted to Roman moral theology:—"It is asked whether an adulteress can deny adultery to her husband, understanding that she may reveal it to him?" The manner of putting these questions is so peculiarly original, that Paley and Jeremy Taylor might well be excused anticipating such probabilities and positions! However, the "most scrupulous and anxiously conscientious and high-minded Italian" does not hesitate to propound the question and give his opinion. His character stands above impeachment or even suspicion. Have not the properly constituted authorities laboured for twenty years to detect a fallacy, and they could not? He says: "She [the adulteress] is able to assert equivocally that she did not break the bond of matrimony, which truly remains. And if, sacramentally, she confessed adultery, she can answer, *I am innocent* of this *crime*." Now mark, ye shades of Paley and Jeremy Taylor, who in your lifetime are accused by Dr. Newman of "laying down the axiom about the lawfulness of lying,"—mark, I say, the reason assigned by this canonized saint, this moralist, this scrupulously conscientious man, for this denial of a fact on oath! "*Because by confession it was taken away.*" So Cardenas, who, however, here remarks, that "she cannot affirm it with an oath, because, in asserting anything, the probability of a deed suffices, but in swearing, certainty is required." But here, again, the "most scrupulous" Liguori comes to the rescue; for he adds, "To this it is replied, that, in swearing, moral certainty suffices, as we said above. Which moral certainty of the remission of sin can indeed be had, when any one morally well-disposed receives the sacrament of penance."

Liguori thinks an adulteress a sufficiently "morally well-disposed person to receive the benefit of the sacrament of penance," in which tribunal, by confession of her guilt, she can get so clearly absolved that she can, with a safe conscience, declare that she is innocent of that crime which she has just confessed to have perpetrated!*

The reader must bear in mind that the theory of the sacrament of penance, in order to obtain absolution by confession to a priest, is that the priest does not require from the penitent a previous *repentance*, or perfect contrition, that is, a repentance of the sin committed, from a hatred of the sin itself, and a love of God; but it is sufficient to have a sorrow for the sin from the fear of punishment—the fear of hell,—and an expressed determination to sin no more. This they call *attrition*, by which, with the confession and absolution, the penitent is supposed to be placed in a state

---

* Dr. Newman knows that I am translating literally; but as my readers, not so well skilled in the *moral theology* of the Roman Church, may think that I am drawing on my imagination, and taking a little—just a little—license with the text, I give it in full :—

"Quæritur 2. An adultera possit negare adulterium viro, intelligens, ut illi revelet? Potest æquivoce asserere, se non fregisse matrimonium, quod vere persistit. Et si adulterium sacramentaliter confessa sit, potest respondere 'Innocens sum ab hoc crimine,' quia per confessionem est jam ablatum. Ita Card. diss. 19, n. 54. Qui tamen hic advertit, quod nequeat id affirmare cum juramento, quia ad asserendum aliquid sufficit probabilitas facti; sed ad jurandum requiritur certitudo. Sed respondetur, quod ad jurandum sufficiat certitudo moralis, ut diximus supra—cum Salm. Lessius, Sanch. Suar. Pal. et communi. Quæ certitudo moralis remissionis peccati potest quidem haberi, quando quis bene moraliter dispositus recepit pœnitentiæ sacramentum."—Tom. ii. p. 322, Mechlin edit. 1845.

of grace. It is in this state of *attrition* that the *morally well-disposed adulteress* can receive absolution, and then swear that she is innocent of the crime! But the case goes beyond this: Liguori tells us that Cardenus admits that if a woman under such circumstances, without confession, is in danger of death, " it is lawful for her to use a metaphor which is common in Scripture, where *adultery* is taken for *idolatry*, as in Ezek. xxiii. 27, " Because they committed adultery, and were guilty of fornication with idols." But he tells us that Busembaum, Lessius, Trullus, Sanches, Soto, Sayrus, Agragius, Tamburini, Viva, &c.—a noble army of uncanonized saints!—"all honourable men," declare their opinion "that if the crime be truly concealed, a woman can deny with an oath, and *say 'I did not commit the crime;'* in the same way that the accused can say to his judge not legitimately interrogating, 'I did not so commit it' that he is bound to manifest it to him." *

Such, then, being the system of lying and perjury sanctioned by the Moral Theology of Rome, will Dr. Newman dare now to assert that the theory is in the most distant manner sanctioned by Milton, Paley, Johnson, Taylor, or any honest Englishman? And does not Dr. Newman endeavour to evade the responsibility of such teaching by laying himself under the charge of putting in practice the very system of equivocation by the line of defence he has chosen to take? Allusion has been made to only one branch of this Moral Theology. Let the inquiring reader turn to the chapter on Confession (tom. ix. p. 37, et seq.); and as to confessions on alleged sins of the married state, from No. 909 to 953. The supposed cases are so horrible that Satan, in company with celibate priests, could only invent such monstrosities; and the evasions of falling into mortal sin by their perpetration could

---

* Liguori's "Moral Theology," tom. ii. p. 323, Mechlin edition, 1845.

only be conceived by prurient-minded priests. The theory is this:—A most fiendish act is proposed; it is freely admitted that that act is a mortal sin to perpetrate. The ingenuity is to determine how close a person may go to the committal of that act, which in itself is a mortal sin to commit,* without being guilty of mortal sin. No one but Satan himself could have devised such a master-piece of ingenuity. It is true that all this is for the priest's private instruction alone; but *cui bono?* In the confessional they have but two rules to lay down to the penitent;—"All unrighteousness is sin," and "Avoid all appearance of evil." The system is the natural result of seeking another moral code or rule of faith than the Holy Scriptures. Dr. Newman admits that the Scriptures have failed to satisfy him. I would ask, can he find the required satisfaction in this moral code of his church?

It is true that Dr. Newman points to books and catechisms which teach a moral Christian code; but in what respect are these better than the like class of books in the church he has left? He adds, "I plainly and positively state, and without any reserve, that I do not at all follow this holy and charitable man [Liguori] in this portion of his teaching." This is candid. But if approved by the Sacred Congregation of Rites and recommended to priests, what right has Dr. Newman to decline to follow Liguori's teaching? It is either right or wrong. If wrong, where is the boasted infallibility on which he so largely dwelt, as one of the inducements which led him to go into the Roman system—an infallibility which demanded his entire submission. Dr. Newman does not follow Liguori. Why?—Because there is sufficient Protestant

* "916.—Quær. I. An peccet mortaliter vir inchoando copulam in vase præpostero, ut postea in vase debito eam consummet? negant [here follow seven names], modò absit periculum pollutionis; quia alias (ut ajunt) omnes tactus etiam venerei non sunt graviter illiciti inter conjugatos."—Tom. ix.: "De Usu Matrimonii." *Vide* No. 909 ad 954.

"leaven" and English honesty left in him to see how opposed this "Moral Theology" is to feelings totally un-English, and contrary to the simple rules laid down in the Gospel for our guide for purity and holiness of life. Were it in my power, I would lead Dr. Newman back to the first principles of our common Christianity, and endeavour to divest his mind of ceremonials and theories, from priest-rule and priest-craft, to CHRIST, and Him alone, as our pattern and our guide; as our one only Mediator and Advocate with the Father, one with Him in glory co-eternal. I would entreat Dr. Newman to recognize the great fact, that God is no respecter of persons, be he Jew or Gentile, bond or free. With Him circumcision availeth not, nor uncircumcision, but a new man. Nor is there any talismanic influence in sacraments, vestures, gestures, and ceremonies. It is not this altar nor that altar that is more highly favoured; but where two or three are gathered together in Christ's name, there is He in the midst of them. Let Dr. Newman extend his charity and conceive the possibility of salvation out of the limited circle within which he has inclosed himself. Let him bring it home to his mind that there is possible salvation without believing that the Pope of Rome is Christ's vicar on earth; that the Blessed Virgin and the Saints are not appointed mediators between God and man; that it is reasonable to believe that Christ instituted the feast of the Last Supper as a *memorial* of His death, of the sacrifice to be offered up on the cross once for all, and not a literal and perpetual and repeated sacrifice of Christ's literal body. Let him consider that perchance purgatory is a fable, and indulgences to remit temporal punishment due to sin drawn from the bank of merits, the celestial treasure of the Church, are myths. If Dr. Newman would for one moment recollect, that for not one of these points has he more than the invention of man to advance in their favour, it might by possibility be more charitable that his church should not curse or anathematize a large, and certainly an intelligent, body of Christians for rejecting them, and that it would be possibly safer to rely on what all accept as admitted truths.

And lastly, I would invite him once again to join us in reciting with heart and soul that beautiful but simple prayer of our Church :—

"O ALMIGHTY GOD, who hast built thy Church upon the foundation of the Apostles and Prophets, JESUS CHRIST himself being the head corner-stone; grant us so to be joined together in unity of spirit by their doctrine, that we may be made an holy temple acceptable unto Thee; through Jesus Christ our Lord. *Amen.*"

DR. NEWMAN AND DR. PUSEY.

"The more I grew in devotion, both to the Saints and to our Lady, the more impatient was I at the Roman practices, as if these glorified creatures of God must be gravely shocked, if pain could be theirs, at the undue veneration of which they are the objects."—*Apologia*, p. 123.

THE perusal of Dr. Newman's letter to Dr. Pusey * will raise in the minds of earnest and thinking men pain mingled with a degree of satisfaction;—pain that a man so decidedly gifted should have had from the beginning no fixed principles of religion, should have allowed himself to be drifted about like a rudderless vessel; satisfaction, that his last production—his letter to Dr. Pusey—has disclosed to us the fact that he is not so far absorbed in the Roman system but that he is bold enough to denounce, in emphatic language, the erratic extravagancies of Mary-worship, as now commonly practised in his church. They appear to him as extravagancies of which we so rightly complain† " as provoking blasphemy," and to " work the loss of souls."‡ They seem to him like a " bad dream." § He reads them " with grief and almost anger;" ‖ and he sanctions but a very modified belief in the late doctrine of the Immaculate Conception. But, alas! what certainty have we that Dr. Newman, this

---

* "A Letter to the Rev. E. B. Pusey, D.D., on his recent Eirenicon," by J. H. Newman, D.D. London, 1866.
† "Letter," p. 114.   ‡ Ibid. p. 121.
§ Ibid. p. 119.   ‖ Ibid. p. 109.

time, is really sincere? We know, that, while in the Church of England, he spoke against his convictions; he was only repeating the opinions of others. What he said was "necessary for his position." In fact he was not sincere in what he did say. What guarantee have we that Dr. Newman is not now also put forward for some ulterior purpose? He does not hesitate to declare his opinion that these condemned writers did not mean what they said;* putting them, therefore, on a level with himself. When and how are we to know that a Roman Catholic divine does mean what he says? Mariolatry is a deep blemish in the Roman system. Perhaps Dr. Newman, as the readiest and most pliant instrument, is used to try the ground — *tâtonner* is the expressive French word — and ascertain how a reformation in this branch of the Roman worship will be accepted. In this view of his mission we bid Dr. Newman "God speed."

Dr. Pusey's "Eirenikon," to which this letter purports to be a reply, has been the subject of comment from all parties. It has satisfied none, and has brought upon the author severe and merited rebuke. But good not unfrequently comes out of evil. If no other good has resulted, it has extracted from Dr. Newman the above encouraging acknowledgments.

The most remarkable part of the "Eirenikon" is the publication, in one continuous series, of the opinions and replies of the various bishops on the invitation of the Pope, previous to his official declaration of the dogma of the Immaculate Conception of the blessed Virgin Mary. We have been led to believe that there was a unanimity of opinion on this subject, on which the Pope founded his decision. It was far otherwise. On this head Dr. Newman, with remarkable dexterity, but with equal inconsistency, repudiates the *genuine doctrine* of the Immaculate Conception, falling back

---

* "Letter," p. 120.

on a diluted theory very far short of the accepted teaching, and as received by all parties in his church.

Dr. Newman is a strange compound. With extensive learning, his writings are too often superficial. With strong religious feelings, he is superstitious. With an apparently strong will, he is vacillating. Though at times eloquent, he is garrulous. Logical and clever in reply, he is at all times unsatisfactory and inconclusive in essentials. Poetic and pathetic, but puerile. With a large loving heart, he is effeminate to a degree. With this strange admixture of opposites, it is not to be wondered that Dr. Newman could never bring his mind to one fixed purpose. He was educated partly at the college de Propaganda Fide, at Rome, partly at Oxford. Ever on the balance between Anglicanism and Romanism. "Alas! (he exclaims) it was my position for whole years to remain without any satisfactory basis for my religious profession, in a state of moral sickness, neither able to acquiesce in Anglicanism, nor able to go to Rome."

While *professing* to be an Anglican, Dr. Newman wrote against Rome and Romanism in a manner to satisfy the most exacting Protestant; but he afterwards told us that, when attacking popery, he was not expressing his own sentiments, he was merely repeating the opinions of English divines, but to which he in no wise pledged his own assent; for "such views (he said) were necessary for our position;" and that necessity he explains as being "a hope of approving himself to persons he respected, and a wish to repel the charge of Romanism." The whole of his anti-papal crusade is now conveniently erased from the tablet of his memory. He tried the Bible, and it came short of his requirement. He frankly admits that he had tried it, "and it disappoints." He also tried the ancient Fathers, and no one knows them better than Dr. Newman. He soon satisfied himself of the hopeless task of squaring modern Romanism (into which he had drifted) with antiquity; so his fertile ingenuity invented a developing theory. Religion, like arts and sciences, grows more complete—"*concrete*," by cultivation;—is like a plant, which shoots forth branches, and will bear extensive engrafting upon. Having embraced his new religion through this specious but deceptive theory (for without this he had no excuse), his book enunciating the same was condemned by the more thoughtful and more consistent Romanists. They held this new theory as totally subversive of the Tridentine declaration which claims Scripture, and all the Fathers in past antiquity, in testimony of these doctrines. But now Dr. Newman excuses himself, and renounces his then pet theory. He tells us that he had not read that work since he published it, and "he has now no doubt at all that he has made many mistakes in it, partly from his ignorance of the details of doctrine *as the Church* of Rome holds them." He finds no difficulty in believing in the existence of a Deity and the doctrine of the Trinity, then why should he find a difficulty in believing in the Supremacy of the Pope? indeed, he tells us that the latter is not half so improbable. He has "no difficulty in receiving the doctrine of the Immaculate Conception. And if he has no difficulty, why may not another have no difficulty also? Why may not a hundred—a thousand?" and so any extravagance may be justified. Yet he now condemns "hundreds" and "thousands" who profess to believe that the blessed Virgin can save sinners; that she is more ready to hear our prayers than Christ himself; and that she is the appointed mediatrix between God and man and the gate to heaven, and can even, by virtue of her authority as Mother, command God himself. He assumed that the Church of Rome is the "Oracle of God," and therefore he had no difficulty in believing the doctrine of Transubstantiation, though he disbelieved it before. And yet he would call the ancient Roman superstitious, who consulted the "Oracle," which *he* believed equally to be the "Oracle of God," and the interpreter of the Oracle an impostor. He professes to believe in the miracles of our Lord, and from this fact he finds no difficulty in believing, with equal certainty, the purposeless legends of his Breviary; of dead men walking with their heads under their arms, or jolly friars navigating oceans on a cloak; and yet he will condemn modern spiritualists as impostors, and their followers, dupes; he will deny the followers of "Joe Smith" the same license he takes himself, who profess to believe the miracles of their Master. Dr. Newman is, in fact, a man purposeless and causeless, shifted about with every wind of strange doctrine. He is one a Hurrell Froude could take up, and out of whom shake the little vestige of Protestantism, as one would shake the dust out of a door-mat; one who professed to be indoctrinated in all the mysteries of "Apostolic succession" in a morning's walk round his college grounds! And now we find him repudiating the genuine doctrine of the Immaculate Conception and Virgin-worship as preached in his church. What are we to expect next? And this is the Rev. John Henry Newman, D.D., formerly of the College of the Propagation of Faith at Rome, afterwards of Oriel College, Oxford, and then Incumbent of St. Mary's, now of the Oratory of Birmingham. Verily, verily, Dr. Newman, you have rightly estimated your own value, when you wrote to Dr. Wiseman, that persons and things look great at a distance, which are not so when seen close; and did we know you, we should see that you were one about whom there has been far more talk for good or bad than you deserve, and about whose movements far more expectation has been raised than the event will justify.*

* "Apologia," pp. 367-8.

Dr. Newman commences his letter to Dr. Pusey by fulsome flattery; but he overrates Dr. Pusey's influence, nor can we subscribe as a fact, "that numbers will be moved by his authority." This might have been so twenty years ago. The "more advanced party" of "a school more recent than Dr. Pusey's" (who I am happy to say are comparatively few), "may, for the occasion, accept Dr. Pusey as their spokesman." But Dr. Newman, speaking of his own party, says that "there is no one among his own body, or, as he supposes, in the Greek Church, who can affect so vast a circle of men, so virtuous, so able, so learned, so zealous, as come more or less under Dr. Pusey's influence."*

Having thus made his peace with his rival, he complains that if he (Dr. Newman) is "dry, hard, and unsympathizing," his "dear Pusey"—"his very dear friend"—is "unfair and irritating." "There was one of old time who wreathed his sword in myrtle; excuse me—you (Dr. Pusey) discharge your olive-branch as if from a catapult."† You have "touched then on a very tender point in a very rude way."‡ The simple question is, are Dr. Pusey's strictures justified by facts? After a laboured essay of evasions and excuses, he comes exactly to the conclusion to which Dr. Pusey arrived; namely, that the worship of the Virgin, as practised by a large section of Romanists, was indefensible, nay, that it "provoked blasphemy" He compares them with the "Covenanters and Ranters."§

Dr. Pusey quotes against Dr. Newman his own words uttered against Romanism in 1841, when in the Anglican Church—that "the Roman Church comes as near to idolatry as can be supposed in a church of which it is said 'the idols He shall utterly abolish.'" This *is* touching him on a very tender point, *rude* Dr.

---

* "Letter," p. 5.   † Ibid. p. 9.
‡ Ibid. p. 121.   § Ibid. p. 122.

Pusey. If Romanism has changed at all, it is, in that Mary-worship has been still more developed; indeed, it is now at the extreme; it is to be hoped a reaction will take place. Dr. Newman is puzzled what to say. "I know not to what authority to go for them,—to Scripture, or to the Fathers, or to the decrees of councils, or to the consent of the schools, to the tradition of the faithful, or to the Holy See, or to reason."* He admits that this Mary-worship has "in times and places fallen into abuse; that it has even become superstition."† As it is "difficult to determine where truth passes into error,"‡ we would put it to Dr. Newman whether it would not be safer to adhere to Scripture and the doctrine of the one Mediator? Avoid all appearance of evil; and this becomes the more necessary if Dr. Newman's estimate of the "Catholic Church" be true. "If we are to have a Catholic Church, we must put up with fish of every kind, guests good and bad, vessels of gold, vessels of earth;"§ and if it be true that "what is abstractedly extravagant, may in religious persons be becoming and beautiful, and only fall under blame when it is found in others who imitate them."∥ One would suppose that we have a case here, above all others, which would require utmost caution to avoid this very evil, since there is such an affinity between religion and superstition.

Before I proceed to the more immediate object of Dr. Newman's letter, I would remark in passing, that he does not appear very particular in defining the real teaching of his church. One of Dr. Pusey's "discharges from a catapult" was the unanimous testimony of the Fathers, that the Scriptures were alone of authority as a rule of faith, and that it was a heresy to maintain their insufficiency. Dr. Newman cannot deny this pregnant fact, so he adroitly avoids the

---

* "Letter," p. 120. † Ibid. p. 93.
‡ Ibid. p. 109. § Ibid. p. 86.
∥ Ibid. p. 85.

question by saying that Dr. Pusey " allows there is a twofold rule,—Scripture and tradition, and this is all that Catholics say."

Indeed! Is that all? The Council of Trent decreed that the oral traditions of the Roman Church should be held with equal piety and veneration to the Scriptures themselves. And the Creed, while it compels all to "firmly admit and embrace apostolical and ecclesiastical traditions," only requires us simply "to admit the Scriptures;" but with this proviso, "according to the sense which the Holy Mother Church has held, and does hold." And as if this were not a sufficient "dead lock,"—the Roman Church never has, never can, and therefore never will, publish any authentic interpretation, since that interpretation, if given, must in every case be "according to the unanimous agreement of the Fathers."

Such being the Roman profession, it is rather astonishing to hear Dr. Newman assert his belief that the difference between Anglicanism and Romanism " is merely one of words." Let us see. Dr. Wiseman, in his " Lectures on the principal Doctrines and Practices of the Catholic Church," lays it down, that " an authority to teach was communicated to the Apostles, and by them to their successors, together with *an unwritten code;* so that, what was afterwards written by them, was but a fixing and recording a *part* of that which was already in possession of the Church."* The Church of England, on the other hand, lays it down, that " Holy Scripture containeth all things necessary to salvation; so that whatsoever is not read therein nor may be proved thereby is not to be required of any man, that it should be believed as an article of faith, or be thought requisite or necessary to salvation." Is it possible to " believe that the difference" between the teaching of the Church of

---

* Lecture V p. 128, vol. i. London, 1851.

England and the Church of Rome on this head "is merely one of words"? Who does Dr. Newman expect to deceive, by holding out such fallacious pretensions? We are required to accept the whole of the alleged apostolical and ecclesiastical traditions of his church, with equal piety and reverence to the Holy Scriptures, and if we were to ask Dr. Newman to define these traditions, he could not do so. If we ask him to produce the Church's interpretation of any one chapter of the Bible, he cannot do so. If we ask him to produce the unanimous agreement of the Fathers on any given text, without which he is precluded from expounding the Word of God, he cannot do so; and yet our belief on this subject does not differ from Rome! Dr. Newman affects great reverence and veneration for Athanasius. "When he became a Catholic, he kissed the volume with delight."—"You are mine (he says), and I am yours beyond mistake." What does his own authority tell him on this very subject? "The Holy Scriptures, given by inspiration of God, are of themselves sufficient towards the discovery of the truth,"* and this we find in the very first page of his voluminous works; and, speaking of the orthodox Catholic Christians of his age, he says, "The Catholic Christians will neither speak nor endure to hear anything in religion that is foreign to the Scriptures, it being an evil heart of immodesty to speak those things which are not written."† But Dr. Newman admits all we can expect of him on this head; for he tells us that "Christians have never gone to Scripture for proofs of their doctrines till there was actual need, from the pressure of controversy;"‡ and that is the very last place a modern Romanist would look to for proofs for

* Athanasii Opera, tom. i. p. 1, edit. Bened. Paris, 1698: Orat. contra Gentes.
† Tom. ii. p. 709: Exhort. ad Monachos.
‡ "Letter," p. 57.

his pecular doctrines. Dr. Newman is a practical illustration of this, for he "has tried Scripture, and finds it disappoints." And this is the key to all Rome's unauthorized and extravagant worship of the Virgin. With this I pass to the real object of the "Letter" itself, namely to clear the writer and "English Catholics," and explain, with reference to the Blessed Virgin Mary, that there "just now seems a call on him, under his circumstances, to avow plainly what he does, and what he does not, hold about the Blessed Virgin, that others may know, did they come to stand where he stands, what they would, and what they would not, be bound to hold concerning her."* Dr. Newman considers the occasion one when a bold front should be assumed, regardless of consequences. With reference to the long series of quotations advanced by Dr. Pusey on the decided and dogmatic acknowledgment of the Fathers, that in matters of faith the Holy Scriptures should be the alone rule of faith and conduct of Christians, and from which an unwritten code is wholly excluded, Dr. Newman treats these with the utmost contempt; but, with strange inconsistency as regards Mary-worship, he boldly avows, that "hopeless as Dr. Pusey may consider it, he is not ashamed to declare that he will take his stand upon the Fathers, and does not mean to budge."† Though gone over to Rome, "history of those times is not yet an old almanac to him;" the Fathers made him "Catholic," and he is not now going to kick down the ladder by which he alleges he ascended into the Church, and "in particular, as regards his Church's teaching concerning the Blessed Virgin, with the Fathers he is content; and to the subject of that teaching he means to address himself at once;"—"and thus (he says) we can join issue on a clear and broad principle." This is a bold challenge.

* "Letter," p. 27.   † Ibid. p. 28.

Now before I proceed, let us understand on what we are engaged. Setting aside for the moment the published and unrebuked acknowledgment of the office and powers of the Virgin Mary, we have the authorized and enjoined worship of the Roman Church, prayers to the Almighty through the mediation of Mary; her merits are pleaded before the throne of grace; prayers are addressed directly to Mary for her intercession and for spiritual and temporal blessings at her hands, which God alone can bestow. They teach that we should depend on her as our hope, the anchor of our soul, the Queen of Heaven, and the Spouse of God; and we find these devotions rewarded by *indulgences*. I now publicly challenge Dr. Newman on the very ground he has assumed. To appeal to the Bible would be to take a vantage-ground, for he has given up that; " he has tried it, and found that it disappoints." I assert, and I challenge Dr. Newman to prove to the contrary, that, taking the records of the early councils and the works of the early Christian writers to the end of the first five hundred years, they all testify, " as with one voice, that these writers and their contemporaries knew of no belief in the present power of the Virgin Mary, and of her influence with God; no practice, in public or private, of praying to God through her mediation, or of invoking her for her good offices of intercession, and advocacy, and patronage; no offering of thanks and praise made to her; no assumption of Divine honour or glory to her name. On the contrary, all the writers through those ages testify that to the early Christians God was the only object of prayer, and Christ the only Mediator and Intercessor in whom they put their trust."

Dr. Newman takes his stand on the Fathers, and does not pretend to fall back on " Development," and so do I. Will Dr. Newman accept this public challenge? He states in his letter to Dr. Pusey, that on this point "the Fathers are enough for him." Then, I maintain, that he must erase from his Breviary and other books of devotion every single prayer to the Blessed Virgin. But Dr. Newman will not accept this invitation, because he cannot. The Roman practice on this head is a novelty.

Dr. Newman, while condemning extravagancies he alleges he never met with, except in Dr. Pusey's books, undertakes to justify the teaching of his Church in her authorized formularies. There is nothing to be condemned "in the Missal, in the Roman Catechism, in the Roman Raccolta, in the Imitation of Christ, in Gother, Challoner, Milner, or Wiseman, as far as he is aware."* I may perhaps be able to disabuse Dr. Newman as to some of these; but it is remarkable that he omits from his catalogue his *Vade mecum*,—the Breviary!

Notwithstanding his protest, Dr. Newman undertakes to defend the *cultus* of the Virgin, in order to evade the fact which stares us in the face, on opening almost every book of devotion of the Roman Church, of the very extravagancies he makes a pretence of repudiating. He tells us that he will have nothing to do with statements which can only be explained by being explained away.† Nevertheless Dr. Newman, with more art than discretion, in fact excuses, if not advocates the system, by trying to explain away, by endeavouring to draw a line of distinction between *faith* and *devotion*, which he alleges "will go far to remove good part of the difficulty of his undertaking, as it presents itself to ordinary inquirers." He fully grants that *devotion* towards the Blessed Virgin has increased among [Roman] Catholics with the progress of centuries; he even goes so far as to admit that it has become an abuse;‡ but he "does not allow that the *doctrine* concerning the Virgin Mary has undergone a growth, for he professes to believe that it has been one in substance,

* "Letter," p. 120. † Id. ibid. ‡ Ibid. p. 93.

and one and the same, from the beginning." That there should be no mistake about his meaning, he says "By *faith*, I mean the Creed and the acceptance of the Creed; by *devotion*, I mean such religious honours as belong to the objects of our faith, and the payment of these honours." "Faith and devotion (he adds) are as distinct in fact as they are in idea." What then is the present creed of the Roman Church on this head? The present creed of the Roman Church declares "that the saints reigning together with Christ *are to be honoured and invocated with* CHRIST." This is a command; and the Trent decree, which is made part of this Creed, declares "that it is useful and good suppliantly to invoke them."* And on this subject we must not confound it with the assertion dwelt upon so forcibly and indeed beautifully by Dr. Newman, that the saints in heaven are occupied in interceding for us on earth. This fact is wholly beyond our knowledge, though we may hope that such is their occupation. Delahogue admits that this worship is a *religious* worship, though "the Tridentine fathers do not use the word."†

That this belief has been in substance one and the same from the beginning, is alleged as a fact, but which I most distinctly, positively, and unequivocally challenge. It has not the slightest sanction in Scrip-

---

* Our subject is the lawfulness of addressing ourselves to the dead *personally*, and that they hear our *verbal* and *mental* prayers; That we can plead their merits before the throne of grace, and employ other mediators besides Christ.

† "Tract. de Mysterio SS. Trinitatis." Autore L. A. Delahogue. R. Coyne. Dublin, 1822. Appendix, de Cultu Sanctorum, p. 218. It is proper here to state, that Veron, in his "Rule of Catholic Faith,' pp. 96-7, Birmingham, 1833, says that it is not an article of Romish faith, that this veneration is to be called a *religious* veneration; but he admits that their "writers differ on the question. Marsilius thinks that the honour which is shown to God and the Saints is the exercise of one and the same virtue," but of different degrees. "Delincourt (he says) goes farther, and maintains, in a pamphlet written expressly on this subject, that a *religious* honour ought to be given to the Blessed Virgin."

ture,* or the confirmation of one single Father of the Church for the first four centuries, nor of any creed previous to 1564. Nor is intercessory prayer or praying for the dead anything to the point. Intercessory prayer is encouraged in Scripture; praying for the dead is an early innovation not sanctioned by Scripture. But I deny Dr. Newman's theory as to "Faith" and "Devotion." When we pray to God through Christ, and express our dependence on the mercy of the all-good and wise Creator, and plead the merits of Christ, our *devotion* expresses our *faith*. We have *faith* that God hears our prayers, that He is able to grant our petition; *faith*, that Christ is our Mediator; and we have *faith* in His merits, and that He is able and willing to intercede for us. When I turn to Dr. Newman's Breviary, and find repeated intercessions made through the Virgin Mary, and her merits also pleaded, the devotion I presume must convey the faith of the utterer. Thus in the octave of Easter, at the Mass, the intercession of the Virgin is made to appear as essential a cause of our peace and blessedness as is the propitiation of Christ. " By thy *propitiation*, O Lord, and by the intercession of the blessed Mary ever Virgin, may this offering be profitable to us," &c. Here the intercession is as much of *faith* as the propitiation. And here let me point to an error into which Dr. Newman has fallen. He says " her name is not heard in the administration of the sacraments."† Again when we read in the Breviary continually : " Pray for us, O holy Mother of God," this devotion is accompanied with the *faith* that the Virgin *hears* the prayer. Let me now quote one of the most favourite prayers in

* "The Sacred Scriptures do not teach, even in effect or by implication, that prayers are to be made to the saints, &c. Therefore it is sufficiently clear, that many things belong to the [Roman] Catholic faith which have no place in the sacred page."—*Dominic Bahnes, in Secundum Secundæ Thom.* Q. i. Art. x. Concil. ii. col. 521. Venet. 1587.

† " Letter," p. 89.

the Breviary. I select the Breviary, because Dr. Newman is bound, under pain of mortal sin, to read the appointed portion every day.

I quote from the Rev. F. C. Husenbeth's edition, Norwich, 1830, and which purports to have received the sanction of the Pope.

Pars Vern. cliii.—"Hail, Star of the Sea, and kind Mother of God, and ever Virgin, Happy Gate of Heaven! Do thou, taking that 'Hail' from the mouth of Gabriel, changing the name of Eve, establish us in peace. Do thou loose their bands for the accused; for the blind bring forth a light; drive away our evils; demand for us all good things. *Show that thou art a Mother!* Let Him who endured for us to be thy Son, through thee receive our prayers. O excellent Virgin! meek among all, *do thou make us meek and chaste, free from fault; make our life pure:* prepare for us a safe journey, that, beholding Jesus, we may always rejoice together. Praise be to God the Father, Glory to Christ most high, and to the Holy Ghost; one honour to the Three. Amen."

Æst. cxlvi.—"Under thy protection we take refuge, Holy Mother of God; despise not our supplications in our necessities, but *from all dangers do thou deliver us,* O glorious and Blessed Virgin."

Æst. cxlv.—"O Mary, Mother of Grace, Mother of Mercy, *do thou protect us from the enemy, and receive us at the hour of death.*"

Æst. cxcviii.—"The Holy Mother of God is exalted above the choir of angels to the heavenly realms. The gates of Paradise are open to us *by thee,* who, glorious this day, triumphest with the angels."—"Rejoice, O Virgin Mary, thou alone hast destroyed all heresies in the whole world. Deem me worthy to praise thee, hallowed Virgin. Give me strength against thy enemies."

Now these are authorized *devotions*, practised by compulsion by Dr. Newman. They are prayers that can with equal propriety be addressed to Christ, except that she is asked to show herself a Mother. Does Dr. Newman believe that the Virgin can drive away evils, make him chaste, free from fault, and deliver him from all dangers? If that is not his *faith*, then his devotions are a mockery. Dr. Newman says "we may believe without feeling devotion." Does Dr. Newman really believe what he prays for, without feeling any devotion, or does he pray without believing in the object of his devotions? And when he has answered, let him show us any like prayers in any Liturgy, Creed, books of the Fathers, for 500 years after Christ!

Dr. Newman cannot shield himself with the excuse that these are "semi-authorized devotions."*

Dr. Newman's remark that "we cannot be devout without faith, but we may believe without feeling devotion,"† is very characteristic. This may be, and probably is, true with Roman Catholics, who have, in their so-called sacrament of Penance, to perform "satisfactory works" by way of punishment; and this is not unfrequently to recite prayers by the gross; and rosaries or beads are invented to regulate the number, not the devotion.‡ The devotee may *believe* that these prayers are efficacious with the Lord, but *devotion* must be out of the question. But what Dr. Newman seeks to establish is, that the forms of prayers addressed to the Virgin Mary are not to be taken as a criterion of the *faith* of the individual who uses such devotions. Nor is a church to be charged with idolatry, or indeed any particular phase of belief, simply from the form of authorized prayers used in that church, though openly practised and unrebuked, and though the printed forms and books of devotion, or other books of explanation, are published by the duly constituted authorities, duly examined, and certified and circulated. "Faith (he says) is everywhere one and the same; but a large liberty is accorded to private judgment and inclination in matters of devotion."§ It is on this leading fallacy that Dr.

---

* "Letter," p. 96.   † Ibid. p. 28.

‡ In the "Garden of the Soul" (Dublin, 1857, p. 357), a book, by the way, on which Dr. Newman challenges us, there is a chapter on "the Fifteen Mysteries of the Rosary." "The method of saying the Rosary of our Blessed Lady, as it was ordered by his Holiness Pope Pius V." There is this explanation: "The Devotion of the Rosary consists of fifteen Paternosters and one hundred and fifty Ave Marias, divided into three parts, each containing five decades, viz., five Paters and fifty Aves." By which we presume we are to measure the relative devotion paid to Jesus and Mary.

§ "Letter," p. 30.

Newman bases the whole of his arguments to excuse the erratic exuberances of members of his church. Dr. Newman himself prefers "English habits of belief and devotion to foreign,"* but he nevertheless adopts and practises the prayers I have cited from his Breviary, and these are orthodox, according to his private judgment. I am bound to explain Dr. Newman's theory, otherwise we cannot possibly account for his subsequent repudiation. "It is necessary for his position."

It is difficult to understand what Dr. Newman does sanction and what he does condemn; he is strong in his condemnation, nevertheless he strings condemned passages together, and says they can all be explained away. "When taken in their literal absolute sense, as any Protestant would naturally take them, they are to be condemned, but not as the writers doubtless intended to use them;" † but, he tell us, these books are happily not known to the vast majority of "English Catholics."‡ "Certain statements may be true under circumstances and in a particular time and place, which are *abstractedly false;* and hence it may be very unfair in a controversialist to interpret by an English or a modern rule, whatever may have been asserted by a foreign or mediæval author."§ "We are not answerable for their particular devotions."‖ "It is clear not one of them is an Englishman."¶ But it seems to Dr. Newman a simple "purism to insist upon minute accuracy of expression in devotional and popular writings."** There "is a healthy devotion to the Blessed Mary, and there is an artificial;"†† and he "supposes that we owe it to the national good sense that English Catholics have been protected from the extravagances which are elsewhere to be found."‡‡ And so satisfied

---

* "Letter," p. 22.   † Ibid. p. 118.
‡ Ibid. p. 119.   § Ibid. p. 110.
‖ Ibid. p. 104.   ¶ Ibid. p. 104.
** Ibid. p. 107.   †† Ibid. p. 105.   ‡‡ Id. ib.

is Dr. Newman with his own explanation that, " on the whole, he is sanguine that we will come to the conclusion that Anglicans may safely trust themselves to English Catholics, as regards any devotions to the Blessed Virgin which might be required of Protestants over and above the rule of the Council of Trent."* We are all indeed very much obliged to Dr. Newman for his condescending consideration of us. To prove his orthodoxy, Dr. Newman boldly says,—" He who charges us with making Mary a *divinity*, is thereby denying the divinity of Jesus."† This has two meanings, which gives the Doctor a means of escape. If we prove that the charge is true, that they make Mary a divinity, then it is we who deny the divinity of Jesus, for she is equally divine; or he may mean that if the charge can be brought home to Romanists, then we also prove that they deny the divinity of Jesus. Now, I invite Dr. Newman to turn to the edition of the " Glories of Mary," " cordially recommended to the faithful " by the late Dr. Wiseman, then Cardinal (London, 1852), and in page 157 he will read, " Whilst all the other saints can do more for their own clients than for others, the DIVINE MOTHER, as Queen of all, is the advocate of all, and has a care for the salvation of all;" and a little lower on the same page this same epithet *Divine* is applied to God,—" the Divine Majesty." Of course, Dr. Newman will find a method of explaining this away. But I may be permitted to doubt whether Anglicans can sufficiently trust themselves to " English Catholics" in matters of devotion to the Blessed Virgin.

This will be a fit place to consider the sort of devotion to the Blessed Virgin which *is permitted* to " English Catholics," who are so peculiarly privileged above their foreign brethren, by having a pure and " healthy *devotion*" offered to them, " without any

---

* " Letter," p. 108.   † Ibid. p. 190.

injury to solid piety and Christian good sense."* Dr. Newman places before us, as examples, "The Garden of the Soul," and he wonders whether we can find anything to displease us in this,† and he says there is nothing objectionable in Milner and Wiseman.

Let us take first the "Garden of the Soul." In every edition we have the "Litany of the Blessed Virgin." Sextus V. is declared to have granted an Indulgence for 200 days to all Christians each time it is repeated. This boon was confirmed by Benedict XIII. This Litany takes four minutes to recite; say five, for extra devotion. *Faith* and *devotion* do not necessarily go together. Suppose we dedicate one hour a day in the devout recital of this Litany. So that an hour a day for one year would give us an indulgence of 2,400 years' relief of punishment due to the sins we have committed in this world. If persevered in for ten years, we obtain a pardon of 24,000 years of punishment. Does Dr. Newman really believe this? But as to the devotions. This Litany is a prayer to the Virgin, in which she is invoked as "Holy Mother of God—Mother of our Creator—Virgin most powerful—Mirror of Justice—Seat of Wisdom—Cause of our Joy—Mystical Rose—Tower of David—Tower of Ivory—Crown of Gold—Ark of the Covenant—Gate of Heaven—Morning Star—Health of the Weak—Refuge of Sinners—Comforter of the Afflicted—Help of Christians." Then there is this prayer:—"We fly to thy patronage, O holy Mother of God! Despise not our petition in our necessities, but *deliver us from all dangers*, O ever glorious and blessed Virgin"! Then we have repeated the hymn, "Hail Star of the Sea!" which I have already quoted in page 143, and also the prayer of "St. Bernard:"—

"Remember, O most Holy Virgin Mary! that no one ever had recourse to thy protection, implored thy help, or sought thy media-

---

* "Letter," p. 105.   † Ibid. p. 106.

tion without obtaining it. Confiding, therefore, in thy goodness, behold me, a penitent sinner, sighing out my sins before thee, beseeching thee to adopt me for thy son, and take upon thee the care of my eternal salvation. Despise not, O Mother of Jesus! the petition of thine humble client; but hear and grant my prayer."

If in all the above we substitute the name of Christ, we could not honour Him more; indeed, most of the titles in the Scriptures applied to Christ, are here applied to Mary. Dr. Newman sees nothing objectionable in all this!

We now come to Dr. Milner, in whom also there is nothing to object. I have before me the

"Devotion of the Sacred Heart, &c.; twelfth edition. Prayers for the use of the Midland *District*. By the R[ight] R[ev.] J[ohn] M[ilner], Bishop of Castab[ala], V[icar of the] M[idland] D[istrict]: London, 1821."

In Section I., page 198, we read—

"As the adorable heart of Jesus was formed in the chaste womb of the Blessed Virgin, and of her blood and substance, so we cannot, in a more proper and agreeable manner, show our devotion to the sacred heart of the Son, *than by dedicating some part of the said devotion* to the ever-pure heart of the mother. For you have two hearts here united in the most strict alliance and tender conformity of sentiments, so that it is not in nature to please the one without making yourself agreeable to the other, and acceptable to both.— Presume not to separate and divide two objects so intimately one, or united together; but ask redress in all your exigencies from the heart of Jesus, and ask this redress through the heart of Mary.

"This form and method of worship is the doctrine and the very spirit of God's Church; it is what she teaches us in the unanimous voice and practice of the faithful, who will by no means that Jesus and Mary should be separated from each other in our prayers, praises, and affections.

"Come, then, hardened and inveterate sinner, how great soever your crimes may be! Come and behold! Mary stretches out her hand, opens her breast to receive you."

Here we are invited to "dedicate some part of the *same devotion* to the ever pure heart of the mother," as accorded to the Son.

In Section II. the Virgin Mary is addressed as "O Holy Mother of God, glorious Queen of Heaven and Earth!" and the following words are not exactly in accordance with the idea that favours are to be obtained through Christ alone:—"Obtain for me at present the gift of a true repentance, and those graces I may stand in need of for the gaining of life everlasting."*

The following four prayers, from the same work, however, place the question in a very clear light. Graces are asked of Mary, which God alone can bestow, and these are *not* asked " through Jesus Christ :"—

"O Holy Mary, our Sovereign Queen! as God the Father, by His own omnipotence, has made thee most powerful, so assist us at the hour of our death, by defending us against all power that is contrary to thine. *Hail, Mary!*

"O Holy Mary, our Sovereign Queen! as God the Son has endowed thee with so much knowledge and charity that it enlightens all heaven, so in the hour of our death illustrate and strengthen our souls with the knowledge of the true faith, that they be not perverted by error or pernicious ignorance. *Hail, Mary!*

"O Holy Virgin, our Sovereign Queen! as the Holy Ghost has plentifully poured forth into thee the love of God, so instil into us at the hour of death the sweetness of divine love, that all bitterness at that time may become acceptable and pleasant to us. *Hail, Mary!*

"Our Blessed Lady herself taught St. Mechtildis the abovementioned triple salutation, promising her certain assistance for it at the hour of her death."†

Again, there is another book, "The Catholic School-Book,"‡ introduced, under the approbation of Dr. Milner, in 1818, as being, in his opinion, "eminently entitled to the patronage of the Catholic public." . . . " As such," he added, he should " not fail to recommend it in those places of education in which he had any authority or influence." I need add but one extract to illustrate Dr. Newman's idea of orthodoxy.

---

* Pp. 201, 202. † Pp. 212, 213.

‡ " The Catholic School-Book; containing easy and familiar Lessons for the Instruction of Youth of both Sexes in the English Language, and in the Paths of true Religion and Virtue." Twentieth edition, with additions. London, 1839. 12mo.

"By her [Mary] we may receive all the assistance which is necessary for us. She is most powerful with God, to obtain from Him all that she shall ask of Him. She is all goodness in regard of us, by applying to God for us. Being Mother of God, He cannot refuse her request; being our Mother, she cannot deny us her intercession when we have recourse to her. Our miseries move her, our necessities urge her; the prayers we offer her for our salvation bring to us all that we desire; and St. Bernard is not afraid to say, 'That never any person invoked that Mother of Mercy in his necessities who has not been sensible of the effects of her assistance.'"

"If you will be a true child, and a sincere servant of the Blessed Virgin, you must be careful to perform four things. [The fourth is:]

"Be mindful to invoke her in temptations, and in the dangers you find yourself in of offending God. You cannot show your respect better than by applying yourself to her in these urgent necessities, *and you can find no succour more ready and favourable than hers*." *

We now come to Dr. Wiseman.

One of the most popular books in England is "The Glories of Mary." It has been translated and re-translated into English for the special devotions of "English Catholics." It is by Liguori, the founder of the Redemptorist order, now so numerous in England. I purchased, when published, the fourth edition, from which I shall take my extracts.† It has come out in several subsequent editions, many of which I have; the last is that of 1852, "approved and cordially recommended by Nicholas, Cardinal Wiseman, [self-styled] Archbishop of Westminster." The translator of this edition, in the Preface, p. xviii., says,—

"Remember that it [the book] has been strictly examined by the

---

* "Catholic School-Book," p. 158.

† Dublin, John Coyne, 1841; fourth edition, entered at Stationers' Hall. John Coyne is the authorized publisher of Romish works in Dublin. The title-page of the work in question is as follows:—"The Glories of Mary, Mother of God; containing a beautiful paraphrase on the 'Salve Regina.' Translated from the Italian of St. Alphonsus Liguori, and carefully revised by a Catholic Priest. Fourth Edition. Hail Mary! full of grace! the Lord is with thee! *Angel Gabriel in St. Luke.* Dublin, printed by John Coyne, 24, Cook-street, 1841."

authority which is charged by God Himself to instruct you, and that that authority has declared that it contains NOTHING [so in original] worthy of censure; that it has been welcomed by all lovers of Jesus and Mary throughout the world, with an enthusiasm which can only be equalled by the scorn and ridicule which, as an invariable rule, attend all that is powerful to snatch from the world its votaries, and from hell its victims."

The "authority" above referred to is the "Sacred Congregation of Rites,"—an authority admitted by Dr. Newman.* The examination of Liguori's works took twenty years' consideration, and we find that with a view to his canonization (the most solemn act of this modern church, and in which Cardinal Bellarmine asserts she is infallible),† Pope Pius VII. confirmed the decree of the Congregation of Rites, which declared‡—

"That all the writings of St. Alphonsus, whether printed or inedited, had been most rigorously examined according to the discipline of the Apostolic See, and *that not one word had been found 'censuræ dignum;'* and that in all these examinations, *undertaken with a view to canonization* of St. Alphonsus, and in the definite judgment of the Sacred Congregation, all agreed, 'voce concordi, unanimi consensu, una voce, unanimiter.'"

And in consequence he was canonized by the late Pope Gregory XVI., A.D. 1839. Again, in the "Lives of Modern Saints," a work approved and specially recommended by two Roman authorities (Bishops of Roman Catholics, one of whom was Dr. Wiseman himself), and dedicated to the regular clergy of the [Roman] Catholic Church in England,§ we find "the precious work, entitled 'The Glories of Mary,'" most particularly mentioned and recommended as a work, the fruit of several years' labour, "in which

* "I am not denying the right of Sacred Congregations, at their will, to act peremptorily, and without assigning reasons for judgment they pass upon writers."—*Letter to Dr. Pusey,* p. 113.
† Bell., "Church Triumphant," tom. ii. p. 871. Cologne, 1671.
‡ See [Roman] "Catholic Calendar for 1845," p. 167.
§ "Life of St. A. Liguori, &c." vol. ii. pp. 19—21. Richardson, London, 1848.

he [Liguori] had employed himself to choose from among the works of holy fathers and theologians the *most conclusive proofs in favour of the prerogatives of Mary*, and the fittest to engage the faithful to devote themselves to her service."* "The applause with which the book was received, or the number of editions through which it has gone, is scarcely to be credited."†

But to place the matter beyond a doubt, that the doctrines and devotions taught by Liguori are or ought to be univerally received by all classes of English Romanists, we find in their own Missal,‡ or Prayer-book, which is in daily use in England, that they must pray, on the 2nd of August in every year, in the following words:—"O God, who by the blessed Alphonsus Maria, thy confessor and pontiff, who was inflamed with a zeal for souls, hast enriched thy Church with a new offspring, *we implore that, taught by his saving admonitions, and strengthened by his example*, we may be able happily to come to thee, through the Lord."§ And in Lesson V. of their Church Service for the same day, the identical book in question is thus expressly named, and specially commended:—"Being an admirable worshipper of the Mother of God, he [Liguori] wrote and published a book upon her praises;" and in the same lesson his writings are stated to be "fraught with sacred erudition and piety."‖

No book, therefore, can possibly come before us with more authority than the "Glories of Mary." It does not come within the category of "foreign or mediæval writers."¶ Dr. Newman can only evade its au-

---

* Ibid. p. 20.   † Ibid. p. 21.

‡ Another book challenged by Dr. Newman ("Letter," p. 120).

§ "Missale Romanum," Mechlin, 1840, p. 402, and "Roman Anglican Ritual." Keating and Brown, London, 1831.

‖ When Dr. Newman repeats the above prayer, does his *faith* follow his *devotion?*

¶ Dr. Newman says he has never read the "Glories of Mary." Let

thority by leaving the Roman Church, for it has become a part of the system. I start with the assertion that Liguori only develops the practical working of the system of Romanism, which, in fact, places the Virgin Mary on a level with, if not above, our blessed Redeemer. We are informed—

"From the moment that Mary *consented* to become the Mother of God, says Bernardine of Sienna, she *merited* to receive sovereignty over all creatures. Mary and Jesus having but one and the same flesh, says St. Arnaud, Abbot, why should not the Mother enjoy *conjointly with the Son* the honours of 'royalty'? As many creatures as obey God, so many obey the glorious Virgin; everything in heaven and on earth which is subject to God, *is also under the empire of His most holy Mother*" (p. 28).

Here is most unequivocal language. The Virgin reigns sovereign over all creatures, enjoys conjointly with the Son all honours of royalty, and everything in heaven and earth is under her empire. Thus we have the Virgin Mary practically incorporated in, or made equal to, one of the Trinity.

This co-operation of Rome's Virgin is much insisted upon by Dr. Newman himself. We are told that—

"It was *by her consent* that Jesus might sacrifice Himself for our redemption" (p. 128).

"Why was not the mystery of the Incarnation accomplished *without the consent of the Virgin?* It is because God wishes she may be *the principal of all Good in the law of Grace*" (p. 88).

"St. Peter Damian (we are told) goes still further, asking himself this question: Why has God, before He became incarnate in Mary's womb, *applied for her consent?* For two reasons (he replies): first to oblige us to be very grateful to her; and, secondly, *to teach us that our salvation depends* on the will of this Blessed Virgin" (p. 123).

As a natural consequence, Abbot Rupert is quoted as exclaiming—

---

him do so now. But he has his misgivings in anticipation, as he says of it, "it never surprises me to read anything unusual in the devotions of a saint. Such men are on a level very different from our own, and we cannot understand them. The spiritual man judges all things, and he himself is judged of no one" (p. 103). But Liguori was *judged* most critically, and approved of.

"O, great Queen! it is by *you the miserable are saved;* and because *their salvation is your work,* they shall form your crown in Heaven" (p. 34).

And it is, therefore broadly stated that—

"It is now the general sentiment of the Church, that the intercession of the Mother of God is not only useful, *but even necessary to salvation*" (p. 122). "God will never save us without Mary's intercession" (p. 131).

Dr. Newman has a remarkable observation on this sentiment in his "Letter to Dr. Pusey,"*

"To say dogmatically that no one can be saved without personal devotion to the Blessed Virgin would be an untenable proposition; yet it might be true of this or that date; and *if* the very statement has ever been made by any writer of consideration (and this has to be ascertained), then, perhaps, it was made precisely under those exceptional circumstances."

For Dr. Newman's information I may state that Liguori is quoting from the writings of the great Cardinal and canonized Saint Bonaventura! But St. Augustine is represented as going a step further—

"Men," he says, "have but one sole advocate in Heaven, and it is you, Holy Virgin" (p. 145).

Dr. Newman, by the way, says, "I should like to know whether St. Augustine, in all his voluminous writings, invokes her once,"† and so should I; but Dr. Newman cannot "deny the right of the Sacred Congregation, at their will, to act peremptorily and without assigning a reason for their judgment,"‡ and so he is bound to believe that Augustine *did* write this passage, though, when he was an Anglican, he knew it was a barefaced forgery; but now he is "bound to believe *white* to be black, if his church so define it to be."§

---

* P. 110. † Ibid. p. 111. ‡ Ibid. p. 113.
§ See Dr. Wiseman's edition of the "Spiritual Exercises of St. Ignatius." London, 1847, p. 180.

If St. Augustine said this, we cannot be surprised that St. Anselm should add—

"Our salvation is often more speedily effected by invoking Mary, 'Beautiful as the Moon,' than in calling on Jesus, the 'Divine Sun of Justice'" (p. 186).

How natural, therefore, is the exclamation—

"Why should Christians feel any scruple in saying to her, with the [Roman] church and the saints, 'SAVE US'?" (p. 130).

Yes, indeed, why should they, if the priests keep the Bible from them?

"St. German then had reason to call Mary the respiration of Christians; for as the body cannot exist without breathing, so the soul cannot live without recurring to the Mother of God" (p. 71). And "she herself warns us [when, and where, and by whom, we are not informed], that she has at her disposal all the treasures of the Divinity" (p. 89).

One would suppose that this was plain speaking enough; but hear St. Anselm; he asks—

"How is it, that we ask many things of God without obtaining them, but when we ask them through Mary they are granted to us?" (p. 104). He had only just before assured us in order "to increase your confidence in Mary, that our prayers will often be more speedily heard in invoking her name than in *calling on that of Jesus Christ*"!

Having thus completely superseded the office of Christ as our Mediator and Advocate, we are shown how necessary is the interposition of the Blessed Virgin: and for what reason, think you?

"God in the Old Law often complained that there was none to interpose between Him and sinners; but since Mary the Mediatrix of peace has appeared on earth, *she restrains His arm, and averts His wrath*" (p. 95).

"That as the Kingdom of God consists in mercy and justice, the Lord has, as it were, divided it, reserving to Himself the dominion of Justice, and yielding to his Mother that of Mercy" (p. 29).

This view of the subject is much insisted upon:—

"An angel told St. Bridget that the prophets of the ancient law leaped for joy when they foresaw that, *in consideration of Mary's purity and humility*, God would be appeased, and turn away His wrath from those who had most irritated Him" (p. 65).

And we are informed that Albertus Magnus says—

"If Ahasuerus heard the petition of Esther through love, will not God, who has an infinite love for Mary, fling away, at her request, the thunderbolts which He was going to hurl at wretched sinners?" (p. 30).

"Mary not only gives, but offers to all men, without exception, milk and wool; the milk of mercy, and the wool of her intercession, the former to reanimate our confidence, and *the latter as a rampart against the thunders of Almighty vengeance*" (p. 31).

Not only is the Almighty represented to us in this revolting character, but Christ, even, is rendered an object of dread.

"Go," says St. Bernard to the sinner, "Go to find the Mother of Mercy; discover to her the wounds of thy soul; and Mary, showing to her Son the breast whence He drew nourishment, *will mollify His anger and appease His wrath*" (p. 64).

Then we have Rome's Virgin presented to us as an independent and self-acting power. To illustrate this, I take one of many similar passages:—

"St. Bernard, asking the question, why the Church calls Mary Queen of Mercy, answers it himself by saying: 'It is because she *opens at pleasure* the abyss of Divine mercy, so that no sinner, *however enormous his crimes may be*, can perish if he is protected by Mary'" (p. 31).

And Mary is supposed to have appeared to St. Bridget, and to have made to her the following revelation (p. 33):—

"I am the Queen of Heaven and Mother of Mercy; I am the joy of the just, *and the gate through which sinners go to God;* to no one on earth have I refused my clemency;—in fine, unless a person be absolutely cursed (this should be understood of the irrecoverable malediction of the damned), *how wicked and reprobate soever he is*, he may obtain grace and mercy through me; and hence, *woe, eternal woe* to him who, having it in his power to profit of my commiseration, does it not, but is lost through his own fault."

Thus we see the Blessed Virgin is made, step by

step, to supplant CHRIST (the sole Mediator and Advocate of the sinner), and even to share with the GODHEAD the glory of His empire and to dispense His mercies. If it had only stopped here, we should have had sufficient to deplore. But alas! Liguori goes still further than this. Mary is represented as having Christ and God Himself at her command, and they obey!

"Yes (says St. Bonaventure) Mary has so loved us, that she has given us her only Son." "She gave Him to us (says Nieremberg) *when, in virtue of her jurisdiction over Him as Mother, she permitted Him to deliver Himself up to the Jews.* God could and did recompense Abraham's generosity; but what can *men render Mary for immolating Jesus? . . . . As she sacrificed for us a Son who was infinitely dearer to her than herself*" (pp. 46, 47). "While we say of virgins that they follow the Lamb, we can say of Mary, on earth, that the Lamb followed her."—"When Mary presents herself before Jesus, the Altar of reconciliation, to mediate for us, she rather *seems to dictate than to supplicate,* and has more the air of a Queen than of a subject" (p. 137).

"We can say of the saints that God is with them; but to Mary it has been given, not only to conform herself to the will of God, BUT THAT GOD HIMSELF HAS BEEN CONFORMED TO HER" (p. 137). "You, O Holy Virgin, *have over* GOD *authority of a Mother*, and hence you obtain pardon for the most obdurate sinners" (p. 140).

And lastly, to crown all, we are told that "all is subject to Mary's empire, even GOD HIMSELF" (p. 137).*

As to visions of the Virgin Mary, and miracles wrought, I need scarcely add they are innumerable.

Dr. Newman is particularly partial to miracles. He

---

* The extracts given are only a few of many of a similar nature.

I would not insult my readers by making any comment on such language and teaching as the above. Dr. Newman may tell us that all must be taken in a "Catholic" sense, and we must understand it as the "Church" does, and that she means nothing more than to honour the Blessed Virgin. But if there is any outspoken honesty in my Roman Catholic readers, they will raise their voices in unanimous reprobation of such blasphemous teaching. The words are too plain for any but their literal interpretation, and the "Church" when approving them vouchsafed none other, anything Dr. Newman may say to the contrary. They were all endorsed by Dr. Newman!

will find enough to satisfy his most exacting appetite in this book. I propose to quote a few narrations, only as samples of the wondrous things which are taught and received as facts by the Romish Church:—

"During the pontificate of St. Gregory the Great, the people of Rome experienced in a most striking manner the protection of the Blessed Virgin. A frightful pestilence raged in the city, to such an extent that thousands were carried off, and so suddenly, that they had not time to make the least preparation. *It could not be arrested by vows and prayers which the Holy Pope caused to be offered in all quarters, until he resolved on having recourse to the Mother of God.*

"Having commanded the clergy and people to go in general procession to the church of our Lady, called St. Mary Major, *carrying the picture of the Virgin, painted by St. Luke, the miraculous effects of her intercession were soon experienced;* in every street as they passed, the plague ceased. And before the end of the processsion, an angel, in *human* form, was seen on the tower of Adrian, named ever since the castle of St. Angelo, sheathing a bloody sabre. At the same moment, the angels were singing the anthem, *Regina Cœli*, &c." (p. 34).

And again—

"We read in the Chronicles of St. Francis, that brother Leo once saw in a vision, two ladders, one red, at the summit of which was JESUS CHRIST; and the other white, at the end of which presided his blessed Mother. He observed that many who endeavoured to ascend the first ladder, after mounting a few steps, fell down; and on trying again, were equally unsuccessful, so that they never attained the summit; but a voice having told them to make a trial of the *white* ladder, they soon gained the top, the Blessed Virgin having held forth her hand to help them" (p. 177).

This is given in page 200 of Dr. Wiseman's edition, and in page 64 he gives us an affecting anecdote related by Bernardine de Busto, the foreign gentleman of whom Dr. Newman is "entirely at fault."*

"Bernardine de Busto relates that a bird was taught to say, 'Hail, Mary!' A hawk was on the point of seizing it, when the bird cried out, 'Hail, Mary!'—in an instant the hawk fell dead. God intended to show thereby, that if even an irrational creature was preserved by calling on Mary, how much more would those who are prompt in calling on her, when assaulted by devils, be delivered from them."

---

* "Letter," p. 103.

And again, in page 196 of Dr. Wiseman's edition:—

"Father Eusebius Nieremberg says, 'that in a city of Aragon, there was a beautiful young lady, of noble birth, named Alexandra, who was courted by two young men. Out of jealousy, they one day fought, and both were killed. Their enraged relatives, considering the young lady as the cause of this sad event, murdered her, cut off her head, and threw it into a well. Some days afterwards, *Saint Dominic* passed by the spot, and, inspired by God, went to the well, and cried out, 'Alexandra, come forth!' In an instant the head of the murdered woman came up, and remained on the edge of the well, and entreated the Saint to hear her confession. The Saint did so, and in the presence of an immense concourse of people, drawn there by the wonderful event, gave her communion. He then commanded her to say for what reason she had received so great a grace. Alexandra replied, that when her head was cut off, she was in mortal sin; but that, on account of the Rosary she was in the habit of saying in her honour, the most Blessed Virgin had kept her alive. The animated head remained for two days on the edge of the well, so as to be seen by all; and, after that, the soul went to Purgatory. A fortnight afterwards Alexandra appeared, beautiful and shining, like a star, to St. Dominic, and said that the Rosary recited for the souls in Purgatory is one of the greatest reliefs that they meet with in their torments; and that, as soon as ever they get to heaven, they pray earnestly for those who have performed this devotion for them. As soon as she had said this, Saint Dominic saw her happy soul ascend with the greatest joy, to the kingdom of the blessed."

I will now draw to a close my quotations, with two examples from Liguori's numerous prayers:—

"*Queen of Heaven and earth! Mother of God! my sovereign mistress!* I present myself before you as a poor mendicant before a mighty Queen. *From the height of your throne*, deign to cast your eyes on a miserable sinner, and *lose not sight of him till you render him truly holy.*

"O illustrious Virgin! *you are Queen of the universe*, and consequently mine; I desire then to consecrate myself more particularly to your service; *dispose of me according to your good pleasure; direct me, I abandon myself wholly to your conduct*, never more let me be guided by myself; chastise me if I disobey you; your correction will be sweet and agreeable; I am then no longer mine, *I am all yours;* SAVE ME, O powerful Queen, save me by your intercession with your Son" (p. 35, edit. 1841).

"Draw me after you, O holy Virgin, that I may run in the odour of your perfumes. Draw me, for I am withheld by the weight of my sins, and the malice of my enemies. As no one can go to your Son, unless the heavenly Father draw him, so I presume to say in the same manner, *that no one can go to the Father*, unless you attract him by *your prayers. It is you who obtain pardon and grace for sinners; you* are the teacher of true wisdom, and the *repository of the treasures of the Most High.* You have found favour with God, being preserved from original sin, filled with the Holy Ghost, and selected as the Mother of His Son. All these graces you have received, O most humble Mary, not alone for yourself, *but also for us, in order that you might be able to assist us in all our wants.* You succour the just by preserving them in grace, and you help the wicked by disposing them to receive the divine mercy; you aid the dying, preserving them from the snares of Satan, and conducting them, after death, to the mansions of the blessed" (p. 182).

Romanists do not cease to complain that they are misrepresented by Protestants of this country. Some few, like Dr. Newman, protest that it is unfair to visit the extravagances of enthusiasts on their church as a body. But I contend that we are justified in asserting that the sentiments of Liguori, as expressed in his acknowledged works, must be those of the modern English Roman Catholic Church and the members as a body.

Bonaventura's Psalter is now well known in England. The Psalms of David, the "*Te Deum,*" and the Athanasian Creed have been so altered, that wherever the name of the Lord occurs, the Virgin Mary is substituted. The reader has thus the whole matter before him. In the "Glories of Mary" this work is repeatedly quoted. Take one instance: in page 190 of Dr. Wiseman's edition, we have, as from the 31st Psalm, "In te *domina* speravi"—"I will always repeat the words of St. Bonaventura, 'In thee, O Lady! have I placed all my hopes,'" &c.

But Dr. Newman has involuntarily led me on to another branch of this same subject. He is not satisfied with the "Glories of Mary," but he must have a "Glories of Joseph." He writes in his "Letter," p. 33:—

"Those names, which, at first sight, might have been expected to enter soon into the devotions of the faithful, with better reason might have been looked for at a later date, and actually were late in their coming. ST. JOSEPH furnishes the most striking instance of this remark; here is the clearest of instances of the distinction between doctrine and devotion. Who, from his *prerogatives and the testimony* on which they come to us, had a greater claim to receive an early recognition among the faithful? A saint of Scripture, the foster-father of our Lord, was an object of the universal and absolute faith of the Christian world from the first, yet the devotion to him is comparatively of late date. When once it began, men seemed surprised that it had not been thought of before; and now they hold him next to the Blessed Virgin in their religious affection and veneration."

Accordingly, the "Queen of Heaven" has her glories recorded, and so has "ST. JOSEPH," presented to us by the most orthodox recommendation of Dr. Newman himself. I have now before me the work entitled the "Glories of Saint Joseph."

The "Glories of Saint Joseph" are entered at large in a volume under that title, stated to be "chiefly from the French of Rev. Father Paul Barrie," in a "second edition, revised, corrected, and improved," and published for the benefit of English and Irish "Catholics," by "Richard Grace, [Roman] Catholic bookseller, 45, Capel Street, Dublin, 1843."

I have stated the peculiar prerogatives of Rome's "*Marie.*" What she enjoyed, Joseph, her spouse, enjoyed too; for we read in pages 14 and 15:—

"Mary, spouse to Joseph, doth in plenitude of grace, surpass both men and angels; and has not her husband, think you, the like endowments, since God judged him a fit match for her, and for this end gave him so great an abundance of grace, virtue, and sanctity, that neither men nor angels ever had the like, whereby to fit him to be the spouse and guide to the Virgin Mother; God judging it fit, that in her right, he should partake of *all her honours*, favours, and dignities? If, therefore, she be a princess, he is a prince, and he also is king, wherever she is queen; for God, who designed to raise Mary to the quality and honours of the Mother of God, at the same time designed her a husband like to herself, whom He loved above all men upon earth, and therefore endowed him with all graces suitable to such a dignity."

A logical deduction, indeed! *If* Mary is Queen of Heaven, then Joseph, of necessity, as her husband, is King of Heaven! A most useful word is *if*. But *if* the Blessed Virgin is not Queen of Heaven, we suppose Joseph would not presume to claim the title of King. I am willing to leave this matter to such alternative; but not so "Father Paul Barrie," and we must presume also Dr. Newman, for we are told in page 16,—

"That the angels who beheld the Son of God, in the bosom of His Eternal Father in Heaven, seeing Him also in the arms of St. Joseph upon earth, might very well cry out with wonder and astonishment: 'Behold the Governor of the Universe, governed by a man,' and address to St. Joseph the same admonition that Methodius did to the Mother of God in these following words: 'O nursing-father to Him who feeds all creatures! O rich Joseph, *to whom God Himself became a beggar!* Thrice happy art thou, who hast Him for thy debtor, who lends to every one whatsoever He possesses, for all creatures are indebted to God for their being, and for everything they enjoy; but to oblige thee, God will become obliged to thee, and make Himself thy debtor.'"

Then, again, what can be plainer than the following acknowledgment in favour of Joseph, by St. Theresa?—

"God by his other saints helped us in some particular cases of necessity; but helps us in all necessities by St. Joseph, as by His plenipotentiary, to let us understand, that as He was subject to him in all things upon earth as to a father, so He was the same in heaven, granting him whatsoever he asked" (p. 47).

He is accordingly called—

"The DIVINE Spouse of our Blessed Lady" (p. 51).

And "if we desire to know what is best to SECURE OUR SALVATION," we are told that there cannot be any doubt but that the Blessed Virgin will advise us to be "devout to St. Joseph" (p. 129). It is not surprising, therefore, that in the "Litanies of St. Joseph" we find thickly and profusely scattered about such expressions as the following, as applied and addressed to him:—

"Advocate of the humble. Defender of the meek. Quintessence of all virtue. Theatre of all glorious privileges (p. 65). Appointed **master of God's household**. Our Intercessor in the hour of danger.

Our patron and protection (p. 155). Whom the Eternal Father made His Vicar on earth," [and we presume, therefore, first Pope, even before St. Peter]. "Prince of all his possessions (p. 156), who [Joseph] dost triumph for ever, shining with ineffable glory: who didst sovereignly despise the world" (p. 157).

Then comes another series of rhapsodic expressions, peculiar to Romish theology. Joseph is declared to be—

"The vermilion rose of charity. Lily of charity. Doctor of humility. Splendour of modesty. Mirror of married persons. Advocate of sinners. Comforter of the afflicted. Protector of the poor. Solace of all who labour. Guide of the wandering. The safety of the shipwrecked. *Father* of the faithful. Who as an angel didst deliver divine oracles. Who as an arch-angel was the companion and guardian of the angel of the Great Council. *To whom the Almighty was subject.* To whose dominion the Queen of Dominations was subject. In whose arms, and bosom, as on a throne, the King of Glory vouchsafed to sit (p. 158). The original guardian of Virgins. Our most holy patron. Our strongest defender. Our most loving father (p. 159). Ensign of our salvation. Heaven of Wisdom (p. 161). Mirror of Divine paternity. *Image of God the Son. Impression of the Holy Ghost*" (p. 160).

But this mighty Joseph condescended to step down for a moment from this lofty pinnacle of greatness, to assist us in all our little troubles, even to effecting "miraculous cures" (p. 112), and that too by the humble means of "a miraculous ointment" (p. 113), far more potent than that of modern nostrums. Dr. Newman is, as I said, most partial to modern miracles. This "miraculous ointment" actually had (if I could only persuade my readers to believe it) so much virtue that it

"Had the power of working miracles, which it likewise communicated to beads, medals, images, and papers that touched it, or the cloth that wiped it off" (p. 115).

If one were tempted to joke, he might be excused—the opportunity is too obvious; but, alas! the heart sickens.

Then St. Joseph cured all sorts of "sore eyes" (p. 120),

"distempers and plagues," "violent headaches" (p. 119). He assisted a nun to pay the "debts which she had contracted" (p. 125). He "also favours marriage, and unites the hearts of married persons, procuring them a true and constant conjugal affection." Also "helps persons pregnant" (p. 127). "He favours also married persons, by giving them children" (p. 128). And we are told that he lifted "a cart out of a rut, which could neither go backwards nor forwards" (p. 131); and he is so obliging as to "help persons even without being asked" (p. 132); and this was exemplified in an extraordinary manner in the case of a young man who had put himself under his protection :—

"As he walked in the fields for his amusement, he met two men unknown to him, one of whom shot at him with a blunderbuss charged with hail shot. All entered his body, without giving him any mortal wound; two or three staid in his belly, and one of them beat flat upon his forehead."

Of course no injury was done, "and he offered a picture (at St. Joseph's church) of this miraculous escape, as a memory of his gratitude" (p. 133). But to sum up; he supersedes any mesmeric medium, for we are told, "when you have lost anything you highly value," you are to have recourse to St. Joseph to beg "his help," and—heigh, presto!—"the lost thing is recovered" (p. 84, *et seq.*).

And to my fair readers St. Joseph shows himself peculiarly amiable; and this is testified on the unimpeachable evidence of Father Barrie himself!—

"I knew (he says) a young woman violently attacked with a passion of love, which she freed herself from by resolving, in honour of St. Joseph, to abstain for nine days from the conversation of the person she loved,"—and upon recommending herself every day to St. Joseph, "she was perfectly freed from this tormenting and dangerous spirit" (p. 108).

Another, more desperate, case is cited on the same evidence. We are surprised St. Joseph did not prescribe a nunnery. But this reminds me that St.

Joseph makes himself generally useful even in this line. A religious "house of nuns" was running dry for want of "novices," and funds as well. The superior, we are told,—

"Had recourse to St. Joseph, to beg his assistance. The devotion was no sooner begun, than a young lady *with a good fortune* offered herself to live and die with them in God's service, which favour will never be forgotten" (p. 68).

My readers may think I am joking; but I solemnly assure them that I transcribe faithfully—and, what is more, Father Barrie declares that he "heard this from the mouth of the superior herself" (p. 67); and we cannot, therefore, resist this evidence!

We must not quit this extraordinary production without calling attention to the fact that JESUS, MARY, and JOSEPH are created into another *Trinity*. The whole of chapter iii. treats of this. Gerson, we are told (p. 25), says,—

"That if the first rank and hierarchy in heaven is that of the Father, Son, and Holy Ghost, so the second is this of *Jesus, Mary, and Joseph*, and that all other saints are of a lower rank, and of a different hierarchy."

The former is stated to be the *uncreated*, the latter the *created* Trinity, but in the image or likeness of the former.

"Mary bears the image of God the Father, Jesus the Son, according to His humanity, in a just likeness to what He is in Heaven, as He is the Word or Son of God; and St. Joseph represented the Holy Ghost, in the quality of Spouse to the Blessed Virgin Mary," &c. (p. 26). And a little further on we are told that "as none can divide their love to the three persons in the uncreated Trinity, *they ought to follow a similar rule in their respect to the created Trinity*," &c. (p. 27).

To sanctify this creation of Popish theology, we are told, that—

"Pius VII. [the same Pope who confirmed the approval of Liguori's 'Glories of Mary'] by a decree of the 28th April, 1807, granted for ever an indulgence of 300 days to the faithful, each time they devoutly repeat the following three aspirations, and if only one of them is said, an indulgence of 100 days, and all applicable to the souls in purgatory:—

"'Jesus, Mary, and Joseph, I offer you my heart and soul.

"'Jesus, Mary, and Joseph, assist me in my last agony.

"'Jesus, Mary, and Joseph, may I expire in peace with you'" (p. 231).

Here let us pause for one moment, fully to appreciate the doctrine thus endorsed by a Pope. The three undivided persons of the uncreated Trinity, the Father, Son, and Holy Spirit, are co-eternal and co-equal; "none, therefore, can (without sin) divide their love," each commanding an *equal* affection. We are offered another Trinity, of whom the same "Son," of the uncreated undivided Trinity, is *one*. This second Trinity is composed of this same Son, and Mary, and Joseph, who, we are told, demand also our "undivided love," to whom we are to " offer our hearts and souls," and to whom we are to pray "to assist us in our last agonies," and that we may expire in *peace* with them! In theology, as in mathematics, " things that are equal to the same are equal to one another." Mary and Joseph are placed in our affection on a level with Jesus, the second person of the Holy Trinity; so, therefore, must Mary and Joseph require from us the same equal and undivided affection which is given to the Father and the Holy Spirit. The consequence is inevitable. A new God and Goddess are thus incorporated into the Divine Trinity, converting Christianity into a Pagan Pantheism, and Pagan temples are erected to their honour.

It is true that this book does not come before us with the same authoritative endorsement as the " Glories of Mary," but we should not overlook the several rules and decrees of Popes that are ostentatiously set out in it, not merely recommending the devotion and Litanies to Joseph, but encouraging them by the offer of extravagant " indulgences " (that imaginary " celestial treasure " composed of equally imaginary superabundant merits of departed saints, and said to be at the free disposal of an ecclesiastical "spiritualist"), applicable as well to the devotee as to "souls in purgatory."

I am anxious, truly anxious, to know what Dr. Newman has to say of all this; evade it he cannot, explain it away it is impossible.

But to return to Dr. Newman's "opinions" on the Mary-worship of his Church. He proceeds, with strange inconsistency, at times justifying the system. Such as it is, I give Dr. Newman's own explanation and justification.

He appeals to antiquity, but does not go far enough back; he should begin at the beginning, the New Testament, the only authentic narrative we have of the history of Mary, the wife of Joseph, and the mother of our Lord. But the Bible, Dr. Newman has already told us, had been tried and disappoints. It is worthy of remark, that in the Gospels, Matthew, Mark, and Luke mention her by name as "Mary;" John, and he alone, names her as "Mother of our Lord." She is never named or alluded to in either of the Epistles of St. Paul, St. James, St. Peter, St. Jude, nor St. John, nor in the Revelation. We are told by St. Luke that Mary was highly favoured in being the chosen servant to give birth to our Lord,—the Lord was with her, and she was blessed among women; and Mary, to whom the announcement of the incarnation was unexpectedly made, with humility declared herself the handmaid of the Lord, and exclaimed "Be it unto me according to thy word." This submission to the Divine will is expanded into a *co-operation by her in the redemption of mankind by her merits*, and that she offered herself up for the purpose. A co-operation is an active interference; the Virgin knew nothing of what had happened,—it was communicated to her, and she believed. To fill up the Roman history, we want the "Immaculate Conception" and the "Assumption." The Evangelists, the Apostles, and

Fathers give no encouragement for belief on these two heads, but the modern Roman Church has appointed a service in commemoration of both as facts. The commemoration of the former was condemned and reprobated as a superstition when it began to be agitated in the 12th century; but it was ultimately established by the present Pope in 1854, and is now accepted as a dogma of the Roman Church. As to the Assumption of the Virgin Mary, this we are told by Alban Butler, in his Lives of the Saints, is the greatest of all the festivals which the Church celebrates in her honour. It has no foundation in the Bible, it rests on no authentic history, nor is it supported by tradition. The time, place, and circumstances of Mary's death are wholly unknown. And the Virgin herself is now only known in carved wood or stone, which are styled the "Blessed Virgin Mary," or in paintings, too often, alas! taken from models of a questionable class. Dr. Newman, as I said, passes by the New Testament, and he is likewise silent on the testimony of the Creeds, and what are called the Apostolic Fathers, those of the first century,—Barnabas, Clement Hermas, Ignatius, and Polycarp; and I pass them over too; not that their works are unimportant on the question, for we meet proofs in their writings that they pointed to one only Mediator between God and Man,—CHRIST JESUS. Of the second century, Tatian, Athenagoras, and Theophilus are also passed over. We now come to the two venerable names of Justin the Martyr, A.D. 150, and Irenæus, Bishop of Lyons, A.D. 165, and also Tertullian, A.D. 190. The passages quoted by Dr. Newman all relate to a supposed parallel between Eve and Mary.

In the passage quoted from Justin, we find that he is commenting on the fact that our Saviour was born of a virgin, and is led to remark how fit it was that, as it was by means of a woman (namely, by Eve's eating the forbidden fruit) that sin entered into the world, so likewise the instrumentality of a woman should be employed in the plan for our redemption, that so disobedience might be destroyed in the same manner it was introduced in the world. What all this has to do with the Roman doctrine of invocation of the Virgin is impossible to be conceived. Tertullian carries out the same idea, and adds, "Mary believed Gabriel; the fault which the one (Eve) committed by believing, the other (Mary), by believing has blotted out." Dr. Newman says that these writers " do not speak of the Virgin as the physical instrument of our Lord's taking flesh, but as an *intelligent responsible cause of it* "(p. 38). I do not see it. But where is the invocation! pleading of merits, &c. &c.? But Tertullian in many passages directs us to offer our prayers to God alone. "These things (he says) I cannot ask in prayer from any other except Him from whom I know that I shall obtain; because He is the one who alone grants, &c."*

The passage from Irenæus is, however, the one dwelt upon more particularly by Dr. Newman.

"For as that one (Eve), by the discourse of an angel, was seduced to fly from God, running counter to his word, so also this one (Mary), by the discourse of an angel recovered the glad tidings that she should bear God. And as that one was seduced to fly from God, in like manner also this one was persuaded to obey God; so that of the Virgin Eve, the Virgin Mary *might become the advocate;* and as the human race was bound to death by a virgin, it *might be loosed* by a virgin, a virgin's disobedience being disposed of in a scale by a virgin's obedience."

Irenæus wrote in Greek, and we have only a somewhat rugged Latin translation. To be strictly critical, therefore, is impossible.

The first feature relied on, is that Mary became the *advocate* of Eve. The question in controversy between us and the Church of Rome is whether it is lawful for Christians to invoke, or call on the name of Mary to

---

* "Apology," p. 27. Paris, 1695.

assist or intercede for us. Is this practice taught or sanctioned by Scripture, or had it the sanction of the Primitive Church? The passage answers neither of these questions, and we fail to discover how the circumstance of Mary becoming the advocate of Eve, who so many generations before Mary's birth had been removed to the other world, can bear on the question. On this Dr. Newman is silent. The word, however, "advocate" is too serviceable to be passed over. He says: "It is supposed by critics, Protestants as well as Catholics, that the Greek word for advocate in the original was *Paraclete;* it should be borne in mind, then, when we are accused of giving our Lady the titles and offices of her Son, that St. Irenæus bestows on her the special name and office proper to the Holy Ghost" (p. 39). Does Dr. Newman approve of this application? If not, why does he not condemn it?

Had not Dr. Newman fully admitted that he had tried the Bible and found it wanting, we might express our surprise that he has not appealed to that authority. We would remind him that in the New Testament, this word Paraclete ($\pi\alpha\rho\acute{\alpha}\kappa\lambda\eta\tau o\nu$) is applied to Christ in His capacity of advocate with the Father:—"If any man sin, we have an ADVOCATE with the Father, Jesus Christ the righteous" (1 John ii. 1); and we want a better authority than an imperfect translation to convict Irenæus of placing the Virgin on a level with our Lord. Christ, then, being our *advocate* with the Father, we come to the conclusion that Irenæus used some word to answer to our word "consolatrix" or "comforter." In our translation of the Bible, a careful distinction is preserved in applying the word $\pi\alpha\rho\acute{\alpha}\kappa\lambda\eta\tau o\nu$ (*Paraclete*) to Christ and the Holy Ghost.*

The Latin Vulgate renders 1 John ii. 1, *advocatus,* and in the other places *Paracletus.* Augustine, as we shall see, uses the word *advocatus;* while Jerome, in

* As in 1 John ii. 1; John xiv. 24; xv. 20; xvi. 7.

his Commentary on Isaiah xi. 1, more properly gives "Consolator," and Tertullian (*cont. Marcion*, iv. 14) translates the words from Isaiah, "to *comfort* those that mourn"—"*advocare lugentes*."

But even supposing the original was Paraclete, no such deduction could be drawn as suggested by Dr. Newman; for we find the substantive and corresponding verb employed both in the Greek Septuagint and the Greek in the New Testament, to describe a mere human comforter, or a mere human act of consolation.* The reason is obvious,—we can have but one *advocate*; but in various gradations of existence, we may have many *comforters*.

If, however, Dr. Newman is attempting to prove, by this passage, that Mary partook the duties and office of Christ or the Holy Spirit, then he comes within the condemnation of the system exposed by Dr. Pusey as idolatrous and unscriptural, and in which he himself subsequently agrees; and we ought not to charge so venerable a personage as Irenæus with idolatry on the authority of Dr. Newman. Indeed it is not creditable to quote a doubtful translation to establish a theory, when we cannot find one single writer for 500 years after Christ who refers to the Virgin Mary as a mediatrix or advocate with the Father, or that it was the custom of the Church to plead her merits or seek her intercession. This is an incontestable fact, which Dr. Newman cannot deny.

The second part of the passage is as follows :—

"And as by a virgin the human race had been *bound* to death, by a virgin it is *loosed*, the balance being preserved, a virgin's disobedience (Eve's) by a virgin's obedience."

Dr. Newman, for *loosed* writes *saved*,—" salvatur"

* The texts, *inter alia*, are 2 Sam. x. 3 ; Job xvi. 2 ; Psalm xvi. 20 ; Eccles. iv. 1 ; Lament. i. 9, 16 ; Nahum iii. 7 ; Isaiah xl. 1, 2 ; 2 Cor. ii. 7 ; Ephes. vi. 22 ; Coloss. iv. 8 ; 1 Thess. iii. 2 ; iv. 18 ; v. 11.

instead of "solvatur."* I had thought that this reading of *solvatur* had been completely established, and my astonishment was great indeed to find Dr. Newman, at this late period, falling back into the Romish cart-rut, without any comment that the reading "*salvatur*" is now quite exploded. But when Dr. Newman professes a desire "to contribute to the *accurate statement*, and the full exposition of the argument in question,"† my astonishment increases as I proceed. Dr. Newman deliberately informs us, "In one place Augustine quotes St. Irenæus' words, as cited above"‡ (p. 44), that is, with the word *salvatur*, and not *solvatur*. I am not aware that in any single edition of Augustine's works is this the fact. The passage is quoted by Augustine as follows, in the place indicated by Dr. Newman himself:—

"Quemadmodum astrictum est morti genus humanum per virginem, *solvitur* per virginem."—*Iren. apud August. cont. Julian. Pelagian.*, lib. i. c. 3, Oper., tom. vii. p. 326. Colon. Agripp. A.D. 1616.

Perhaps Dr. Newman may think it worth while to save his credit and correct his extract from Irenæus and this reference to Augustine. He has the credit, at least, of being well read in the Fathers; it is a pity this advantage should be forfeited. I am quite aware that Dr. Wiseman, in an article in the *Dublin Review* of June, 1844, fought hard for the "salvatur;" but either his memory was very short, or he had profited by experience, for in 1852 a translation of Liguori's "Glories of Mary" was put forward under his express authority, and in the translator's preface we read: "I have carefully compared and corrected all these quotations with the *original* from which they are taken,"§ and to which edition I have already alluded. In page 82 we have this very passage from Irenæus

---

* "Letter," p. 37, and p. 126, notes. † Ibid. p. 27.
‡ His reference is "Adv. Julian, i. 4." § P. xix.

quoted, and the Latin is given in note 1:—"Et quemadmodum astrictum est morti genus humanum per virginem, *solvatur* per virginem."* Here, then, we have the translator's evidence of the word *solvatur* being in the original. But I do Dr. Wiseman an injustice. It may be said that his approval extends to the *translation only*. " We approve of *this* translation of 'Glories of Mary,' and cordially recommend *it* to the faithful. (Signed), Nicholas Card. Wiseman, Archbishop of Westminster." And in referring to the translation, we read : " And as the human race was bound to death through a virgin, it is *saved* through a Virgin." So Dr. Wiseman saves his credit for consistency at least at the expense of his powers of translation, though we cannot compliment him for " that keen apprehension" which Dr. Newman alleges to be " his characteristic" (" Letter," p. 16).†

The following passage from the same work by Irenæus, cited by Dr. Newman, may throw some light on his *doctrine*, if not his *devotion* :—

" Nor does it [the Church] do anything by invocation of angels, nor by incantations nor other depraved and curious means ; but with cleanliness, purity, and openness, directing prayers to the Lord who made all things, and called upon the name of Jesus Christ our Lord, it exercises its powers for the benefit, and not for the seducing of mankind."‡

Dr. Newman passes over Origen (A.D. 230), who, as he is aware, is a most powerful opponent of his theory, and who, as he is also aware, condemned Mary for want of faith. He passes over also Gregory Thaumaturgus (A.D. 245), Cyprian (A.D. 258), Methodius and

* The reference given is " S. Iren. *adv. Hæres.*, lib. v. c. 19."

† While these sheets were going through the press, I drew Dr. Newman's attention to the misquotation, and he has politely acknowledged it, proposing to correct it in a third edition of his Letter ; but he alleges that the force of the passage is in no wise impaired by the alteration.

‡ Oper., lib. ii. c. 35, sec. 5, p. 1666. Paris, Bened. edit. 1710.

Lactantius (A.D. 317), Eusebius (A.D. 314), the "Apostolic Constitutions," the great Athanasius (A.D. 350), and all the ancient Liturgies. Not one word in his favour can Dr. Newman extract from any one of these. One word of the Liturgies. Dr. Newman says: "It would be preposterous to pray for those who are in glory."* But in these Liturgies, and in the works of Epiphanius and Cyril of Jerusalem, we find prayers *for* the Blessed Virgin, but none *to* the Virgin, which, to my mind, totally overthrows all Dr. Newman's theories.

We come then to Cyril of Jerusalem (A.D. 315).

"Since through Eve, a virgin, came death, it behoved that through a virgin, or rather from a virgin, should life appear; that, as the serpent had deceived the one, so to the other Gabriel might bring good things."

But Dr. Newman's theory of the Virgin's active co-operation in our redemption is somewhat disturbed by Cyril's subsequent expression,—"This is that Holy Spirit which came upon the Holy Mary. *He made her holy, that she might* have power to receive Him by whom all things were made."†

To the like effect is quoted Ephrem, Epiphanius, Peter Chrysologus, and Fulgentius. The passages are all equivalent in effect. The theory, or "rudimental view," as he calls it, cannot be driven further; therefore comments on them would only be repetitions, though I may be permitted to observe that Dr. Newman ought to have reminded—not Dr. Pusey, for though the letter is addressed to him, it is not intended for him—the general reader of the two well-known passages with which I shall close my comments on this phase of Dr. Newman's theory. Epiphanius was alluding to certain heretics who worshipped the Virgin; the passages are peculiarly appropriate to the present controversy:—

* "Letter," p. 75.
† Catech. xvii. B. 6, M. 4. Edit. Oxford, 1703.

"Nay, [some will reply] but the body of Mary is holy! Yes, but not a deity. Nay, but the Virgin is a virgin, and honoured! Yes, yet not given for us to worship, but herself worshipping Him who was born of her in the flesh. For this reason the Gospel confirms us, saying (in the words of our Lord), 'Woman, what have I to do with thee?' Lest any one should think that the holy Virgin was a *being of superior excellence*, He calls her woman—as if He prophesied on account of those divisions and heresies which were to take place on the earth—in order that no one by *admiring the holy Virgin in excess* might fall into this folly of heresy. The whole story (he continues) is full of absurdity. For what Scripture speaks of it? Which of the prophets ever suffered a man to be worshipped, not to say a woman? She is a chosen vessel, but she is a woman, and not at all changed in nature, though, as to her mind and sense, she is held in honour; as the bodies of the saints, or whatever else in point of honour I might mention more excellent; as Elijah, a virgin from his birth, and continuing so throughout, and, being taken up, did not see death; as John, who lay upon the bosom of our Lord, whom Jesus loved; as the holy Thecla; and as Mary, honoured above her, because of the dispensation of which she was deemed worthy. But neither is Elijah, though among the living, an object of worship; nor is John an object of worship, though by his own prayer, or rather by receiving grace from God, he made his death wonderful; nor is Thecla, nor any one of the saints, an object of worship. For the old error shall not lord it over us, that we should leave the Living One and worship things made by Him, for they served and worshipped the creature more than the Creator. For if He willeth not that the angels be worshipped, how much more is He unwilling that worship should be paid to her who was born of Anna, and was given to Anna from Joachim—given to the father and mother by promise; but, nevertheless, not born differently from the nature of man?"

If this is not sufficiently precise, let us proceed with the extract:—

"God the Word, as a Creator and of authority over the thing, formed himself from the Virgin as from the earth, having clothed Himself with flesh from the Holy Virgin; but, nevertheless, not a Virgin to be worshipped, nor that He might make her a deity—not that we might offer in her name; not that after so many generations women should become priestesses. God willed not this to take place in Salome, nor in Mary herself. He suffered her not to administer baptism, nor to bless the disciples. He did not commission her to rule upon earth; but only appointed this, that she should be a holy thing, and be deemed worthy of His kingdom. Whence, then, is the coiling serpent? Whence are his crooked counsels renewed? *Let Mary be in honour; but let the Father, Son, and Holy Ghost, be* *worshipped.* Let no one worship Mary. The mystery [that sacred thing religious worship] is assigned, I do not say, to no woman, but not even to any man: it is assigned to God. Neither do angels receive the ascription of glory [that doxology]. Let these errors written in the hearts of the deceived be wiped away. Let the evil generated at the tree be obliterated from our sight. Let no one eat of the error which has arisen by means of holy Mary; for though the tree be beautiful, yet it is not given for food; and though Mary be most beautiful, and holy, and honoured, yet she is not intended to be worshipped. Let Eve, our mother, be honoured, as having been formed by God; but let her not be listened to, lest she persuade her children to eat of the tree and transgress the commandment. And how many more things might be said? for these silly women offer to her the cake, as either worshipping Mary herself, or they take upon themselves to offer their rotten fruit on her behalf! The whole thing is foolish and strange, and is a device and deceit of the devil. But, not to extend my discourse further, what I have already said will suffice. *Let Mary be in honour. Let the Lord be worshipped.*"[*]

It may be answered that "we do not worship the Virgin." That may be true; but you pray to her, and ask of her gifts which God alone may bestow; and if such were the practice of Christians in the days of Epiphanius, he could not, while condemning the *worship*, have failed to refer to the limits to which prayers might lawfully be addressed to her. But he allows her nothing but a pure honour, which we all admit to be due to her.

"What dignity," exclaims Dr. Newman, "can be too great to attribute to her who is so closely bound up, as intimately one with the Eternal Word as a mother is with a Son?" "What exuberance of merits must have been hers. Men sometimes wonder that we call her Mother of life, of mercy, of salvation [add to this, Gate of Heaven, Refuge of Sinners, &c., &c.]; what are all these titles compared to that one name MOTHER OF GOD."[†] He goes further; he calls her "Mother of her Creator." "It extends to express that God is her Son as truly as any one of us is son of his mother." If we admit the spirit of Dr. Newman's

---

[*] Epiphanii Opera, p. 1064. Paris edit. 1622.
[†] "Letter," p. 67.

argument, no title, no attributes, would be sufficiently great or sufficiently exalted to meet the occasion. But what example did our Lord himself give with regard to any special reverence to be given to Mary from the fact of her being his mother? On the occasion mentioned by St. Matthew, of her seeking her Son to speak to Him, His example before the multitude does not encourage the idea of the Roman Church that our Lord *is* ready to listen to her, and grant all she may wish. Instead of pointing out Mary to His disciples as an object of special veneration, Christ showed that her place in His favour was determined not by being His mother, not by the closeness of earthly relationship, but by readiness to do the will of His Father.* Dr. Newman's deduction is by no means supported by the only *authority* to which appeal can be made; but as he prefers to " stand upon the Fathers," let us for a moment examine what they say of this incident; for, remember Mary is here before us in the character of Mother of our Lord. Tertullian (Dr. Newman's own authority), commenting on these words from St. Matthew, says:—

" Christ with reason felt indignant, that whilst strangers were bent intently on His discourse, persons so nearly related to Him should stand without, seeking, moreover, to call Him away from His solemn work."†

Ambrose (A.D. 397), Bishop of Milan, commenting also on these words of our Lord, said:—

" They ought not to stand without who seek Christ; for if parents themselves, when they stand without, are not acknowledged (and perhaps they are not acknowledged for an example to us), how shall we be acknowledged if we stand without?"‡

Chrysostom (A.D. 405) comments in still stronger terms. He points out that the lesson to be learnt

---

* Matt. xii. 46, 50.
† Tract. *adv. Marcionem*, iv. 19, p. 433. Paris, 1675.
‡ Tom. i. p. 1392, ed. Bened. 1686.

from this incident is, "Not even the conceiving of Christ in the womb, and bringing forth that wonderful birth, hath any advantage, if there be not virtue." And he adds that "Christ said this, not because He felt ashamed of His mother, but to show that she would derive no advantage from that, unless she did her duty in everything." And Chrysostom adds,— "What she was then undertaking was the effect of *excessive ambition*, for she wished to show to the people that she commanded and controlled her Son;" and concludes: "Now see the foolish arrogance both of herself and of them."*

On yet another occasion Mary interfered with our Lord. I refer to the marriage feast, where He performed His first miracle.† He chid her for her interference. "Woman, what have I to do with thee." Irenæus remarks that "the Lord repelled her *untimely hurrying*."‡ Chrysostom speaks of her "foolish arrogance." But perhaps St. Augustine's (A.D. 430) remarks are the best reply to Dr. Newman, when he presses that Mary was "Mother of God," and therefore no praise can be sufficient for her station. Augustine said:—

"His mother required Him to perform a miracle; but He, as it were, does not acknowledge His human origin, [or others translate the words *viscera humana non agnoscit*, 'does not recognize parental authority,'] when about to effect a Divine work, as though He said, 'To that part of me which works the miracle thou didst not give birth.' 'Thou didst not give birth to my divinity, &c.' Therefore, because she was not the mother of His divinity, that the miracle was about to be performed, He answered, 'What have I to do with thee?'"§

Cyril of Alexandria (A.D. 400) uses precisely the same language,‖ and Epiphanius expressly informs us

---

* Tom. vii. p. 407, edit. Benedict. 1718.
† John ii. 3, 4.
‡ Lib. iii. c. 18, p. 206, edit. Benedict.
§ August., tom. iii. pt. ii. pp. 354, 355, 357, &c., ed. Paris, 1700.
‖ Tom. iv. pp. 135, 1064. Paris, 1638.

that our Lord made use of the word "Woman" on this occasion, "lest any one should think that the Blessed Virgin was a being of superior excellence."*

Now, compare all this with the language of Dr. Newman, a specimen only of which we have given above, brought in comparison with the very authorities to which he himself appeals, but quotes only just so much as suits his purpose. Having made the comparison, we can appreciate his conclusion, which he makes in the following words:—" And what are we to say of those who, through ignorance, run *counter to the voice of Scripture;* to the testimony of the Fathers; to the traditions of the East and West; and speak and act contemptuously towards her whom the Lord delighted to honour."—(" Letter," pp. 65, 66.)

Roman Catholics are fond of accusing us of speaking "contemptuously" of Mary. This is a libel. We do not *pray* to her, but that is no reason for saying that we do not hold her in honour.

Before I pass on to the conclusions Dr. Newman arrives at in quoting from the Fathers, as we are on the expression " Mother of God," as applied to the Virgin Mary, I would make a few observations on the introduction by him of the word *theotokos*—θεοτοκος, as applied to her. Dr. Newman uses the expression as meaning " Mother of God." Dr. Newman is a scholar, and it is with considerable diffidence that I speak. But, nevertheless, I maintain that θεοτοκος is *not* the word that would have been used by persons who spoke the Greek language, to express what the Church of Rome now means by " Mother of God." I will not go into the question under discussion at the Council of Ephesus; it is too well known. They had to maintain that the very person who was born of Mary was also the Son of God, and therefore God. They did this by calling her θεοτοκος, which means, " she who brought forth

* Epiph., pp. 1056-1064. Paris, ed. 1622.

Him who was God." "Mother of God" is not the proper translation of that word, or its Latin equivalent, "deipara." The Council would have used the word Θεου-μητηρ, or *Dei-Mater*. They seemed to shrink from using these terms, but invented rather another word to convey what they desired to express. The latter expression conveys a maternal authority; the former the fact that God was born of a woman; but the modern reading makes the two equivalent terms. It is an error, conveyed by Dr. Newman's remarks, that the Council of Ephesus decreed that the Blessed Virgin should be called *Theotokos*. The Synod *never* itself used the word but once, and then only as the name of a church in Ephesus.* The letter of Cyril to the Church of Alexandria makes this evident. The essence of the Christian religion is to hold that He who was born of a virgin is truly God, and so the essence of the modern religion of Rome is to hold that the Blessed Virgin is the "Mother of God," and they rely chiefly on this council for their theory; but the reader will not have forgotten the marked expression of Augustine, that Mary did not give birth to the Divinity.

I gladly quit this part of my subject, as it is one little bearing on the controversy, while it affords a handle for scoffers and unbelievers.

To return to the citations from the Fathers. They testify that sin was brought into the world by a virgin —Eve; and the world was loosed again from sin by a virgin—Mary, bringing forth a Saviour. Dr. Newman strains the passages, and concludes that we are *saved* through a virgin. We can have no objection even to this, if it is taken no further, for it is equivalent to the language used by St. Paul (1 Tim. ii. 15), Σωθήσεται δὲ διὰ ΤΗΣ τεκνογονίας; that is, as the definite article τῆς fixes the reference, "She shall be

---

* See Labb. et Cossart., tom. iii. Synodical Epistle, col. 574, ed. Paris, 1671.

saved through *the* child-bearing of the Virgin." From this "rudimental view, which the Fathers have given us of Mary" as the second Eve, "Mother of the Living," Dr. Newman deduces two leading doctrines (p. 48).

1. That Mary co-operated in the redemption of the world, which gives a significance to the salutation, "Hail, full of grace," which is a real inward condition or superadded quality of the soul.

2. "And if Eve had this supernatural inward gift given her from the moment of her personal existence, is it possible to deny that Mary, too, had this gift from the very first moment of her personal existence? and this is simply and literally the doctrine of the *Immaculate Conception*. It is in its substance this, *and nothing more or less than this*, putting aside the question of degrees of grace;" and it really does seem to him (Dr. Newman) "bound up in the doctrine of the Fathers, that Mary is the second Eve"! (p. 49).

On these two assertions the whole of Dr. Newman's theories of Mary-worship depend. As to the *first* head, Dr. Newman declares the translation, "full of grace," as undoubtedly the right interpretation of the original word, as soon as they resist the common Protestant assumption that grace is a mere external approbation of acceptance, answering to the word "favour;" whereas, it is, as the Fathers teach, a real inward condition or superadded quality of the soul. Dr. Newman is an Oxford scholar; but, previous to his "going over," he admitted, as critically correct, our authorized version, "highly favoured." One of the effects of this "going over" seems to throw some new light on classical as well as spiritual attainments. I have shown elsewhere (*antè*, pp. 5, 132), that when Dr. Newman discovered that the Church of Rome was "the oracle of God," he at once believed in transubstantiation, and now to this implicit belief are added all her erroneous translations of the New Testament. The sequence is inevitable. I was asked the other day why I lost my time in controversy with Roman Catholics, as they all belong to a *dogmatic Church;* the Pope says "*Ba, ba,*" and the people dare not for their lives say "*Bo, bo!*" though they prefer the latter. In this case we can make an exception in the learned Dr. Lingard, a Roman Catholic divine, who published a "New Version of the Four Gospels, with Notes" (London, 1851). He follows our authorized version, rendering "Hail, thou favoured of God;" and adds this note: "κεχαριτωμένη—*gratia plena.*" These words are explained by the angel himself, v. 30: "Thou hast found favour (χαρὶν, *gratiam*) with God." The grace or favour was not *inherent* in the Virgin, but *imparted to her* by God. The same word we find applied by St. Paul (Ephes. i. 6) to all Christians—ἐχαρίτωσεν ἡμᾶς, and translated in the Roman Catholic version, "He hath graced us;" and, according to Dr. Newman, we have St. Paul's authority that we are all immaculately conceived. As, however, Dr. Newman rests the whole on an "if"— "*If* Eve has this supernatural gift, &c."—he must not find fault if we take "benefit of the doubt" and agree to differ; and certainly we decline to rest so important a dogma on, to say the least for it, a text of admittedly doubtful meaning.

2. As to the IMMACULATE CONCEPTION, Dr. Newman in 1866 sets himself up to interpret the meaning of the Pope's decree of 1854! He declares that this doctrine is nothing more than a "supernatural inward gift given her from the moment of her personal existence, exactly as was received by Eve." Authority for this there is absolutely none; but, nevertheless, he declares it to be "a strange phenomenon that so many learned and devout men stumble at this doctrine," and he can only account for it by supposing that, "in matter of fact, they do not know what we [Romanists] mean by the Immaculate Conception" (p. 49). He asserts that "it has no reference to her parents, but simply to her own person. It does but affirm that, together with the

nature which she inherited from her parents,—that is, her own nature,—she had a supernatural fulness of grace, and that from the first moment of her existence" (p. 49); and a consequence of this is, that she was "innocent and sinless" (p. 47). And it is a "great consolation to Dr. Newman to have reason for thinking that in some sort the persons in question [who disbelieve] are in a position of those great saints in former times, *who are said to have hesitated* [mark these words] about it when they could not have hesitated at all if the word 'conception' had been clearly explained in that sense in which it is now usually received" (p. 49). He denies "that Mary had original sin" (p. 51). She "never came under the original curse;" and he adds that he "has drawn the [this] doctrine of the Immaculate Conception as an *immediate inference* from the primitive doctrine that Mary is the second Eve." The argument seems to him "conclusive;" of course, according to his own "private judgment." But what if he differed from his co-religionists? Why, then, he says, "if it has not been universally taken as such, this has come to pass because there has not been a clear understanding among Catholics what exactly was meant by the Immaculate Conception"! (p. 52). We have here the admission that there has not been a clear understanding among "Catholics" as to what this "Immaculate Conception" after all does mean; and Pope Pius IX., while decreeing it as a matter of belief, left that essential in an unhappy state of haze. Dr. Newman gives it as his further opinion—and "much virtue—I repeat—is there in an *if*"—

"IF controversy had in earlier days so cleared the subject as to make it plain to all that the doctrine meant nothing else than that in fact, in her case, the general sentence on mankind was not carried out, and that by means of the indwelling in her of divine grace from the first moment of her being (and this is all the decree of 1854 has declared), I cannot believe that the doctrine would have ever been opposed; for an instinctive sentiment had led Christian jealousy to put the Blessed Mary aside, when sin comes into discussion" (p. 52).

This is the explanation Dr. Newman now "thinks it necessary for his position" to offer. But it will be scarcely endorsed by his co-religionists, and he may possibly find *himself* accused of a "want of a clear understanding of the subject," if not heresy.

Dr. Johnson defines *immaculate* as "spotless, pure, undefiled;" *conception*, "conceiving or growing quick with pregnancy." Our Lord was conceived in the womb of Mary without the agency of man, and was in fact sinless; so, when we speak of the Immaculate Conception of Mary, it means that she also was conceived in the womb of her mother without the agency of man, and, being born sinless, they declare that she lived and died sinless. A very different theory to that advanced by Dr. Newman.

If there is one point on which the Scriptures seem to dwell more than another, it is that we have *all*, without exception, sinned (Rom. iii. 23; Gal. iii. 22). "Wherefore, as by one man sin entered into the world, and death by sin; and so death passed upon all men, for that all have sinned" (Rom. v. 12). If Mary had been conceived without sin, why had she to undergo the penalty of sin—death? That Mary *died*, the Roman ritual on the feast of the Assumption clearly admits. Augustine commenting on these texts, applied them expressly to the Virgin Mary. "Mary sprang from Adam, died because of sin; Adam died because of sin; and the flesh of our Lord, derived from Mary, died to take away sin."* Dr. Newman professes a great reverence for the Fathers, when it is convenient for his position, and I dwell on Augustine, as Dr. Newman has given one doubtful passage, to the effect that when treating of sin, for the honour of the Lord, he desired to exclude the Virgin Mary. Augustine was not

---

* "Maria ex Adam mortua propter peccatum; Adam mortuus propter peccatum; et caro Domini ex Maria mortua est propter delenda peccata."—*August. Opera*, Enarr. in Psalm. XXXIV. serm. ii. tom. iv. col. 240. Paris, 1691.

speaking of *original sin* but of *actual* sin; but as a fact, Augustine does repeatedly treat of sin, and does not exclude the Virgin Mary from *actual sin*. Why cannot Dr. Newman tell the whole truth,—it must come out? We must fill up the hiatus, and I am rather curious to see what Dr. Newman can say in reply. Augustine further says:—

"He *alone*, being made man, but remaining God, never had any sin; nor did He take on Him a flesh of sin, though *from the flesh of sin of his mother*. For what of flesh He thence took, He either, when taken, immediately purified, or purified in the act of taking it."*

Again—"Mary, the mother of Christ, from whom He took flesh, was *born of the carnal concupiscence* of her parents; not so, however, did she conceive Christ, who was begotten, not by man, but of the Holy Ghost."†

There are numerous other passages in Augustine to the like effect, showing Augustine's opinion that Mary was born in sin.‡

I have already quoted the opinion at length of Epiphanius (A.D. 370), where he says that Mary was " a

* "*Solus* ergo Ille etiam, homo factus, manens Deus, peccatum nullum habuit unquam; nec sumpsit carnem peccati, quamvis de maternâ carne peccati. Quod enim carnis inde suscepit, id profecto aut suscipiendum mundavit, aut suscipiendo mundavit."—*St. Augustini Opera*, tom. x. p. 61 B, Benedict. ed. Paris, 1690. "De Peccatorum Meritis et Remissione," lib. ii. c. 24, § 38.

† "Maria, Mater Christi, de qua carnem sumpsit, de *carnali concupiscentia parentum nata est*, non autem Christum sic ipsa concepit, Quem non de virili semine sed de Spiritu Sancto procreavit."—*Idem. Oper. imperf. contra Julian.*, lib. vi. tom. x. p. 1334 A.

‡ "*Virginis caro* etiamsi de *peccati propagine venit*, non tamen de peccati propagine concepit. . . . Proinde corpus Christi, quamvis ex carne *fœminæ* assumptum est, *quæ de illâ carnis peccati propagine concepta fuerat*, tamen quia *non* sic in eâ conceptum est quo modo fuerat *illa* concepta, nec ipsa erat caro peccati, sed similitudo carnis peccati."—*S. Aug. de Genesi, ad Literam*, lib. x. cap. xviii. tom. iii. pp. 268-9.

"Apparet illam concupiscentiam per quam Christus concipi noluit, fecisse in genere humano propaginem mali, quia *Mariæ corpus* quamvis *inde venerit*, tamen eam non trajecit in corpus quod non inde concepit."—*S. Aug. contra Julian. Pelagian.*, lib. v. xv. tom. x. p. 654 E.

chosen vessel, but was a woman not at all changed in nature," and declares that she "was not born differently from the nature of men" (*antè*, pp. 175-6).

Passing over the Fathers, whose works are replete with testimony against this doctrine, I would draw the attention of Dr. Newman to Melchior Canus, the professor of divinity at Salamanca, and bishop, who assisted at the Council of Trent. He admits, in express terms, that "*all* the Fathers who have at all made mention of this matter, have asserted with one voice that the Blessed Virgin was conceived in original sin."

He gives a long list of Fathers and Roman Catholic divines of the very highest repute who held this doctrine; he names Augustine, Chrysostom, Eusebius, Bernard, Antoninus (a canonized saint), Bonaventura, the great Thomas Aquinas, and many others; and winds up with these emphatic words, "cui nullus sanctorun contravenerit."*

But surely the opinions of Popes ought to have some weight :—

---

* Melchior Canus, "Loci Theologici," p. 348. "De Sanctorum Auct.," lib. vii. cap. 1. Col. Agrip. 1605. "*Sancti omnes*, qui in ejus rei mentionem incidere, *uno ore asseverarunt, Beatam Virginem in peccato originali conceptam.* Hoc videlicet Ambrosius astruit super Psal. 118, concione 6. Hoc Augustinus super Psalmum 34, in illum versiculum, 'Ego autem cum mihi molesti,' &c., et lib. secundo de baptismo parvulorum capita 24 et 10, super Genesim ad literam, caput 18 et lib. 53, contra Julianum, cap. 9. Hoc Chrysostomus super Matthæum; hoc Eusebius Emisenus in 2. Concione Nativitatis Domini; hoc Remigius super Psalmum vicesimum primum, et Maximus in Sermone de Assumptione Beatæ Virginis astruxere. Idem quoque affirmat Beda in Homilia super '*Missus est*,' Anselmus in libro, 'cur Deus homo,' caput 16. Bernardus in Epistola ad Lugdunenses, 174. Erhardus episcopus, et martyr, in concione quadam de Nativitate Beatæ Virginis, Sanctus Antonius Paduanus in concione etiam de Nativitate ejusdem sanctæ Virginis, Sanctus Bernardinus in sermonum suorum opere tertio, in tractatu de Beata Virgine, concione 4. Divus Bonaventura 3. sent. distinctione 3, quæstio 1, artic. 2. Divus Thom. 3. parte, quæstio 27, articul. 2. Divus Vincen. in Sermone de Conceptione Beatæ Virginis. Divus Anto. 1. parte, titu. 8. Damas. lib. 3. sententiarum suarum. Hugo de Sancto Victore de Sacram. part. 2, cap. 4."

Pope Leo, A.D. 440, says—"Therefore the Lord Jesus Christ *alone* among the sons of men, was born immaculate."*

Pope Gelasius I., A.D. 492, says—"It belongs alone to the immaculate Lamb to have no sin at all."†

Pope Gregory the Great, A.D. 600, says—"For though we be *made* holy, we are nevertheless not born holy. But He alone was truly born holy who, in order that He might overcome this condition of corruptible nature, was not conceived after the manner of men."‡

Dr. Newman dwells much on the comparison between Eve and Mary: now hear what Pope Innocent III. said, in his second discourse on the Assumption:—

"Eve was produced without sin, but she brought forth in sin; *Mary was produced in sin*, but she brought forth without sin."§

I transcribe the following short history of the doctrine from my late work, "Novelties of Romanism."‖

The festival of the Conception of the Virgin Mary was first introduced at Lyons about the year 1140, but was opposed by Bernard (now a canonized saint of the Roman Church) as a novelty, without the sanction of Scripture or reason. Bernard said that it was a

---

* " Solus itaque inter filios hominum Dominus Jesus innocens natus est, quia solus sine carnalis concupiscentiæ pollutione conceptus."—*St. Leonis Magni Opera*, tom. i. p. 160, ed. Paris, 1675, Sermo 24, in Nativitate Domini, v. cap. 5.

† " Immaculati agni proprium est nullum prorsus habuisse peccatum."—*Gelasii Papæ I., Tractatus III.*, dicta adversus Pelagianam Hæresim. Labbe et Coss. Conc., tom. iv. col. 1241, Paris, 1671.

‡ "Nos quippe etsi sancti efficimur, non tamen sancti nascimur, quia ipsa naturæ corruptibilis conditione constringimur, ut cum Propheta dicamus: ' Ecce enim in iniquitatibus conceptus sum, et in delictis peperit me mater mea.' Ille autem solus veraciter sanctus natus est, qui ut ipsam conditionem naturæ corruptibilis vinceret, ex commixtione carnalis copulæ conceptus non est."—*S. Gregor. I. Papæ cognomento Magni Opera*, Ben. ed. Paris, 1705, tom. i. p. 598. Moralium, lib. xviii. in caput xxviii. Beati Job, cap. lii. § 84.

§ " Illa [Eva] fuit sine culpâ producta, sed produxit in culpam; hæc [Maria] fuit in culpâ producta, sed sine culpa produxit."—*Innocent. III. Sermo II. de Festo Assumptionis Mariæ*. Colon. 1552, fol. LXVII. b.

‖ Religious Tract Society, Paternoster Row, price 4s.

"false, new, vain, and superstitious" idea.* According to Fleury, it was John Scott, commonly called Duns Scotus, at the beginning of the 14th century, who seriously broached the doctrine of the Immaculate Conception.†

At the thirty-sixth Session of the Council of Basle, A.D. 1439—a council condemned and rejected by the Church of Rome—it was declared that the doctrine which asserts that the Virgin Mary was actually subject to original sin, should be condemned; but that the doctrine that she was always free from all original and actual sin, and both holy and immaculate, should be approved, and should be held and embraced by all Catholics, as being pious and agreeable to ecclesiastical worship, to Catholic faith, to right reason and the Scriptures, and that it should not be lawful for any one to teach or preach to the contrary.‡ The festival was directed to be celebrated on the 17th December. The Council of Avignon, A.D. 1457, confirmed this act of the Council of Basle, and forbade, under pain of excommunication, any one to preach anything contrary to the doctrine.§

The doctrine created a sore division in the Church of Rome; the Dominicans following their leader, St. Thomas Aquinas, combated the new dogma most vehemently, as *contrary to the Scriptures, tradition, and the faith of the Church;* while it was as vehemently supported by the Franciscans. The scandal became so great at each returning festival-day, that Sixtus IV. (A.D. 1483) issued a Bull, wherein he, of his own accord, and unsolicited, condemned those who called

---

* Fleury's "Eccl. Hist.," tom. xiv. p. 527, Paris, 1769. "Nulla ei ratione placebit contra ecclesiæ ritum præsumpta novitas, mater temeritatis, soror superstitionis, filia levitatis."—*S. Bernard. Ep.* 174, tom. i. col. 393. Paris, 1839.

† "Eccl. Hist.," tom. xix. p. 150. Paris, 1769.

‡ Lab. et Coss. Concl., tom. xii. cols. 622, 623. Paris, 167.

§ Ibid., tom. xiii. col. 1403. Paris, 1671.

the doctrine a heresy, the celebration of the festival a sin, and that those who held the doctrine were guilty of mortal sin, and subjected those to excommunication who acted contrary to this decree. By the same Bull he enacted the like penalty against those who maintained the opponents of the doctrine to be in heresy or mortal sin, declaring as a reason, that " this doctrine had not yet been decided by the Roman Church and the Apostolic See."* Despite this Pope's Bull, the discord continued, to the great scandal of religion; and when the doctrine of " original sin " came to be argued at the Council of Trent, the Dominicans and Franciscans ranged themselves on opposite sides and re-fought the battle. The debate became so warm, that the Pope ordered, through his legates, that the Council should "not meddle in this matter, which might cause a schism among Catholics, but endeavour to maintain peace between the contending parties, and to seek some means of giving them equal satisfaction; but, above all, to observe the brief of Pope Sixtus IV., which prohibited preachers from taxing the doctrine [of the Immaculate Conception] with heresy." †

The Council of Trent (A.D. 1546) expressly excluded from its decree on original sin the Virgin Mary, the papal legate being directed not to meddle with the subject, lest it should cause a schism; but declared " that the constitutions of Pope Sixtus IV., which it revives, are to be observed under the penalties contained in those constitutions." Thus, both parties claimed the victory. The theological contest raged as violently as ever. In the seventeenth century, Spain was thrown into the utmost confusion by these miserable disputes; and it was sought to bring them to a close by an appeal to the supposed infallible head of the Church, who was asked to issue his Bull to deter-

* This decree is found in the appendix of every authorized edition of the Decrees of the Council of Trent.
† Paul Sarpi's Hist. Conc. Trid., lib. ii. c. 68. Geneva, 1629.

mine the question. "But (observes Mosheim) after the most earnest entreaties and importunities, all that could be obtained from the Pontiff by the Court of Spain was a declaration intimating that the opinion of the Franciscans had a high degree of probability on its side, and forbidding the Dominicans to oppose it in a public manner; but this declaration was accompanied by another, by which the Franciscans were prohibited in turn from treating as erroneous the doctrine of the Dominicans."[*]

Alexander VII., A.D. 1661, while reviving the constitution of Sixtus IV., vainly endeavoured to allay the feud; but admitted that the Church had not decided the vexed question, and that he by no means desired or intended to decide it.[†]

Clement XI. appointed a festival in honour of the Immaculate Conception, to be annually celebrated by the Church of Rome; but the Dominicans refused to obey this law.[‡]

Eventually Pope Pius IX. undertook to decide, as he thought, for ever, the much-vexed question.

In December, 1854, the Pope, in an assembly of bishops, from which all non-contents were excluded, issued his Bull, declaring the doctrine as a matter of faith.[§] "Let no man (says the decree) interfere with this our declaration, pronunciation, and definition, or oppose or contradict it with presumptuous rashness. If any should presume to assail it, let him know that he will incur the indignation of the Omnipotent God, and of his blessed apostles Peter and Paul." Hence the *Tablet* observed, that "whosoever should thenceforth deny that the Blessed Virgin was herself, by a miracu-

---

[*] Mosheim's "Eccl. Hist.," cent. xvii. sec. ii. part i. c. i. s. 48.

[†] Alex. Sept. A.D. 1661. *Mag. Bull. Romanum*, tom. vi. p. 158. Edit. Luxemb. 1727.

[‡] Mosheim's "Eccl. Hist.," cent. xvii. sec. ii. pt. i. c. i. s. 48.

[§] The *Univers*, Paris, 20th January, 1855; the *Tablet*, London, 27th January, 1855.

lous interposition of God's providence, *conceived without the stain of original sin*, is to be condemned as a heretic." This appears very much as if Dr. Newman's theory was heretical, and he himself condemned as a heretic.

Such is a brief history of the doctrine of the Immaculate Conception; but it is a popular fallacy to suppose that it is a *doctrine* of the Roman Church. The Pope of Rome, according to the orthodox principles of that church, cannot create doctrines of faith which have not emanated from a General Council of the Church.

The invited bishops gave their opinions on the subject; and Dr. Pusey has shown us the "happy discord" that still existed in 1849, in the bosom of the self-styled "centre of unity," notwithstanding the Pope, in 1854, declared the Immaculate Conception of the Virgin Mary to be a doctrine of the Roman Church. And Dr. Newman is only repeating the "Ba, ba, ba" of the Pope of a dogmatic church, because he dare not say "Bo, bo, bo"! But when Dr. Newman has the boldness to assert "that it is true that several great Fathers of the fourth century *do* imply or *assert* that on one or two occasions she did *sin venially*, or showed infirmity," we can only counter-assert that he is gifted with an extraordinarily short memory, and with a genius for invention, or that he is really ignorant of the merits of the question on which he presumes to school us.

Passing on from this painful subject, Dr. Newman, failing all other proofs from Scripture, falls back on his old idea that the "woman clothed with the sun and moon," described in the 12th chapter of the Revelation of St. John, is the literal Virgin Mary herself! but he saves his reputation by admitting, that in the first degree the symbol does mean to represent the Church. How it can represent the Blessed Virgin in the second degree is difficult to make out; but as Dr. Newman is bound by his creed not to interpret Scripture " except according to the unanimous consent of the Fathers," we will pardon him for his erratic fancies, if he can find one *genuine* reliable authority to support his theory. I emphasize *genuine*, for the idea springs from a notoriously spurious discourse attributed to Augustine. But I am not at all surprised at this application of Scripture. Dr. Newman's "daily companion," the Breviary, in the church lessons and offices, and in the "Glories of Mary," &c., where the Scriptures introduce epithets and prophecies relating to Christ, all these are applied directly to the Blessed Virgin.*

Dr. Newman, with considerable art, mixes up subjects wholly distinct, and draws conclusions, which are disputed, from admitted premises.

The question is not one of intercessory prayer for the living; this is encouraged by Scripture. Nor is it whether the departed in heaven offer up their prayers for us who are on earth. This may or may not be their occupation. We have no information on the matter, except that we are expressly informed "that the dead know nothing more; neither have any part in this world, and in the work that is done under the sun."† "The *seven spirits* that are before the throne of grace," to which Dr. Newman refers as favouring his theory, according to Augustine, are the seven graces of the *one* Holy Spirit;‡ and Gregory Nazianzen gives the same interpretation.§

Nor is the question whether we may lawfully pray *for* the departed. This was one of the earliest inno-

* The reader may profitably consult on this head Foye's "Romish Rites, Offices, and Legends." London, 1850.
† Eccl. x. 5, 6, *Douay version*.
‡ August. Ennar. in Ps. cl. tom. iv. p. 1693. Bened. edit. Paris, 1685.
§ Oratio XLI. p. 733. Bened. edit. Paris, 1778.

vations in Christianity, but has no sanction in Scripture. Nor can Dr. Newman come to any certain conclusion that Onesiphorus was dead, as presumed by him, when St. Paul sent messages to his *household*, and prayed " he might find mercy in the Lord," which is quite compatible with the idea that he was alive.

All these, I say, are beside the question, which is, whether we are justified, by any revelation or apostolic instruction, in praying to saints, as intercessors, or pleading their *merits* on our behalf. To presuppose that they " hear our mental and verbal prayers," as alleged by the Trent Council, is not only prying into those things which it has not pleased God to reveal to us, but endows those creatures, if they be in heaven, with two of the great attributes of the Divinity, —*Omniscience* and *Omnipresence*. Is the medium appointed by Scripture insufficient? Dr. Newman will not dare to assert it. Then I would earnestly entreat him to consider whether the limited license which he permits amounts only to a question of degree; and if with imaginative dispositions those excessive demonstrations for a creature, which, he admits, amount to blasphemy, are not a natural consequence of the system. And I would call Dr. Newman's attention to his own expressions, uttered in a sober and thoughtful moment, when his mind was not controversially bent, and which conveyed sentiments in which Protestants and Roman Catholics can join with heart and hand.

One of the lamentable consequences of this devotion to the Virgin Mary is the superstitious use of the scapular, rosaries, and beads which Dr. Newman sanctions " as mediums of divine manifestations of grace," and are indigenous to this country, and not of foreign importation. He tells us " large liberty is accorded to private judgment and inclination in matters of devotion" (p. 30). These devotees " pursue independently a common end, and by paths distinct, but converging, present themselves before God." And these, among others, are "confraternities attached to the Church—of the Sacred Heart or the Precious Blood—devotions connected with the brown, blue, or red scapulars." And it is this phase of Romanism, thus admitted as orthodox by Dr. Newman, to which I shall finally address myself.

I have now before me "the Manual concerning Scapulars, &c.," published "permissu superiorum;" London: Richardson and Son, with the "imprimatur, 18th January, 1864, N. Cardinal Wiseman;" and this edition is, "by kind permission," dedicated to him. The object of the Manual is stated to be to "supply those who are invested with the five scapulars with a sure guide," and "the greatest care has been taken to admit nothing but what is *most authentic;*" and the Bishop of Tournai testifies that "he has found in it nothing contrary to the doctrine of the Church upon indulgences." "The extraordinary and miraculous graces, of which the scapulars have been the instrument, and the formularies approved by the Church for the blessing of scapulars and other objects of piety," are here laid before the reader.

The scapular is described as being composed of two pieces of cloth, to be hung over the shoulders and over the breast (p. 9), back and front. They are called "religious habits" (p. 11), and "instruments of mercy" (p. 34). "There are five principal scapulars" (p. 10). The scapular of the "Discalced Trinitarians *must be* white linen or cloth;" of the "Carmelites, *must be* brown, or chesnut-coloured;—black cloth, however, is allowed." That of the "Servites," or Servants of Mary, "*must be* of black woollen cloth." "Theatines," or of the Immaculate Conception, "*must be* of woollen cloth of azure or light blue colour;" and the "Vincentians," or of the Passion, "is of scarlet woollen cloth, &c."

Why they *must* be of a particular cloth is not explained. The "strings do not form any essential part of the habit, excepting perhaps the red scapular."

"They must be suspended upon the shoulders, and not pinned to the dress, or in the pocket." "By this dress the wearers are placed under the special protection of the Mother of God; and without any doubt it shields them from many dangers, corporeal as well as spiritual." The Blessed Virgin is said to have personally appeared to St. Simon Stock, an Englishman, and presented him with a brown scapular, with a promise that " whoever dies whilst devoutly wearing this habit shall be preserved from eternal pains. It is a sign of salvation, a safeguard from danger, and a pledge of eternal peace and alliance which I contract with you" (p. 40). And the Blessed Virgin has promised to relieve those from Purgatory who should die wearing one of these "holy habits."

Each particular scapular is stated to have been presented to the founder of the particular Order by special and miraculous interposition of an angel or the Blessed Virgin herself, and numerous miracles are recorded as having taken place solely by virtue of the blessed scapular. One example is sufficient. A man in a duel, actually committing a mortal sin, "was hit at ten paces by a ball; but happily the ball hit against his scapular, and he only received a slight bruise, although the said ball had pierced his coat and his shirt, and was found flattened against his stomach at least three inches below the ribs, the scapular adhering close to the bruise." This particular kind of scapular is declared to be a "defence against bodily dangers, as may be abundantly proved by numerous examples." The above is one; but it is added: "Nor is this all. It is a passport to heaven, and preserves them [the wearers] from eternal damnation" (p. 40). The same system is carried on to beads and rosaries, and, in order to obtain the benefit of indulgences, they must be blessed by a duly-authorized priest. Conceive Father Newman, a professed Christian minister, blessing pieces of rag and then pretending that they are miraculous! What a solemn mockery! The indulgence appears to attach to the article itself; for we are gravely told that "indulgences cannot be applied to engravings, paintings, crosses or crucifixes and medals of tin or lead; but by *special decree* crucifixes of iron may be indulgenced, also ivory ones, glass or crystal beads, if the grains be compact and solid" (p. 108). "The beads ought to be held in the hand; but if several persons say them together, it is sufficient that one only hold the beads, and all the rest participate in the indulgence, provided they are in possession of an indulgenced rosary—this condition is necessary" (p. 110).

A leading feature in this system is the ease with which *indulgences* are obtained through wearing these pieces of rag,—that is, a remission is thereby obtained, either partial or plenary, of the temporal punishment due to sin, remitted as to their guilt, by the presumed power of the keys, *but without the Sacrament* (of penance) by the application of the satisfactions which are contained in the treasury of the Church.* It presupposes the existence of this fabulous treasure of superabundant merits of Christ and the saints. Did ever any one hear of such a delusion? We are told that it was the opinion of Thomas Aquinas and others that the devising of indulgences was a kind of pious fraud and a harmless deceit, that by a devout kind of error people may be brought to godliness;† cheating people into piety,—say superstition. But we are reminded that the devotees of the scapular, in

* "Quid est indulgentia?—R. Est pœnæ temporalis peccatis, quoad culpam remissis, debitæ remissio, facta potestate clavium, *extra sacramentum*, per applicationem satisfactionum quæ in thesauro Ecclesiæ continentur."—*Dens Theologia*, tom. vi.; Tract. de Indulg., No. 30; De Indulgentiarum Natura. Dublin, 1832.

† "Num tibi leves .... causæ videntur, quibus ab hac nova Indulgentiarum assertione patres ante Albertum et Thomam discesserunt, asserentes nihil esse nisi piam fraudem ac dolum non malum, quo plebs officioso," &c.—*Wessel. Farrag. Rer. Theolog.* Basil, 1522. Epist. contra Tac. Hock. de Indulgent., cap. i. fol. 106.

order to receive the benefit of indulgences, must be "in a state of grace." There must be previous sacramental confession and absolution, communion and certain prayers. As to the prayers, "it is sufficient to say five *Paters* and five *Aves*, or the Litanies of our Lady, or of the holy name of Jesus, or some decades of the rosary, or other equivalent prayers" (p. 21); except to the wearers of the " scapular of the Blessed Lady," who " are not bound by any *particular* obligation in order to gain the indulgence attached" (p. 38). The process to arrive at a state of grace (according to the Roman standard) is as easy as the subsequently imposed terms. It is not necessary to have *true repentance* or *contrition* (as they call it, and to which I have before adverted), but simply *attrition*, or imperfect repentance, arising principally from the fear of punishment, and a promise to sin no more. The theory is well defined in a catechism or compendium of faith, compiled and approved by the Cardinal Archbishop of Paris, where we read that—

"There are two kinds of *contrition*, the one *perfect* and the other *imperfect*, which is called *attrition*. Perfect *contrition* is sorrow for having offended God, because He is supremely good. The effect of perfect contrition is to justify the sinner *without absolution;* but nevertheless with the desire or obligation * to receive it. *Attrition* is sorrow for having offended God, from remorse for having committed the sin, *or* from fear of enduring its penalty. *Attrition* does not of itself justify the sinner, but prepares him to receive the blessing of justification by means of absolution, in which principally consists the force of the Sacrament of Penance."†

---

* "Or obligation" is an unwarrantable addition, found neither in the Decree of Trent, nor in the Catechism.

† "Il y a deux sortes de contritions ; l'une parfaite, et l'autre imparfaite, que l'on appelle *attrition*.—La contrition parfaite est une douleur d'avoir offensé Dieu, parcequ'il est souverainement bon.—L'effet de la contrition parfaite est de justifier le pécheur *par elle-même sans l'absolution*, avec le désir néanmoins et l'obligation de le recevoir. L'attrition est une douleur d'avoir offensé Dieu, par la honte d'avoir commis le péché, *ou* par la crainte d'en recevoir le châtiment. L'attrition ne justifie pas le pécheur par elle-même, mais

And Dr. Delahogue, the Professor of Maynooth College, puts it still plainer:—

"Perfect repentance," he says, "is not required in order that a man may obtain the remission of his *mortal sins* in the Sacrament of Penance."*

And this is only confirmatory of the Decree of Trent, which declared, by the fourth chapter passed at the 14th session, that,—

"Although this *attrition cannot of itself, without the Sacrament of penance,* bring the sinner unto justification, yet does it dispose him to obtain the grace of God *in the Sacrament of Penance.*"

Such is the process for bringing a person in mortal sin to what they call a "state of grace." But the advantages do not rest here. "Many indulgences may be gained on the same day; in that case it is well to apply one to ourselves, and the others to the souls in purgatory." Nay, further, "all indulgences attached to scapulars, rosaries, crosses, or medals, may be applied to the dead, except perhaps those of the scapular of the Passion" (p. 77). Enough for yourself, and to spare, too, for departed friends! Is it possible to conceive a greater delusion and a more wicked device of the priests, who teach this doctrine, since they cannot believe in it themselves?† The

---

elle le dispose à recevoir la grâce de la justification par l'absolution, *dans laquelle consiste principalement la force du Sacrement de Pénitence.*"—*Catechisme, ou abrégé de la Foi,* dressé par l'ordre de Mgr. de Harley, approuvé par M. de Baumont, et par S. E. Mgr. le Cardinal de Belloy, Archevêques de Paris, pour être seul enseigné dans son Diocèse. A Paris. Chez Th. Morinval, Imprim.—Libr. des Frères des Ecoles Chrétiennes. 24mo. 1828, cap. ix. p. 25 *et seq.*

* "Contritio perfecta non requiretur ut homo, in sacramento pœnitentiæ, peccatorum mortalium remissionem obtineat."—*Tract. de Sacr. Pœnitentiæ,* autore Lud. Ægid. Delahogue; Dublinii, ex typ. N. Coyne, 1825.

† One of the works specially named by Dr. Newman as containing nothing extravagant or heterodox, is the *Raccolta*. I have not seen this book; but in this "Manual," bearing the *imprimatur* of

scapular of the "Immaculate Conception," and to which the greatest number of indulgences is attached, stands the most prominent as affording the greatest facilities to enable us to march straight to heaven.

But why pursue this painful and humiliating subject,—deeply humiliating to us as Christians! And oh! how sad to find a man like Dr. Newman, possessing otherwise a cultivated intellect, who, while in our Church, taught that God is a Spirit, and must be worshipped in spirit and in truth, should now have fallen so low as to conceive it necessary to have recourse to such external and senseless means to excite devotion. Well may he say that *faith* and

the late Dr. Wiseman, in January 1864, is the following, under the Title "*The Angelic Trisagion*" (pp. 28, 29).

"'Holy, Holy, Holy, Lord God of Hosts, all the earth is full of Thy glory. Glory be to the Father, Glory be to the Son, Glory be to the Holy Ghost.'

"This prayer was revealed by the angels in the year 446 to a child at Constantinople. The people of this great city began at once to recite it with devotion, and were immediately delivered from a succession of terrible earthquakes, from which they had suffered for six months previously.

"Pope Clement XIII. granted, and Pope Clement XIV. confirmed afresh *for ever*, the following Indulgences to those of the faithful who, with contrite heart, should recite the above '*Trisagion*.'

"i. An Indulgence of 100 days once a day.

"ii. The same Indulgence three times every Sunday, as well as on the Festival and during the Octave of the Most Holy Trinity.

"iii. A Plenary Indulgence for ever, once a month to all those who, throughout the said month, shall have said daily the Angelic Trisagion as above.

"This Indulgence may be gained on any one day when, after Confession and Communion, they shall visit some Church or Oratory and pray according to the intention of the Sovereign Pontiff.—*Raccolta*, etc. i. p. l."

Is Dr. Newman prepared to endorse this? 1. Does he believe that a penitent with a contrite heart requires any such indulgences as here enumerated? 2. Does he really believe that this prayer was revealed as stated? 3. Does he really believe that on recital of this *Trisagion*, the reciter obtains each day a remission of 100 days' punishment, which would be otherwise consequent on his sins? If he does, where is his authority? If he does not, then is this not a *pious fraud*, which he now justifies?

devotion are distinct principles, and do not necessarily go together. The faith of the devotee of the scapular may be of a certain order, but it is not that faith which ennobles the Christian. Dr. Newman says that "there are but two alternatives—the way to Rome and the way to atheism." Say rather, that the way to Rome is the high road to *infidelity*.

Dr. Newman endeavours to shield his church by advancing as a fact that the Greek Church carries the worship of the Virgin even beyond the Roman. If the Greeks are right in principle, then Romanists fall short in their duty; if wrong, then the evil is one of degree only, and the example cannot be pleaded in justification.

With these authorized devotions before us, Dr. Newman has the boldness to tell us that the Roman Church

"Allows no image of any sort, material or immaterial, no dogmatic symbol, no rite, no sacrament, no saint, not even the Blessed Virgin herself, to come between the soul and his Creator. It is face to face, 'solus cum solo,' in all matters between man and his God. He alone creates; He alone has redeemed; before His awful eyes we go in death; in the vision of Him is our eternal beatitude." *

But is this true? I appeal to Dr. Newman himself. What explanation can he give to the statement in the "Manual" to which Dr. Wiseman gave his sanction in 1864, that "God, who has given His holy mother to be our mediatrix, desires that we have recourse to her assistance"? (p. 33). Truly may we apply the words of Jeremiah the prophet to this perverse generation:—

"*They have committed two evils; they have forsaken Me, the fountain of living waters, and hewed them out cisterns, broken cisterns, that can hold no water.*"

* "Apologia," p. 318.

LONDON, 1865.

Popular Tracts and Books on Social and Religious Subjects, etc.,

PUBLISHED BY

JOHN F. SHAW & Co.,

48, PATERNOSTER ROW, E.C.

THE PEOPLE'S LIBRARY.

A GOOD JACK MAKES A GOOD JILL; or, John's Remedy for a Bad Wife. By the Author of "What Put my Pipe out," etc. Boards, 1s. With Four Illustrations.

HOUSEHOLD PROVERBS FOR MEN. Boards, 1s. Illustrated with a Coloured Frontispiece, and numerous Illustrations.

HOUSEHOLD PROVERBS FOR WOMEN. Boards, 1s. Illustrated with a Coloured Frontispiece, and numerous Illustrations.

HOUSEHOLD PROVERBS FOR EVERY ONE. Boards, 1s. Illustrated with a Coloured Frontispiece, and numerous Illustrations.

HOUSEHOLD NAMES, AND HOW THEY BECAME SO. Boards, 1s. Illustrated with a Coloured Frontispiece, and numerous Illustrations.

STORIES FOR WOMEN. Boards, 1s. Illustrated with a Coloured Frontispiece, and numerous Illustrations.

HEARTH AND HOME; or, Men as they are, and Women as they ought to be. Cloth boards, 1s. 6d. Illustrated with a Coloured Frontispiece, and numerous Illustrations.

"A series of plain and simple tales, all likely to do good, especially among the humbler classes, for whom the work is chiefly intended."—*City Press.*

"A capital collection of stories, all interesting, and true to the life. The language used is precisely that of the working classes, and the author is evidently thoroughly acquainted with the habits and customs, the petty troubles and household cares of those for whose use the Tracts are intended."—*Athenæum.*

HOUSEHOLD PROVERBS;

OR,

TRACTS FOR THE PEOPLE.

PRICE ONE PENNY EACH.

1. TAKE CARE OF THE PENCE, AND THE POUNDS WILL TAKE CARE OF THEMSELVES.
2. A MAN IS WHAT A WOMAN MAKES HIM.
3. HE THAT GOES A-BORROWING GOES A-SORROWING.
4. HE THAT SERVES GOD SERVES A GOOD MASTER.
5. A CAT IN PATTENS CATCHES NO MICE.
6. WASTE NOT, WANT NOT.

(*Continued on next page.*)

Nos. 1 to 12 may be had in One Volume, price 1s. 6d. cloth.
Nos. 13 to 24 ,, ,, price 1s. 6d. cloth.
Or, complete in One Volume, price 2s. 6d.

A Specimen Packet (1 to 24) sent Post Free for Two Shillings.

Tract Societies and District Visiting Societies supplied with Numbers at a great reduction, by applying direct to the Publishers.

These striking Narrative Tracts are eminently adapted for reading at Mothers' Meetings, Social Gatherings of the Poor, and for general circulation among the Working Classes. The truths sought to be enforced are such as must commend themselves to all, and the narratives illustrating these truths bring them so forcibly home to the readers and hearers, that they cannot fail to discern and appreciate them. From long and intimate acquaintance with the Working Classes, the Author has been thoroughly able to enter into all the peculiar characteristics of their lives and homes. The testimony borne by persons of every class both to the faithfulness of these narratives, and their great usefulness, has been most gratifying. The Series has circulated to the unprecedented extent of more than HALF A MILLION in the short space of fifteen months.

48, Paternoster Row, London, E.C.

HOUSEHOLD PROVERBS;

OR,

TRACTS FOR THE PEOPLE.

PRICE ONE PENNY EACH.

7. ILL WEEDS GROW APACE.
8. BIRDS OF A FEATHER FLOCK TOGETHER.
9. WILFUL WASTE MAKES WOEFUL WANT.
10. LIGHTLY COME, LIGHTLY GO.
11. GOD HELPS THEM WHO HELP THEMSELVES.
12. RIGHT WRONGS NO MAN.

(Continued on next page.)

Nos. 1 to 12 may be had in One Volume, price 1s. 6d. cloth.

Nos. 13 to 24   ,,   ,,   price 1s. 6d. cloth.

Or, complete in One Volume, price 2s. 6d.

A Specimen Packet (1 to 24) sent Post Free for Two Shillings.

Tract Societies and District Visiting Societies supplied with Numbers at a great reduction, by applying direct to the Publishers.

From Rev. Dr. MARSH, Beddington.

"Dr. Marsh will be glad of 400 'Tract No. 2,' as he has invited the wives of all the workmen to tea. He hopes the 'Household Proverbs' have a great circulation."

From Rev. W. MORLEY PUNSHON, London.

"The Tracts appear to me admirable. I hope a very wide circulation for this wholesome literature of thrift and morals."

"We advise clergymen, district visitors, and managers of tract societies, to put them on their list at once."—*Record*.

48, Paternoster Row, London, E.C.

John F. Shaw & Co.,

HOUSEHOLD PROVERBS;
OR,
TRACTS FOR THE PEOPLE.

PRICE ONE PENNY EACH.

13. MORE ARE DROWNED IN BEER THAN IN WATER.
14. STORE IS NO SORE.
15. WHEN POVERTY COMES IN AT THE DOOR, LOVE FLIES OUT OF THE WINDOW.
16. MARRY IN HASTE AND REPENT AT LEISURE.
17. IT IS NEVER TOO LATE TO LEARN.
18. FINE FEATHERS MAKE FINE BIRDS.

(Continued on next page.)

Nos. 1 to 12 may be had in One Volume, price 1s. 6d. cloth.
Nos. 13 to 24   ”   ”   price 1s. 6d. cloth.
Or, complete in One Volume, price 2s. 6d.

A Specimen Packet (1 to 24) sent Post Free for Two Shillings.

Tract Societies and District Visiting Societies supplied with Numbers at a great reduction, by applying direct to the Publishers.

From Rev. C. H. SPURGEON, London.
"I highly approve of them."

From Mrs. BAYLY, Author of "Ragged Homes," "Workmen and their Difficulties," etc.

"Their value has been long known and appreciated by us, and we have distributed some hundreds of them in this neighbourhood. The work of sanitary and domestic reform, so deeply needed among our people, owes much to the gifted writer of 'Household Proverbs.'"

From Mrs. WIGHTMAN, Author of "Haste to the Rescue," "Annals of the Rescued," etc.

"The Tracts are most admirable, and I very gladly aid in making them known."

"We recommend 'Household Proverbs' to all those who are striving to ameliorate the condition of the masses."—*Atlas.*

"They are written in a pleasing style, are healthy in tone, and calculated to do great good among 'the People,' whose welfare they are intended to promote.'—*United Methodist.*

"A series of plain and simple tales, all likely to do good, especially among the humbler classes, for whom the work is chiefly intended."—*City Press.*

48, Paternoster Row, London, E.C.

HOUSEHOLD PROVERBS;

OR,

TRACTS FOR THE PEOPLE.

PRICE ONE PENNY EACH.

19. CLEANLINESS IS NEXT TO GODLINESS.
20. IT IS BETTER TO CRY OVER YOUR GOODS THAN AFTER THEM.
21. WELL BEGUN IS HALF DONE.
22. USE THE MEANS AND TRUST TO GOD FOR THE BLESSING.
23. THERE IS NO MIRTH GOOD BUT WITH GOD.
24. PAY AS YOU GO, AND KEEP FROM SMALL SCORE.

Nos. 1 to 12 may be had in One Volume, price 1s. 6d. cloth.
Nos. 13 to 24   ,,   ,,   price 1s. 6d. cloth.
Or, complete in One Volume price 2s. 6d.

A Specimen Packet (1 to 24) sent Post Free for Two Shillings.

Tract Societies and District Visiting Societies supplied with Numbers at a great reduction, by applying direct to the Publishers.

From Rev. J. B. OWEN, St. Jude's, Chelsea.

"I believe their circulation, by the Divine blessing, will be very useful."

From Rev. S. MARTIN, Westminster.

"These Tracts are very good in every respect, and admirably adapted to benefit the class of persons for whom they are intended."

"These 'Proverbs for the People' deserve to be brought under the notice of all who wish to have at command, for any purpose, a series of excellent morals conveyed in an entertaining and attractive form. We cannot do better than strongly recommend the series to general notice."—*English Churchman.*

"A capital collection of stories, all interesting, and true to the life. The language used is precisely that of the working classes, and the author is evidently thoroughly acquainted with the habits and customs, the petty troubles and household cares of those for whose use the Tracts are intended."—*Athenæum.*

48, *Paternoster Row, London, E.C.*

By the Author of "HOUSEHOLD PROVERBS," etc.,

HEARTH AND HOME;
OR,
MEN AS THEY ARE AND WOMEN AS THEY OUGHT TO BE.

PRICE ONE PENNY EACH.

1. THE WIDOWER.
2. THE WIDOWER'S CHILDREN.
3. TRUTH.
4. TEMPER.
5. RESIGNATION TO THE WILL OF GOD.
6. GOSSIPING.
7. WOMAN'S WORK AND WOMAN'S RIGHTS.
8. EMULATION AND COMPETITION.
9. FAITH.
10. SELFISHNESS.
11. SYMPATHY.
12. WOMAN'S INFLUENCE.

Nos. 1 to 6 in a Packet price 6d.
Nos. 7 to 12, in a Packet, price 6d.
Or, in One Volume, cloth, with Coloured Frontispiece, price 1s. 6d.

It is an old saying, but a very true one, "that a man's happiness depends more upon his inner self than upon his *outward circumstances*." It is to illustrate this truth that these stories have been written, and they will not have been written in vain if they make only one family the happier by persuading its members to try for themselves whether their own comfort, and the comfort of all about them, is not best promoted by the cultivation of a spirit of genuine piety towards God, which must of necessity show itself towards man, by bringing forth the fruits of the Spirit, love, joy, peace, longsuffering, gentleness, goodness, faith.

THIS SERIES IS ESPECIALLY ADAPTED FOR READING AT MOTHERS' MEETINGS, AND SOCIAL GATHERINGS OF THE WORKING CLASSES.

By the Author of "HOUSEHOLD PROVERBS," etc.

HOUSEHOLD NAMES,

AND HOW THEY BECAME SO.

A SERIES OF ILLUSTRATED BIOGRAPHICAL TRACTS FOR THE PEOPLE.

Showing that there is no royal road to honour and distinction, but that the great and good men of all times and all stations have achieved their success, and earned their fame, by serving God faithfully, by doing their duty to their fellow-men steadily, and by employing diligently, perseveringly, untiringly, their best powers, whether of mind or body, to the prosecution of their own allotted work, whatever that work might be.

PRICE ONE PENNY EACH.

1. GEORGE STEPHENSON, the Mechanic.
2. ROBERT STEPHENSON, the Engineer.
3. MARTIN LUTHER, the Reformer.
4. JOHN F. OBERLIN, the Village Pastor.
5. JOHN HOWARD, the Prisoners' Friend.
6. BERNARD PALISSY, the Potter.
7. BERNARD GILPIN, the Preacher.
8. HUGH LATIMER, the Martyr.

Nos. 1 to 6, in a Packet, price 6d.

Complete in One Volume, with Coloured Frontispiece, price 1s.

The Series to be continued.

John F. Shaw & Co.,

NEW SERIES OF TRACTS,

BY THE AUTHOR OF

"HOUSEHOLD PROVERBS," "HOUSEHOLD NAMES," ETC.

STORIES FOR WOMEN.

PRICE ONE PENNY EACH.

1. THE WANDERER.
2. LIZZIE PARKER. Part I.
3. LIZZIE PARKER. Part II.
4. ALICE LESLIE'S DECISION.
5. THE PROMISE, AND HOW MARY LESTER KEPT IT.
6. SUSAN WESTON'S CHOICE, AND WHAT CAME OF IT.
7. ELLEN WARNER, THE GOOD SERVANT.
8. MILLIE'S TEMPTATION.

48, Paternoster Row, London, E.C.

WORDS OF LIFE; a Series of Plain Tracts on Important Subjects. By the Rev. JOHN W. LESTER, D.D. Price 1d. each, or in a Packet, price 1s.

1. DO YOU LOVE GOD?
2. YET THERE IS ROOM.
3. I HEARKENED AND HEARD.
4. THE WATERS WEAR THE STONES.
5. WHO SHALL ROLL US AWAY THE STONE?
6. SCARCELY SAVED.
7. MAN'S TRUE DWELLING-PLACE.
8. WILL A MAN ROB GOD?
9. FAINT, YET PURSUING.
10. THE LAME TAKE THE PREY.
11. WATCHMAN, WHAT OF THE NIGHT?
12. THE MOUNTAIN BURNED WITH FIRE.

"Mr. Lester's Tracts are admirable, and should be circulated by tens of thousands. They combine all the requisites of Tracts in these days, for lack of one or more of which we, in large parishes, find so many Tracts all but useless. Full of Gospel Truth, they a e striking in title, cheap in price, and in matter pithy and salient."—*Rev. Canon Miller, Birmingham.*

LARGE TYPE TRACTS FOR WOMEN.

LOVING WORDS PLAINLY SPOKEN TO POOR WOMEN. By Mrs. J. ADDISON. In a Packet, price 6d.

1. DO YOU READ THE BIBLE?
2. ON CHASTITY.
3. GOSSIP.
4. DRESS.
5. CONTENTMENT.
6. HOME COMFORT.
7. INFLUENCE.
8. DEATH AND ETERNITY.

"Most admirably adapted to their purpose."—*British Mother's Journal.*

"We cannot breathe a better wish, than to desire that the Tracts might be circulated by thousands."—*Christian Witness.*

KIND WORDS TO MOTHERS, SONS, AND DAUGHTERS. By Mrs. J. ADDISON, Author of "Loving Words to Poor Women." In a Packet, price 6d.

1. TAKE THIS CHILD AND NURSE IT FOR ME.
2. HOW TO LIVE CHEAPLY AND WELL.
3. KIND WORDS TO BOYS ON TRUE MANLINESS.
4. KIND WORDS TO GIRLS ON GOING OUT TO SERVICE.

48, *Paternoster Row, London, E.C.*

BY REV. JOHN CUMMING, D.D., F.R.S.E.

SMALL WORKS: Personal, Practical, and Pointed.

In limp cloth, 6d. each.

- VITAL QUESTIONS.
- QUESTIONS FOR THE ENQUIRING.
- QUESTIONS FOR YOUNG CHRISTIANS.
- QUESTIONS FOR DOUBTING BELIEVERS.
- GLAD TIDINGS FOR SINNERS.
- GLAD TIDINGS OF CHRIST.
- GLAD TIDINGS TO CHRISTIANS.
- VITAL TRUTHS.

Full of momentous truths, admirably adapted for general circulation.

URGENT QUESTIONS: Personal, Practical, and Pointed. Price 1d. each, or 7s. per 100.

- WHAT THINK YE OF CHRIST?
- WHAT MUST I DO TO BE SAVED.
- HOW SHALL WE ESCAPE?
- WHO IS ON THE LORD'S SIDE?
- LOVEST THOU ME?
- WHAT SHALL IT PROFIT?
- WHAT IS YOUR LIFE?
- WHY ART THOU CAST DOWN?
- WHAT WILT THOU HAVE ME TO DO?
- WILT THOU BE MADE WHOLE?
- WHO CAN BE AGAINST US?
- O GRAVE, WHERE IS THY VICTORY?

A Packet, containing a Set, price 1s.

GLAD TIDINGS: A Series of 12 Tracts, Personal, Practical, and Pointed. Adapted for general circulation. Price 1d. each, or 7s. per 100.

- "IN CHRIST."
- "TO WHOM SHALL WE GO?"
- SOVEREIGN GRACE.
- THE WIDE WELCOME.
- THE HEAVENLY APPLICANT.
- HUMAN RESPONSIBILITY.
- FORGIVENESS OF SINS.
- THE LIVING WAY.
- THE EXALTED LORD.
- THE CROSS OF CHRIST.
- WARNING WORDS.
- CHRIST "ALL AND IN ALL.

A Packet containing a Set, price 1s.

48, Paternoster Row, London, E.C.

BY REV. JOHN CUMMING, D.D., F.R.S.E.

CHRIST RECEIVING SINNERS. Twenty-second Thousand. Fcap. 8vo, 2s. 6d. cloth.

"Most heartily do we commend this volume."—*Christian Lady's Magazine.*
"A valuable little work."—*Christian Times.*

⁎ At the earnest solicitation of many persons, a cheaper edition of this valuable work is now published, price 1s., or 12 for 10s. 6d.

THE CHRISTIAN PILGRIM. Cloth, gilt edges, 1s.

THE BLESSED OF THE LORD. Royal 32mo, 3d. gilt edges.

PEACE WITH GOD. Royal 32mo, 4d. gilt edges.

THE CHRISTIAN NURSERY. Fcap. 8vo, 6d.

SAVED OR UNSAVED. A Word for the New Year. 32mo, 2d.

"ALL THE WAY." A Word for the New Year. 32mo, 2d.

SET THINE HOUSE IN ORDER. A Word for the New Year. 32mo, 2d. sewed.

LIVING WATER FROM THE WELLS OF SALVATION. A Word for the New Year. 32mo, sewed, 2d.

"I AM WITH THEE:" the Promised Reward. Royal 32mo, 3d. gilt edges.

FRIENDLY INQUIRIES. Price 6d. per packet.
Gospel Truths in the very words of Scripture. A series of Cards for enclosure in letters and general distribution. They are also printed on Paper, price 6d. per 100.

FEAR NOT. By S. BUNBURY. Limp cloth, 6d.

PLEASANT STORIES FOR THE YOUNG. By the Author of "Old Peter Pious," "Have You ——?" and others. In a packet, 1s.; in a handsome box, 1s. 6d.

48, *Paternoster Row, London, E.C.*

PENNY LETTER TRACTS.

1. WHAT I WAS AND WHAT I AM.
2. PRAY WITHOUT CEASING; or, Jesus on Olivet.
3. THE HAPPY HOME; or, Jesus at Bethany.
4. EARTHLY CARE; A Heavenly Discipline.
5. GOSPEL HYMNS.
6. THE OMNIPOTENT HELPER. By J. H. Evans.
7. HYMNS OF COMFORT.
8. ONE HOUR. By the Author of "Have You ———?"
9. FORGETTERS OF GOD. By HENRY MARTYN.
10. THE HOLY AND HAPPY DEAD. By Dr. CUMMING.
11. GOD'S TENTH. A True Incident.
12. HYMNS OF JESUS.
    AND A SORTED PACKET.

The above are printed on Tinted Paper, for enclosing in envelopes, and sold in packets containing 13, price One Shilling.

90,000 of this Series have already been printed.

RICH TOWARD GOD; or, My Trust Money,
How shall I Dispose of it? A word to Christians. 32mo, sewed, price Twopence.

WAIT: A WATCHWORD FOR THE
LORD'S PEOPLE IN DAYS OF DARKNESS. Royal 32mo, 3d. sewed, 6d. cloth.

PETER'S KEYS. By GORDON FORLONG, Esq.
"I will give unto thee the keys of the kingdom of heaven."—Matt. xvi. 19. Price One Penny.

"JEWELS GATHERED;" or, Scenes from Life.
Limp cloth, 6d.

SHE WILL NEVER DIE. A True Narrative.
Limp cloth, 6d.

THE PITMAN'S PRAYER. By G. W.
McCREE. With wrapper, price 2d.

A SONG FOR LIFE AND DEATH. By G.
W. McCREE. Price 3d. sewed, 6d. cloth.

UNEXPECTED CONVERSIONS: a Book for
Discouraged Workers. By G. W. McCREE. Price 3d. sewed, 6d. cloth.

SMALLER PUBLICATIONS OF
REV. O. WINSLOW, D.D.

Price 4d. each, 32mo, gilt edges,

- DIVINE PREDESTINATION AND EFFECTUAL CALLING.
- ALONE WITH JESUS.
- THE CHASTENING OF LOVE.
- THE SICK ONE WHOM JESUS LOVES.
- THE HOLY SPIRIT THE AUTHOR OF PRAYER.
- THE SYMPATHY OF THE ATONEMENT.
- ON DECLENSION IN PRAYER.
- ON GRIEVING THE HOLY SPIRIT.
- ON DECLENSION IN LOVE.
- THE LORD THE KEEPER OF HIS PEOPLE.
- ON DECLENSION IN FAITH.
- THE FRUITLESS AND FRUITFUL PROFESSOR.
- THE SEALING OF THE HOLY SPIRIT.
- THE FREENESS OF THE ATONEMENT.
- THE WITNESS OF THE HOLY SPIRIT.
- THE HOLY SPIRIT A COMFORTER.
- ACQUAINTANCE WITH GOD.
- DIVINE RESTORINGS.

Price 2d. each,

- WALKING WITH JESUS.
- CHRIST IS EVER WITH YOU.
- MY FATHER'S WAY RIGHT.
- LIVING TO THE LORD.
- NONE LIKE CHRIST.
- TRUST IN PROVIDENCE.
- THE LORD'S DAY.
- MY TIME'S IN GOD'S HAND.
- ONLY TRUST ME.
- ALL FOR THE BEST.
- THE DANGER OF REJECTING THE ATONEMENT.
- IT IS WELL.
- GO AND TELL JESUS.
- THE WIDOW AND HER PRODIGAL SON.

Price 1½d. each,

- SOWING AND REAPING.
- THE BOSOM OF THE FATHER.
- GOING HOME.
- SEEKING JESUS.
- THE WORM JACOB AND JACOB'S GOD.

THE UNTRODDEN PATH. Price 1d.

WORDS ADDRESSED TO AN ANXIOUS SOUL. Price ½d.

Any of these choice little Books to the amount of One Shilling sent post free on receipt of 12 stamps.

48, *Paternoster Row, London, E.C.*

SMALLER PUBLICATIONS OF
REV. O. WINSLOW, D.D.

HONOURING GOD, AND ITS REWARD.
6d. sewed, 8d. cloth.

HUMAN SYMPATHY, A MEDIUM OF DIVINE COMFORT, an incident in the Life of David. Eighth Thousand. Royal 32mo, 8d. sewed; 1s. cloth, gilt edges.

THE COMING OF THE LORD, THE HOPE AND CONSOLATION OF THE BEREAVED. Fcap. 8vo, sewed, 4d.

IS THE SPIRIT OF THE LORD STRAITENED? A Plea for a National Baptism of the Holy Ghost. 1s. sewed.

SELECT PIECES. Series One to Four. Cloth gilt, 1s. each.

These choice volumes, containing some of the gems of Dr. Winslow's writings, are admirably adapted for pocket companions for the Christian reader.

WORDS TO THE SICK AND AGED. Limp cloth, 1s. 6d.

WORDS OF COUNSEL AND ENCOURAGEMENT. 1s. 6d., limp cloth.

DR. WINSLOW'S PACKETS OF TRACTS.

LARGE TYPE TRACTS FOR THE SICK AND AGED. 1s. per packet.

PRACTICAL AND EXPERIMENTAL TRACTS. 1s. per Packet.

ANNUAL ADDRESSES. 1s. per Packet.

ADDRESSES AND NARRATIVES. 1s. per Packet.

BY REV. E. H. BICKERSTETH, M.A.

THE BLESSED DEAD: What does Scripture Reveal of their state before the Resurrection. By Rev. E. H. BICKERSTETH, Incumbent of Christ Church, Hampstead. Third Thousand. Price 9d., limp cloth.

WINGED WORDS. By the Rev. E. H. BICKERSTETH, Christ Church, Hampstead. Price 1s.

HOW TO BE SAVED; or, The Sinner Directed to the Saviour. By J. B. 18mo, sewed, price 6d. A Small Edition of the above, price 3d. sewed.

WAYMARKS OF THE PILGRIMAGE; or, Teaching by Trials. By G. B. CHEEVER, D.D., Author of "Lectures on the Pilgrim's Progress," etc. New Edition. 18mo, 1s. sewed, 1s. 6d. cloth.

THE BIBLE: What is it? Whence came it? How came it? Wherefore came it? To whom came it: How should we treat it? By A. J. MORRIS. Third Thousand. 1s. sewed, 2s. cloth.

"Clear in style, candid in the statement of difficulties, and direct in the answers, it is just the kind of book which is likely to please readers whose wish is to obtain a general view of the subject discussed."—*Athenæum*.

HYMN BOOK FOR POPULOUS DISTRICTS.

PSALMS, HYMNS, AND SPIRITUAL SONGS. Selected and Arranged by Rev. JOHN KNAPP, Incumbent of St. John's, Portsea. Royal 32mo, sewed, 2d.; cloth, 3d.; cloth gilt, 6d.

This Hymn Book (containing 150 of the choicest Hymns) has been specially compiled for the use of congregations where the use of larger and more expensive collections is impracticable. The sale of many large editions has abundantly testified to its acceptance by those for whom it was prepared.

48, Paternoster Row, London, E.C.

DAILY TEXT BOOKS.

THE DAILY PROMISER. 64mo, cloth, price Sixpence.

THE BOY'S OWN TEXT BOOK. Containing a Text from the Old Testament, and a Corresponding verse from the New, for every day in the Year. Selected by a LADY. Royal 64mo, January to June, price 6d., cloth extra—July to December, price 6d., cloth extra—or in 1 vol., 1s. cloth; 1s. 6d. roan tuck.

THE GIRL'S OWN TEXT BOOK. Containing a Text from the Old Testament, and a corresponding verse from the New, for every day in the Year. Selected by a LADY. Royal 64mo, January to June, price 6d., cloth extra—July to December, price 6d., cloth extra—or in 1 vol., 1s. cloth; 1s. 6d. roan tuck.

A TEXT BOOK FOR THE SICK AND AFFLICTED. Selected by a LADY. Royal 64mo, 1s. cloth; 1s. 6d. roan tuck.

A BIBLE CALENDAR FOR YOUNG PEOPLE, designed to encourage the habit of daily perusing the Scriptures. By WILLIAM OLDING. Second Edition, price One Penny, in wrapper Twopence.

A VOICE TO MOTHERS. By Mrs. HENRY STACE. With a Preface by Rev. W. PENNEFATHER, Barnet. Twelfth Thousand, revised and corrected. Price 6d.

"In this little work an earnest loving voice is heard, and we only hope the tiny volume will find its way into the hands of high and low, rich and poor."—*Rev. W. Pennefather.*

48, *Paternoster Row, London, E.C.*

HARRILD, PRINTER, LONDON.

www.ingramcontent.com/pod-product-compliance
Lightning Source LLC
LaVergne TN
LVHW061308060426
835507LV00019B/2062